# Sir Walter Scott

## A LIFE IN STORY

# Sir Walter Scott

## A LIFE IN STORY

### Eileen Dunlop

National Museums Scotland

First published in 2016 by
NMS Enterprises Limited – Publishing
a division of NMS Enterprises Limited
National Museums Scotland
Chambers Street
Edinburgh EH1 1JF
www.nms.ac.uk

**British Library Cataloguing in
Publication Data**
A catalogue record for this book
is available from the British Library.

ISBN: 978 1 905267 93 4

Cover design by Mark Blackadder.
Cover images
   Front (top), spine and rear cover: Sir
   Walter Scott from a private lender.
   Front (below): postcard of Abbotsford
   © National Museums Scotland.

Printed and bound in the United Kingdom
   by Bell & Bain Ltd, Glasgow.

For a full listing of titles from NMS Enterprises
Limited – Publishing, and related merchandise:
**www.nms.ac.uk/books**

# Contents

# Acknowledgements

I HAVE MANY people to thank for help and encouragement in the writing of this book. They have answered questions, given advice, lent and gifted books and fed my enthusiasm by their own great knowledge and love of Scott. I am glad to acknowledge in particular Prof. Douglas Gifford, Marina Branscombe, Louise Brodie, Wilna Bryce, Alison Coutts, Hamish and Ali Dunlop, Jennifer Dunlop, Dairmid Gunn, Ian and Mary Love, Dr Richard Kamm, Alison Kinghorn, Jennie Milligan, Sheriff Isobel Anne Poole, Mark Ridley, Susan Robertson, Irene Smorthit, Anna Bennett and James Hamilton (Signet Library), Aileen Heggie (Stirling University Library), John Summerscales (Summerscales Technology Services, Alloa), Marion and Ray Brunton (Central Peripherals, Dollar). I owe special gratitude to my splendid publisher Lesley A. Taylor and editor Lynne Reilly, to Dr Bob Cowan for generous help in understanding the medical history of Scott and his family, and to John and Mary Robertson for companionship and encouragement in hard times, warm hospitality at Kelso and shared love of Scottish literature.

*Eileen Dunlop, 2016*

*For the memory of my husband*
*Antony Kamm*
*1931–2011*
*for whom I wrote everything*

# CHAPTER 1
# Pedigree

*Every Scottish man has a pedigree. It is a national prerogative, as
inalienable as his pride and his poverty.*

~ *Memoirs*, 1837 ~

THESE WORDS, WRITTEN by Sir Walter Scott in 1808 and published in
1837, tell a partial truth about Scottish identity. Among indigenous
Highlanders, the pride of clan unity and kinship with the chief has always
been strong but, until recently, it is unlikely that many Scots were quite as
obsessed as was Scott by their personal line of descent. For ordinary
people in the past, burdened by long hours of exhausting work, leisure
for research was scanty. Access to historical records was limited, and for
the descendants of the 'small folk' who played a part in the Scots victory
at Bannockburn in 1314, ancestors gone beyond living memory were
known chiefly by carved inscriptions on gravestones. Perhaps it might be
recalled in the family circle that a great-grandfather had fought at
Waterloo, or emigrated to Australia in the days of sail. More frequently,
when wind and rain had erased the names on the simple memorials in the
churchyard, individuals passed into a collective rather than a personal
past, sharing the 'folk memory' of communities the world over. Pedigrees
were the preserve of royalty and the aristocracy, marked by pride of
descent and continuity of wealth, land ownership and power.

Only in recent times has the researching of one's ancestors become
fashionable among ordinary people. There are various reasons for this:
curiosity and the desire, in a period of rapid social change, to anchor
ourselves by references to our own past; the influence of popular television programmes in which 'celebrities' seek their roots and seldom fail
to make dramatic discoveries; the availability of DNA profiling and the
opening up of public records on the internet, making research easier and

less demanding of time and expense. Perhaps there is a sneaking desire, even among the staunchest egalitarians, to discover a connection to a royal or aristocratic person of the past, although descent from a highwayman, pirate or transported convict may also provide satisfaction of a kind. Even if such connections are so remote and tangential as to be virtually meaningless, the desire to know and celebrate heredity can be compelling. Yet it remains true that for most people who pursue it, genealogy is a hobby, a spare time interest separate from their ambitions and perceptions of their everyday lives. They are less concerned with establishing a grand pedigree than with compiling a family tree to pass on to their children. For Walter Scott, aged 37 in the year 1808, it was all much more serious than that.

*     *     *

Scott is an ancient Border name. Originally from Lanarkshire and Upper Tweeddale, by the end of the thirteenth century the extended family, which at that time cut no great dash compared with Bruces, Hamiltons and Douglases, had settled in the valleys of Teviot and Ettrick. There they became known as 'the rough clan', distinguishing themselves principally as cattle reivers, freebooters and terrorisers of their defenceless neighbours. Only their unwavering loyalty to the Scottish Crown, noted in high places, gave them freedom to combine violent and lawless occupations with intermittent service as 'March Wardens' policing the 'debatable lands' on either side of the as yet undefined border between Scotland and England.

In 1606, three years after the Union of the Crowns, the family's loyalty was rewarded. The Sir Walter Scott who rescued Kinmont Willie in the ballad (published by his eponymous kinsman in his *Minstrelsy of the Scottish Border* in 1802) was created Lord Scott of Buccleuch. In 1619 his son became the first earl. Two generations later Anne, Countess of Buccleuch and owner of vast estates in Lothian and the Borders, married James, Duke of Monmouth, the illegitimate son of King Charles II, who created them Duke and Duchess of Buccleuch. The marriage was terminated by Monmouth's rash rebellion against his uncle King James VII & II and execution in 1625; his dukedom of Monmouth was forfeited, but since his widow was Duchess of Buccleuch in her own right, her title was unaffected. Fortunate in other alliances, by the end of the eighteenth century the Scotts had inherited lands from the houses of Montagu and Argyll, and finally, in 1810, the estates and titles of the dukedom of Queensberry.

An offshoot of the powerful Scotts of Buccleuch was named first Scott of Synton and later of Harden; their ancient tower still stands near Hawick on the Borthwick Water. It was the head of this house that Walter Scott the author acknowledged as his chief, since he traced his descent, with more pride than was decent, from Sir Walter Scott, 'Auld Wat of Harden', an amoral, murderous, cattle-rustling thug who flourished around the turn of the sixteenth century. Auld Wat married Mary Scott, the 'Flower of Yarrow', whose fabled beauty and gentleness seem to have belied her nature. It was she who, whenever the larder was empty, presented her husband with a dish containing only a pair of spurs – a none-too-subtle hint that it was time to get out and literally rustle up the next dinner.

Wat's son William inherited his father's preference for dining on other men's beef. He too made a notable marriage, though to someone less immediately attractive than, in her youth, his mother. Margaret Murray, 'Muckle Mou'd Meg', was allegedly so hideous that her parents despaired of her ever finding a husband. Thus, when William Scott, out on the rampage, was captured by Meg's father, he seemed like an answer to prayer. The young thief was given a stark choice – marry Meg, or be hanged. Walter Scott the author gives a gleeful account of what followed:

> *The lady was so very ugly that Sir William, the handsomest man of his time, positively refused the honour of her hand. Three days were allowed him to make up his mind; it was not until he found one end of a rope made fast to his neck and the other knotted to a sturdy oak bough that his resolution gave way …. It is said, they were afterwards a very happy couple.*

Such stories may well be apocryphal, but William and Meg's remote descendant never lost his enthusiasm for them; Scott the author even claimed to trace a resemblance between Meg's 'muckle mou' and his own. In conversations, letters, journals and fragmentary autobiography, his boasting of his ancestors' exploits continued uncritically throughout his life. They were men who 'for three hundred years before the union have murdered, stolen and robbed like other Border gentlemen … hunted, drank claret, rebelled and fought duels, right down to the time of my father and grandfather'.

One of the problems of disentangling Scott the author's family tree is the prevalence of the name Walter. But to state his later descent simply:

the William Scott who married 'Muckle Mou'd Meg' died in 1655. His second son Walter, who became the first Laird of Raeburn, briefly broke with tradition by marrying Margaret Makdougall [sic] of Makerstoun and embracing her religious beliefs. Thus he became a pacifist and a Quaker – a startling aberration in such a belligerent family. Their son Walter (1653–1729), however, who was Scott the author's great-grandfather, reverted spectacularly to type. A man of some learning, he was a keen Jacobite, known as 'Beardie' from his refusal to shave – a token of mourning for the royal house of Stuart, banished after the 'Glorious Revolution' of 1688. In 1689 Beardie fought at Killiecrankie with John Graham of Claverhouse, Viscount Dundee, against the new king, William III, and was on the losing side in the Jacobite Rising of 1715. As a result of the latter adventure he had his lands confiscated and was only saved from hanging by the intervention of his kinswoman Anne, Duchess of Buccleuch. Unsurprisingly, this larger-than-life warrior was second only to Auld Wat of Harden in his great-grandson's affections, and his extravagantly hirsute portrait was given a prominent place on the author's study wall.

Fortunately, since Beardie's warlike exploits had ruined him: his sons appear to have learned a lesson from his example. The second, Robert (1699–1775), who was Scott the author's grandfather, became a farmer – although even of him his grandson found a flamboyant tale to tell. Originally intended by Beardie for a naval career, Robert was rather ingloriously shipwrecked within sight of Dundee on his first voyage, an experience which so scunnered him that he absolutely refused to set foot on a ship again. Beardie, unused to contradiction, took this defiance badly. Father and son fell out and Robert was left to make his own way in life. According to his grandson's *Memoirs* he accepted this change of fortune philosophically: 'He turned Whig upon the spot and fairly abjured his father's politics, and his learned poverty.' Since 'Whig' was a term used politically in the early eighteenth century for a Protestant supporter of the royal house of Hanover, this filial rebellion could not have been more offensive to the old Jacobite Beardie.

Robert now did what his grandson would do throughout his life; he used family connections. From his cousin, Walter Scott of Harden, he obtained the lease of Sandyknowe Farm at Smailholm, six miles from Kelso (the nearby tower had been leased to Beardie before his fall from grace). Here Robert hired a shepherd, an old man named Hogg who 'out of respect for his family' and, presumably, in order to have some sheep to herd, lent his master his entire life savings of £30 to buy a flock. Scott and Hogg set off for a livestock fair at Wooler, where Hogg examined sheep and eventually selected a flock he thought suitable and affordable. His horror can only be imagined when, returning to his master, he discovered that Robert had blown his entire fortune on a racehorse. The fact that this purchase turned out well – the horse was sold for twice as much, sheep bought and the shepherd repaid – hardly absolves Robert Scott of irresponsibility. He had risked a poor man's savings and, if the outcome had been otherwise, would have been guilty of an unpardonable breach of trust. Such rash selfishness, uncritically admired by his grandson Walter, presaged the author's own cavalier attitude to money many decades later.

* * *

Writing in 1938, the critic Sir Herbert Grierson wisely observed that the life of Auld Wat of Harden and his like, 'when stripped of feudal glamour, does not really differ essentially from that of the gun-men of Chicago'. So why was his relationship to these colourful but disreputable characters so important to Walter Scott, born into much more respectable and law-abiding circumstances in 1771? One reason, perceived by his son-in-law and biographer John Gibson Lockhart in the 1830s, now seems psychologically obvious. Scott, a physically disabled youth brought up during the Napoleonic Wars, dreamed (as did his contemporary Lord Byron and the novelist Robert Louis Stevenson more than a century later) of being a soldier. His pride in kinship with strong, boisterous hooligans like Auld Wat and William Scott was a kind of compensation for his own frustration at his inability to win military glory.

Another reason, essential to an understanding of Scott, is that for all their flaws, his ancestors were gentlemen. Scott, who was no literary head-in-air, was quick to see that such a descent established his claim to the same status, opening doors that would have remained closed to one of lower rank in society. If this attitude seems snobbish and even slightly distasteful in a more egalitarian age, it is only fair to remember that the structure of eighteenth-century society was very different from our own. The aristocracy did hold great power in the land, and for an ambitious young lawyer, which Scott was long before he became a famous writer, the quest for patronage was not so far removed from the social and professional networking of the present day.

The most important reason, however, for Scott's obsession with his ancestry is that he loved and lived through stories, his own as much as those that sprang from his imagination. His friend Robert Shortreed, who accompanied him on youthful excursions into the Borders in search of old ballads, said that even in early manhood the future novelist was 'aye makin' himsel', which means 'growing in maturity' or 'getting on in the world', but which can also be read as 'inventing himself'. There are many stories in the invention of Walter Scott. There is the story that he told of himself, the story written after his death by his son-in-law, and the reminiscences of those who knew him. All contribute to the legend, if not the entire truth of Walter Scott. Most importantly there are the poems and novels he wrote, which reveal his view of history and the influences that made him. These influences were many, but none mattered more in Scott's invention than the stories of the Border lands and the exploits of his ancestors, which all his life were vital to his sense of place and sense of self.

## CHAPTER 2

# Fathers and Sons

*Punctual as the clock of St Giles' tolled nine, the neat, dapper form of the little hale old gentleman was seen on the threshold of the court hall, or at furthest, at the head of the back stairs, trimly dressed in a complete suit of snuff-coloured brown, with stockings of silk or woollen, as suited the weather, a bobbed wig and a small cocked hat ... silver shoe buckles and a gold stock buckle. A nosegay in summer and a sprig of holly in winter completed his well-known dress and appearance.*

~ *Redgauntlet*, chapter 1, 1824 ~

THIS VIVID DESCRIPTION of Edinburgh solicitor Mr Saunders Fairford, in one of Scott's greatest novels, is widely believed to be a pen-portrait of the author's father, another Walter Scott. He was a son of Robert Scott, the farmer of Sandyknowe.

Robert had done well for himself since his youthful fling with his shepherd's savings. A judicious marriage in 1728 to Barbara Haliburton, daughter of a rich Berwickshire farmer, had brought money to the farm. Robert sold sheep and his surplus produce at market, and in time developed a useful ancillary career as a cattle drover, moving livestock from the Highlands to the north of England. He had early proved himself an astute judge of horseflesh, and his proficiency in riding and field sports earned him the respect of his neighbours.

Perhaps his grandson the author found this douce middle-class life something of a comedown after the aristocratic shenanigans of Beardie and his ilk. In his *Memoirs*, he would be at pains to point out that Robert's birth, 'admitted as *gentle*, gave him access to the best society in the county', while John Gibson Lockhart, who never lost an opportunity to talk up his father-in-law's connections (and, by implication, his own) devoted some space in his *Memoirs of the Life of Sir Walter Scott, Bart.* (1837–38) to the grand descent of the family of Barbara Haliburton, who enjoyed 'among other patrimonial possessions the parts of Dryburgh ... comprehending the ruins of the Abbey'. There was one particular, however, which may have mattered more to Robert Scott than his descent, since it clouded his own claim to the status of 'gentleman'. Despite his prosperity, it appears that he was never wealthy enough to buy his own land.

According to Lockhart, Robert had 'numerous progeny'. It has been suggested that some of these were born before his marriage and so, according to the mores of the time, were illegitimate. Robert's highest ambition, however, concerned Walter, his eldest son with Barbara Haliburton, for whom he clearly wanted a station in life more exalted than that of a 'tacksman' or tenant farmer. A second son, also called Robert, became a naval officer; and only the youngest, Thomas, stayed on the land.

Born in 1729, ten months after his parents' wedding, Walter was destined for a career in law, a prestigious profession in Scotland then, and now. Robert was no doubt aware of the possibility of patronage from his kinsmen the Scotts of Buccleuch – his own father, after all, had been saved from the gallows by the personal intervention of the Duchess – and may have harboured a hope that, should his son make money and invest it in land, his own ambition to make Sandyknowe a family property might yet be realised. The young man was educated in Latin, the lawyers' language, and in due course was apprenticed to George Chalmers, an Edinburgh writer, or solicitor. When his initial training was completed, Robert bought him – probably at considerable further cost – a partnership with Chalmers.

Yet if Robert looked to Walter to raise his family to the position of landed gentry, he was doomed to disappointment. Walter was studious and hard-working, and in 1755, at the age of 26, achieved the designation of Writer to the Signet. Edinburgh was the hub of the legal profession and, as a member of the highest rank of solicitorship, not far below the status of Advocate, he had the right to appear (though not to plead) in the Court of Session, the highest tribunal in the land. The conditions for making useful professional and social contacts were perfect and, with his powerful family connections, the tacksman's son might have made a fortune. In fact, in a career spanning more than forty years, Walter Scott WS (the initials his qualification permitted him to write after his name) was never to achieve more than a modest, comfortable prosperity. And, although he seems briefly to have owned a small estate in Kelso, he never showed any interest in owning land; it was a sore point with his famous son that he refused even to buy the burial ground at Dryburgh when it was put up for sale. Instead it was 'sold for a trifle [about £3000]' to the Earl of Buchan, reserving only the right of Walter Scott WS and his two brothers, as the descendants of the Haliburtons, to be buried there.

Although Lockhart dutifully reproduces some testimonials to the good character and professionalism of Walter Scott WS, most of what we know about him comes through the writings of his more famous son, with whom he had a mutually irritable though not unaffectionate relationship. Writing his recollections of family life in 1808, only ten years after his father's death, the younger Scott's exasperation over the muddle in which his father had left his affairs (the Writer to the Signet's estate took an incredible 15 years to settle) was still high. The old man's refusal to approve his choice of a wife still rankled, and the future novelist seemed determined to expose every flaw, as he saw it, of his father's character and conduct of his affairs. The failure of Walter Scott WS to keep records and collect fees, his scrupulous refusal to put his own interest before that of his clients, his tendency to allow the same clients first to cheat him and then to pick quarrels with him, all incurred the censure of his son. Another source of indignation at this time was the memory of the father's extreme Calvinism, which impacted on a family doomed to endure Scottish Sabbaths more rigorous and demanding than any day at work or school.

Psalm-singing and tedious sermons in the chilly Greyfriars Kirk had to be endured in the morning. In the afternoon, more amusing books had to be laid aside in favour of the Puritan John Bunyan's *The Pilgrim's Progress* and *Letters Moral and Entertaining* by a long-forgotten religious prig, Elizabeth Rowe. Evenings brought stern quizzing by the father on the content of the morning's sermon and memory-testing on the Catechism (part of the *Confession of Faith* adopted by the Church of Scotland and the bane of many generations). Still to come were lengthy Bible readings by the Writer to the Signet before merciful night fell on another Sabbath. These tedious exercises, not to mention *cold dinners*, left the Scotts – like families the length and breadth of Scotland – exhausted by the 'day of rest' and eager for Monday morning.

Scott the author had even more bones to pick with his father, accusing him of fostering a repressive and undemonstrative regime at home, and of a personal abstemiousness in keeping with his personal beliefs, but both laughable and occasionally embarrassing to his children. One anecdote describes a dinner party at the Scotts', where someone politely but ill-advisedly praised the richness of the broth. 'Aye, too rich,' replied the Writer to the Signet sourly as, to the mortification of his children, he grabbed a jug of cold water and diluted his own portion.

This section of Scott's *Memoirs*, taken out of context, has been used to argue a complete lack of empathy between father and son. This is, however, to misunderstand the nature of eighteenth-century parenting. The author's slightly younger contemporary Henry Cockburn (1779–1854), although he too would disagree with his father in adult life, remembered that in earlier years: 'He was one of many good fathers who, from mere want of consideration or method, kept his children at a distance.' Walter Scott WS was one of the same kind. At a deep level, his son understood this; it is notable that even at his most resentful the younger Scott – normally the most good-humoured and equable of men – could not entirely condemn his father. In the same manuscript, he admitted that his father was 'uncommonly handsome, with an expression of sweetness of temper, which was not fallacious; his manners were rather formal but full of genuine kindness, especially when exercising the duties of hospitality' (provided, presumably, that one did not mention the broth).

By 1824 the young man's impatience with an old man's ways had cooled. In his great novel *Redgauntlet,* Scott incorporated traits of his father, both kindly and comical, into the character of Saunders Fairford, the buttoned-up but anxiously loving father of Alan, one of the joint heroes of the tale. No one who has read this book needs the stiff portrait that hangs at Abbotsford, attributed to Robert Harvie, to evoke the Writer to the Signet, Walter Scott.

\* \* \*

In the year when his portrait was painted, 1758, Walter married 26-year-old Anne Rutherford who, according to her grandson-in-law Lockhart, was 'short of stature, and by no means comely, at least after the days of her early youth'. This does not seem to have been a disqualification in the eyes of her fiancé; it is unlikely that he chose her solely on the strength of the money and useful connections she brought to the marriage. Indeed, it says much for Walter's perceived prospects at this time that he was considered a good match, since the social disparity between the couple was considerable. His new father-in-law, Dr John Rutherford (1695–1779), was a man of status and reputation. He had degrees from the universities of

Edinburgh and Rheims, and had studied at Leyden in the Netherlands under the great pioneer of clinical medicine Herman Boerhaave (1668–1738). On his return to Edinburgh, Rutherford founded the School of Medicine at the University of Edinburgh, holding the post of Professor from 1726 until 1765. He had married twice; his daughter Anne was the only surviving child of his marriage to Jean Swinton who, according to her pedigree-obsessed grandson, belonged to a family 'which for antiquity and honourable alliances might rank with any in Britain'.

Anne Rutherford had been educated at a private school for young Edinburgh ladies, where she learned history and literature as well as needlework, household accounting and polite manners. When school-days were over, Anne was sent off to be 'finished' by an aristocratic lady, the Honourable Mrs Ogilvie. This personage, according to Scott's contemporary and early biographer Robert Chambers, taught 'a style of manners that would nowadays be considered intolerably stiff', but which impressed Scott's mother so much that, even in old age, she never allowed her spine to touch the back of her chair. A striking portrait, painted in her later years by Sir John Watson Gordon, shows a strong Scots face, surrounded by the lavishly beribboned bonnet favoured by elderly ladies of the period. There is humour around her mouth and in her eyes confidence, an awareness of her place in society and knowledge that she had survived all the sorrows and trials that life had dealt her.

Writing late in his own life a new introduction to *Chronicles of the Canongate*, first published in 1827, Scott claimed that Mrs Martha Bethune Baliol, an exquisite specimen of an elderly Edinburgh gentle-woman of the eighteenth century, was 'designed to shadow out ... the interesting character of a dear friend of mine, Mrs Murray Keith'. Lockhart, however, discerned that this was only partly true. 'I am assured,' he wrote, 'he had mixed up various features of his own beloved mother.' The notion that a fictional character is 'based on' any one person must be treated with caution; the act of creation is much more complicated than that. No doubt traits of Mrs Murray Keith find their way into Scott's depiction of Mrs Bethune Baliol. Yet for those who have seen her portrait, it is the kindly, generous face of Mrs Anne Scott that comes most vividly into the mind's eye.

\*   \*   \*

Professor John Sutherland, in *The Life of Walter Scott* (1995), suggests that there was a culture clash, and by inference friction, between Walter Scott WS and his wife, which had a bearing on their son's development and life choices. In this reading, Scott the author's sense of alienation from his father led him to rebel against everything the older man stood for – Presbyterianism in religion, Whiggism in politics and philistinism in culture – in favour of his mother's less rigid Episcopalianism and love of secular literature. Sutherland makes an interesting case, but hard evidence of domestic discord is hard to find. One may conjecture the distaste of Mrs Scott as she watched her less genteel husband ostentatiously pouring water into his soup, but as far as records are concerned the couple had a conventional eighteenth-century marriage. Their chief mutual concern was the raising of children, and their own interests – Walter's church history and Anne's poetry and drama – were pursued in the scanty leisure time their busy lives afforded.

The younger Walter did reject Presbyterianism in favour of Episcopalianism, but not until he had left home and married an Episcopalian wife. He did inherit his mother's love of poems and plays, but all his life he was fascinated by his father's beloved Covenanters and wrote movingly of their obstinate courage. And, despite the father and son disputes acted out in the novels, quite hilariously in the instances of Frank Osbaldistone in *Rob Roy* and Alan Fairford in *Redgauntlet*, Scott stated in his *Memoirs* that he loved his father and wanted to please him. It is worth noticing too that his recollections of his father really belong to his adolescence and young manhood. During his son's earliest and most formative years, Walter Scott WS was a distant and mostly absent figure.

# CHAPTER 3

# College Wynd

*I was born, as I believe, on the 15 August 1771 in a house belonging to my father at the head of the College Wynd …. I showed every sign of health and strength until I was about eighteen months old. One night, I have often been told, I showed great reluctance to be caught and put to bed, and after being chased around the room was appre-hended and consigned to my dormitory with some difficulty. It was the last time I was to show such personal agility. In the morning I was discovered to be affected by the fever which often accompanies the cutting of large teeth. It held me three days. On the fourth when they went to bathe me as usual it was discovered that I had lost the power of my right leg.*

*~ Memoirs, 1837 ~*

AFTER THEIR MARRIAGE in 1758, Walter Scott WS and his new wife settled first in Anchor Close, one of many narrow lanes running at right angles to Edinburgh's High Street. From there they moved to an apart-ment at the top of the College Wynd. This was a steep alley, subsequently demolished, which ran uphill from the Cowgate to emerge opposite the Town College, forerunner of the present University building on the south side of Chambers Street. In these quaint but incommodious places, they set about the serious and often dispiriting business of raising a family.

Paintings, engravings and prints of the 'Old Town' of Edinburgh abound, many dating from the early to mid-nineteenth century, but some even older. A picturesque city lures artists, and Edinburgh was certainly picturesque. What such images often fail to convey is the squalor lurking beneath the charm, a seediness largely eclipsed by the refurbishments of the late twentieth century. Although the structure of the town remains intact and the restoration is in the main sympathetic, it is difficult to walk in the gentrified streets of today and imagine the grimy tenements, the reek of burning fuel that famously hung over them, the sinister closes and atmosphere of decay that defined the area well into modern times.

Until the eighteenth century, this Old Town of Edinburgh was the only town. Abandoned by the royal court when King James VI departed for London on his succession to the English throne in 1603, and by the parliament at the Treaty of Union in 1707, Edinburgh was a capital only in name; the real business of government was carried on elsewhere. By the time Anne and Walter Scott were bringing up their children, it was a long, narrow city with roughly 70,000 inhabitants. Rich and poor lived cheek by jowl in vertiginously high 'lands', closely packed on the swamp-encircled volcanic 'tail' running from the Castle, downhill through the Lawnmarket, High Street and Canongate to the Palace of Holyroodhouse, the shabby and partly ruinous seat of a long-absent king. Hygiene was appalling, with human excretions routinely tipped from windows into the pavements beneath. The teetering tenements, romantic only to the distant eye, were so rickety that it was not unknown for one to collapse into the street.

It is true that the city accommodated the socially mixed population which modern town planners have tried in vain to recreate. Dukes, earls, law lords and their families lived in apartments sandwiched between the attics and cellars of tradesmen, artisans, publicans, scavengers, paupers and thieves. Aristocratic and common children played together among dunghills and rooting pigs, and no doubt there was a sense of community among the filth, but it is hard to imagine any other advantage to be had from such a press of human beings. The stink of the place was carried for miles on the wind. Plague made ghastly visitations, as did cholera, typhoid, smallpox, diphtheria and the viral illness which Sir Walter Scott mistakely attributed to a 'teething fever'.

The house at the head of the College Wynd was better than many, and certainly better than the hovel in Anchor Close. The Scotts were moving up in the world, and could now afford accommodation on the relatively salubrious third and fourth floors. Below them, according to Scott's biographer Robert Chambers, lived the family of another Writer to the Signet, Mr Keith, the father of Sir Alexander Keith of Ravelston and grandfather of a future Knight Marischal of Scotland. The Scotts' apartment was accessed by a private stair at the rear of the building. The exteriors of such 'mansions' suggest that all the rooms must be tiny and cramped, yet in his novel *Guy Mannering* Scott, describing the quarters of Mr Paulus Pleydell the lawyer in just such a tenement, contradicts this. Although the odour of the 'scale stair' was 'not sweet' and the wainscotted entrance 'narrow and mean', Colonel Mannering found the library 'a complete contrast to these unpromising appearances. It was a well-proportioned room, hung with a portrait or two of Scottish charac-ters of eminence, by Jamieson, the Scottish Vandyke, and surrounded by books, the best editions by the best authors.'

It would be wrong to suppose that because all classes of society inhabited the same building, they all lived in equal squalor, and it is likely that the Scotts' dwelling possessed at least one such 'well-proportioned room'. The rest would have had more in common with the dark, wainscotted entrance mentioned in *Guy Mannering*, a jumble of tiny, interconnected rooms used for cooking, eating, washing, nursing, reading and letter-writing during the day. Beds, built into the recesses of the walls, were discreetly shuttered when not in use. Since these had to accommodate father, mother, children and servants, it is unlikely that the sick child was the only occupant of the 'dormitory' to which he was consigned. Walter Scott WS has been castigated for trying to rear children in such an unhealthy environment, but in the first years of marriage he had little choice. Although by the early 1760s the Town Council had decided on expansion and had made a start by draining the Nor' Loch, the swampy area to the north of the city which was the dumping ground for most of its sewage, the first houses of the 'New Town', designed by the architect James Craig, were not built until the end of the decade. Brown Square and George Square, a smaller development on the south side of the area reclaimed from the Burgh Loch and renamed the Meadows, were still under construction when Walter Scott the author was born. College Wynd was near the Law Courts where the Writer to the Signet did much of his work, and within easy reach of Greyfriars Kirk, where he held the office of elder. Its proximity to the College gave it respectability; many of the Scotts' neighbours were professors and doctors, and the Wynd was regarded as a good address.

The inescapable unhealthiness of the city, however, took its toll. Anne Scott bore twelve children; of the nine who were born in Anchor Close or College Wynd, six were either stillborn or died in childhood. Lockhart recounts that when Scott the author died, his family found in his desk a little package containing six locks of baby hair and a faded note in Anne Scott's handwriting.

1. *Anne Scott, born March 10, 1759*
2. *Robert Scott, born August 22, 1760*
3. *John Scott, born November 28, 1761*
4. *Robert Scott, born June 7, 1763*
5. *Jean Scott, born March 27, 1765*
6. *Walter Scott, born August 30, 1766*

*All these are dead, and none of my present family was born until some time afterwards*

There has been a tendency among some modern social critics, following the lead of the late twentieth-century historian Lawrence Stone, to suggest that in the pre-modern period parents became so hardened by loss that they failed to bond with their infants and scarcely mourned their passing. As if in evidence of such a degraded mindset, the Scotts have been censured for giving surviving children names already assigned to the dead. In fact, it was common practice at a time when the passing on of a name was of almost sacred importance, and there are many recorded instances of families where two, or even three surviving children were given the same forename. The pathetic relics of Anne Scott's dead children give the lie to impertinent assumptions; no doubt like the rest of their generation the Scotts tried to understand their affliction as the mysterious will of God, and the need to care for the living forced them to repress their grief. Yet such experience of loss could not but make them fretful about the health of their surviving offspring, and when little 'Wattie' succumbed to the fever which left his right leg paralysed, their pain and anxiety may be easily imagined.

\* \* \*

Despite his boast that he was an 'uncommonly healthy child', Scott mentions in his *Memoirs* that before his 'teething fever' he had already had one close encounter with death. It was usual for women who could afford it to delegate the task of breastfeeding their babies to a 'wet nurse', a less affluent woman who had milk to spare, and one had been found for Wattie. What no one realised was that the chosen nurse was suffering from tuberculosis, a notoriously infectious disease, common to cattle and human beings and spread by coughing and sputum. Only when the alert doctor she consulted tipped off Walter Scott WS was the baby hastily removed to the breast of a 'healthy peasant'.

This fright could scarcely have faded from his parents' memory when Wattie succumbed to another potentially fatal disease. Although the cause of the child's affliction was mysterious at the time – he himself never understood the reason for his lameness – it is now generally agreed that he suffered an attack of infantile paralysis, more commonly known today as poliomyelitis or 'polio'. The disease was improperly understood before 1840; it was not until 1908 that a causative agent was identified, and no protective vaccine was developed until the 1950s. Polio is a viral illness leading to severe paralysis and often death, and in the eighteenth century it was endemic; every child in Edinburgh was exposed to the virus, but only the unfortunate developed symptoms. Despite their crowded living conditions the older Scott children were unaffected, and polio epidemics seem not to have occurred before the twentieth century.

In the panic that followed their alarming discovery, the Scotts' first thought was to summon Wattie's grandfather, the eminent Dr Rutherford, but in the first weeks other distinguished members of the University Faculty of Medicine were also called in. Depressingly, none had a clue what was wrong. After a sprain or dislocation had been ruled out, the barbaric but universal applications of blistering (causing blisters to rise by burning the skin) and bloodletting were tried. Not for the last time in Scott's life, the pain of unproven treatments must have been as terrible as it was in vain. It is evidence of his parents' deep distress that even when the baffled doctors had washed their hands of the case, they went on desperately seeking help. As Scott remembered later:

> *During the course of many years* [they] *eagerly grasped at every prospect of a cure which was held out by the promise of empirics, or of ancient ladies and gentlemen who conceived themselves entitled to recommend various remedies, some of which were of a nature sufficiently singular.*

In the short term, however, it was the pragmatic advice of Dr Rutherford which was to give Wattie his best chance of health and a partial recovery. The little boy, he opined, should be sent to live in the country where fresh air, wholesome food and exercise could not fail to do him good. So, escaping from unsalubrious Edinburgh and the never-ending attentions of doctors, quacks and interfering old ladies, Wattie was transported in 1773 to the farmhouse at Sandyknowe where his father had been reared, to be cared for by his grandparents and his unmarried aunts.

# CHAPTER 4

# Borderlands

*And still I thought that shatter'd tower*
*The mightiest work of human power;*
*And marvell'd as the aged hind*
*With some strange tale bewitch'd my mind*
*Of forayers, who, with headlong force*
*Down from that strength had spurr'd their horse,*
*Their southern rapine to renew,*
*Far in the distant Cheviots blue …*

~ Marmion, Introduction to canto III, 1808 ~

IN 1831, WHEN Sir Walter Scott was one of the most famous people on the planet, his publisher Robert Cadell invited the great English painter Joseph Mallord William Turner to supply watercolours to be engraved for a new edition of Scott's *Poetical Works*. Terms were agreed, and at Scott's invitation Turner paid a summer visit to Abbotsford. Following the journey made by the eponymous hero of Scott's early narrative poem *Marmion*, he made 15 sketches, which included one titled 'Smailholm Tower'; this he later used as the basis of a watercolour now in the collection of Vassar College, New York. Although Scott did not live to see the 'Magnum Opus' of his work completed, he would surely have responded warmly to Turner's vision of the place where he spent most of his early childhood years.

In the right corner of the foreground (usually reversed in engravings) stands the unpretentious farmstead of Sandyknowe, enlarged by Robert Scott when he became tenant in the 1720s. A lane leads from the house to a meadow busy with cattle and milkmaids, watched by a woman in a plaid dress and a recognisable small boy. So far, so pastoral, but from this scene the eye is drawn swiftly upward, across a burning blue lake to a high rock where the tower of Smailholm rears proudly into a turbulent Turnerian sky. It is substantial yet ethereal, grim but alluring, its slightly eerie atmosphere heightened by the daylight shining of a single star. Turner was responding as only he could to Scott's romantic vision, but he was not painting reality.

Although it remains one of the most prominent landmarks in southern Scotland, Smailholm is more chilly than romantic. The hills around it are less precipitous than Turner made them. The tower itself, a starkly utilitarian Border peel, stands solidly within its ruined barmkin, scowling down on the farmhouse folded into the hillside below. Turner's shining lake is a dark, reedy lochan, the surrounding grey-green slopes cropped to the bone by grazing sheep. What Smailholm does convey is immutability, a feeling that little has changed since the arrival of the sickly child, tired out after an eight-hour journey from Edinburgh, more than two and a half centuries ago.

No greater contrast can be imagined than that between cramped, suffocating College Wynd and the Border hills, with their bluster of wind, restless clouds and sudden, piercing shafts of sunshine. The house where Robert Scott, now in his seventies, lived with his wife and middle-aged spinster daughters, had long been a child-free zone, and the arrival of Wattie was greeted with delight by all. He was the centre of attention, loved and indulged by the whole family, but particularly by his aunt Janet, known as Jenny, who found in him the only child she would ever have to love.

Once Wattie had settled in, the bizarre attempts to cure his lameness continued, perhaps on parental insistence. One of his earliest memories was of being wrapped, according to some folklorish remedy, in a newly flayed sheepskin; he recalled lying on the parlour floor in this 'tartar-like habiliment' while his grandfather, 'a venerable old man with white hair', used 'every excitement' to persuade him to crawl. His grandfather's elderly cousin, Sir George MacDougal of Makerstoun, joined in the fun, going down on his creaking knees in the parlour, coaxing Wattie to stretch his limbs by dragging his watch along the carpet. It is a touching picture, but more good was done by the farm servants who carried the child out of doors and laid him on the grass, where boredom and curiosity compelled Wattie to move around. It is known that polio responds to physiotherapy and, gaining strength from wholesome food and fresh air, Wattie eventually pulled himself upright. His grandfather made him a crutch-headed stick and, although his right leg was permanently shortened, he learned to walk on the ball of his foot. Dr Rutherford's advice had proved sound.

The household at Sandyknowe did not aspire to grandeur. Its way of life was comfortable but unpretentious, and none of the family had leisure or much inclination for printed literature. There were a few books in the parlour besides the family Bible, a random collection among which the grown-up Scott remembered Josephus's *The Jewish War* and a now-forgotten tale published in 1745 by John Kirkby, a Church of England vicar and tutor of the great English historian Edward Gibbon. This was advertised as '*Automathes: the story of a Young Nobleman who was accidentally left in his Infancy upon a Desolate Island, and continued Nineteen Years in the Solitary State, separate from all Human Society. A Narrative Abounding with Surprizing* [sic] *Occurrences ...*'. When the weather was too severe to go out of doors, the adventures of Automathes, 'the self-taught', was read aloud to an appreciative Wattie by Aunt Jenny.

Another favourite was Allan Ramsay's *A Tea-table Miscellany*, a book of old and not-so-old ballads. Scott eventually fell heir to the Sandyknowe copy, noting in a margin that it had belonged to his grandfather. In his *Memoirs* he recalled a visit to Sandyknowe by the local minister, 'a tall, emaciated figure, his legs encased in clasped gambadoes [riding gaiters] and his face of a length that would have rivalled the Knight of Lamancha's [*Don Quixote*'s], during which he wrecked the adult conversation by shouting out verse after verse from his favourite ballad, 'Hardyknute'. 'One may as well speak in the mouth of a cannon as where that child is,' complained the minister. It is hard to believe that such an incident would have been tolerated in College Wynd, but at Sandyknowe Wattie could do no wrong.

It might be thought, nonetheless, that for an intelligent child the dearth of reading material was a disadvantage. Wattie, like many children who enjoy being read to, was slow to learn to read by himself. What saved him from boredom was that the older Scotts' lack of book-learning was more than compensated for by a rich oral culture. In the long winter evenings in the parlour, literally a 'talking-place', his grandfather would tell stories handed down to him in his youth from the previous generation. Robert, born in 1699, could remember the Jacobite Rising of 1715, when his father Beardie had got himself into hot water, and the even greater excitement of the Rising led by 'Bonnie Prince' Charles Edward Stuart thirty years later. Wattie's championing of the doomed House of Stuart dated from this time; he was whipped into a frenzy of indignation by tales of the cruel Hanoverian commander, the 'Butcher' Duke of Cumberland, the suppression of the Highland clans and the brutality, after Culloden, of the ringleaders' executions at Carlisle. 'One or two of our own distant relations had fallen on that occasion, and I remember hating the name of Cumberland with more than infant hatred.' Maturity would modify his loathing, yet the sufferings of the Stuarts would be the wellspring of some of his greatest creative work.

From his grandmother, the former Barbara Haliburton, 'in whose youth the old Border depredations were a matter of recent tradition', Wattie learned of Auld Wat of Harden and Muckle Mou'd Meg, and of the Scotts and Haliburtons who had played a real or apocryphal part on the wild and tragic stage of Border history. It was at Sandyknowe that his pride of descent took root, before he was four years old.

Just as influential were the Border ballads, with their spare, compelling narratives of heroic deeds, battles, betrayals and supernatural events. Rarely written down before the eighteenth century, they had been transmitted by word of mouth through many generations, recited to entertain rich and poor in halls and farm kitchens on dark nights when the day's work was done. Wattie heard tales of Otterburn and Kinmont Willie, Tam Lin and Thomas the Rhymer, and was enchanted by the glamour of heroic deeds and eerie encounters. It was this heady atmosphere that informed his adult vision of Smailholm Tower, and which he fondly recalled in the introduction to the third canto of *Marmion*:

> *And ever, by the winter hearth,*
> *Old tales I heard of joy and mirth,*
> *Of lovers' slights, of ladies' charms,*
> *Of witches' spells, of warriors' arms …*
> *While stretch'd at length upon the floor,*
> *Again I fought each combat o'er,*
> *Pebbles and shells in order laid,*
> *The mimic ranks of war display'd;*
> *And onward still the Scottish Lion bore,*
> *And still the scatter'd Southron fled before.*

David Daiches, in *Sir Walter Scott and his World*, suggests that even if Scott had never lived at Sandyknowe he would still have developed a historical imagination, but that the peculiar experiences of his early childhood 'gave a very special cast' to the kind of historical imagination he had. Rooted in the topography of the real Border landscape, it was for ever coloured by his passionate identification with figures from the borderlands between history and folklore, the natural and the supernatural. The mature Scott's attitude to history was more nuanced, but the passion and childish prejudice excited by his early exposure to tales of wonder found their way into the poetry and novels he would write forty years later. Without Sandyknowe, we would have a different Walter Scott.

Scott had an extraordinarily capacious memory; he could recite all manner of lengthy texts, and had a clear recall of events from a period of his life when most human memories are fragmentary and unreliable. The introduction to the third canto of *Marmion* gives the most vivid insight into Scott's childhood imagination, his unfinished *Memoirs* the best account of his actual experience. In shaping the story of himself, however, he occasionally recounts incidents which even he could not possibly have remembered, and which must have come from hearsay. The story of his rescue from the tubercular wet nurse is one of these. He did not claim to recall his arrival at Sandyknowe some twenty months afterwards, but he did think 'an odd incident worth recording':

> *It seems my mother had sent a maid to take charge of me, that I might be no inconvenience to the family. But the damsel sent on that important mission had left her heart behind her, in the keeping of some wild fellow .... She became extremely desirous to return to Edinburgh, and as my mother made a point of her remaining where she was, she contracted a sort of hatred of poor me. This rose, I suppose, to a sort of delirious affection for she confessed to old Alison Wilson, the housekeeper, that she had carried me up to the craigs, meaning under a strong temptation of the Devil, to cut my throat with her scissors and bury me in the moss .... She was dismissed, of course, and I have heard became afterwards a lunatic.*

Perhaps it is the coincidence of two such narrow escapes from death, both connected with dangerous young women, in such a short period that raises a question in the mind. Perhaps it is the heightened language and melodramatic tone of the second incident, quite different from the down-to-earth tone of the rest of the text. Is it factual or 'creative' writing? The way the *Memoirs* were written may give a clue, though not a complete answer to this question.

Scott wrote the first draft of his *Memoirs* in 1808, when he was living at Ashiestiel, between Selkirk and Innerleithen, in what he would later describe as the happiest period of his life. The colossal success of *Marmion* had stimulated public interest in the author, and Scott's intention was to let his readers know 'from good authority all they are entitled to know of an individual who has contributed to their amusement'. Although the 'right to know' was not enshrined in the popular culture of the period as it is today, Scott was not the first or last author to imagine that his admirers' interest could be so easily curbed. Other tasks, however, interrupted his flow of reminiscence, and although he revisited the existing text in 1826, revising and adding to it, its scope was never extended beyond his 22nd year. Eventually it was published in 1837, when it became the first chapter of John Gibson Lockhart's biography of his father-in-law. By then, any claim to privacy was long gone, and what the public was entitled to know had been expanded into seven massively detailed volumes.

Lockhart was aware of the 1826 revisions and simply appended them to the original text. It was not until the 1970s, when interest in Scott was reviving after a long period of neglect, that Professor David Hewitt spent time examining Scott's original manuscript and working out where the revisions fitted into it. In a scholarly but accessible book titled *Scott on Himself* (1980) Hewitt published a new version of the text, showing clearly what Scott had altered, and where he had made additions to his first draft. One of the additions was the story of the homicidal young woman, so unhinged by desire for her lover that she came within an inch of murdering a helpless child, before being despatched into a limbo of madness.

It is, of course, possible that the story is true, and that the strange echo of a Border ballad is an instance of life imitating art. Or it may be based on a less dramatic incident repeated, in a family of storytellers, with increasingly macabre detail. More probably it is fiction, inserted to emphasise the drama of the author's infancy, his several brushes with death and his survival to embrace his destiny. In a writer of Scott's inventive power, reared in borderlands where history and legend are inextricably mingled, occasional enhancement of the truth may be less deliberate lying than the irresistible impulse to spice up a story.

# CHAPTER 5

# No Fixed Address

*The play was* As You Like It; *and the witchery of the whole scene is alive in my mind at this moment. I made, I believe, noise more than enough, and remember being so much scandalized by the quarrel between Orlando and his brother in the first scene that I screamed out, 'A'n't they brothers?' A few weeks at home convinced me, who until then had been an only child in the house of my grandfather, that a quarrel between brothers was a very natural event.*

~ Memoirs, 1837 ~

IN JANUARY 1775 Robert Scott died aged 76. The distress of adults, the rituals of death and atmosphere of gloom, are always disturbing to children; Wattie, aged three and a half, was no exception. Years later he told Lockhart that he remembered the writing and sealing with black wax of the funeral invitations, and the sad procession leaving Sandyknowe for the churchyard in the darkness of a winter day. But he could not have understood the grief and anxiety of his grandmother; Robert had been a tenant, not the owner of the farm, and new arrangements of the lease had to be agreed. Mrs Scott, though herself seventy, was determined to keep running the business with the help of her youngest son Thomas, a farm manager at Crailing near Jedburgh. But while the future was being settled, she may have felt that the care of her lively grandson was rather more than she could handle. It is not known whether Wattie travelled back to Edinburgh with his father after the funeral, but go he did, and not to College Wynd. In 1774 his family had moved to a new house at 25 George Square.

The first of the new housing developments in eighteenth-century Edinburgh, George Square and adjoining Brown Square stood half a mile beyond the old city, with the reclaimed parkland of the Meadows to the north and to the south open fields flowing away to the foothills of the Pentlands. That the Scotts had really stepped up in the world is indicated by the status of their neighbours. In College Wynd they had rubbed shoulders with doctors and professors; in George Square they exchanged greetings with the Countess of Sutherland, the Lord Justice Clerk Lord Braxfield, and Henry Dundas, Lord Advocate, MP for Midlothian and the future Lord Melville. Their three-storied, grey sandstone terraced house had large, high-ceilinged rooms, sash windows, elegant furniture and amenities undreamt of in College Wynd. To the older Scotts, spaciousness was a luxury, but the rather chilly splendour of George Square could only have added to the bewilderment of the country child.

Although he is entirely absent from his son's account of the Sandyknowe years, it would be strange if Wattie had never seen his father. The Writer to the Signet had clients to visit in Roxburgh and Ettrick Forest, and it seems unlikely that he would pass close to the farm without calling in to see his parents and check up on the progress of his disabled child. But to a two year-old he would have been just another occasional visitor, and when Wattie returned to Edinburgh it was to a house full of strangers – father, mother, siblings and the staff necessary to run the new establishment. His older brothers, Robert and John (born 1767 and 1769), were now eight and six, while two more children, Anne and Tom (born 1772 and 1774), had arrived since his departure. A final addition to the family, Daniel, would arrive the following year, 1776.

Scott has little to say specifically about this period at George Square, but it could not have been a happy one. His mother, who to the end of her days called him 'Wattie, my lamb', was kindly and arranged for him to sleep in her dressing room, presumably to protect him from his boisterous brothers, who slept on the top floor. But she was burdened by household duties and the care of her even younger children, and she was pregnant again. Wattie spent much of his time with sharp-tongued, town-bred servants, who saw him as a nuisance and gave him none of the affection he was used to at Sandyknowe. To the end of his life, he could not cross the Meadows without a pang of bitterness on seeing the stile where a 'cross child's-maid' had made an impatient remark about his lame leg as she hoisted him 'roughly and carelessly over the steps which [his] brothers traversed with a shout and a bound'.

However busy they were at the time of their move to George Square, Mr and Mrs Scott were far from calling it a day in their search for a cure for Wattie's mysteriously impaired leg. Lockhart tells of a Dr Graham whose electrical and earth-bath treatments were all the rage; and according to Robert Chambers, there was also in Edinburgh around this time 'an ingenious mechanist in leather' named Gavin Wilson, who facetiously advertised himself as 'Leather leg-maker *not* to His Majesty'. 'Gavin, on the application of his parents, did all he could for Sir Walter, but in vain,' says Chambers, discreetly leaving the details to the imagination. That the boy found these useless treatments painful and embarrassing is certain, but his parents, undaunted, moved on to the next piece of advice – that the thermal waters at Bath, a spa town in the south west of England, might be beneficial to their son.

To send and maintain Wattie so far from home would involve a considerable financial outlay, and it is evidence of the Scotts' intense anxiety about their son's future that they decided it was worth trying. Aunt Jenny, free now from the care of her father, was recruited to accompany him, and in the late summer the reunited pair sailed from Leith to London on the *Duchess of Buccleuch*. After a brief stay in the capital to visit Westminster Abbey, the Tower of London and other 'common shows exhibited to strangers', aunt and nephew travelled on to Bath. As the coach clattered through the streets, Jenny Scott may have noticed similarities to Edinburgh's rising New Town in the architecture of this alien city; a glance at its gaily dressed inhabitants would have suggested an ambience almost unimaginably different.

The belief that mineral water has beneficial properties, especially in the treatment of rheumatic disease, is an ancient one. The Romans who invaded Britain in AD 43 quickly recognised such therapeutic quality in the waters in the region of Bath, which they named *Aquae Sulis*, 'Waters of Sul' – Sul being a Celtic deity whom they had incorporated into their Pantheon. With typical efficiency they drained a swamp, built a temple in honour of Sul and their own goddess of healing Minerva, and nearby a complex of magnificent thermal baths. In the 1720s the rediscovery of these buildings, long buried under medieval streets, helped to boost the sleepy little town into a fashionable 'watering place'. During the eighteenth century its size increased tenfold as the aristocratic and fashionable flocked to it, some genuinely seeking a cure, others to enjoy the pleasures of urbane society. Terraces of golden sandstone arose around the new Pump Room and Assembly Room, their Palladian beauty a mellow counterpart to the sterner grey streets of the new Edinburgh. By the 1770s Bath was in its heyday, thronged with wealthy socialites intent on promenading and shopping by day and dancing, music and gambling at cards late into the night. It was the modish world evoked by Jane Austen in *Northanger Abbey* and *Persuasion*, but to the countrified Scotts it must have seemed like another planet.

Considering her importance to her nephew's development, Jenny Scott remains an unsatisfactorily shadowy figure. Reduced to a rustic stereotype in the foreground of Turner's painting of Smailholm Tower, her function was more important than her presence. Scott remarks that even in her forties she was good-looking, with fine eyes and good teeth, yet she never married. She was literate, but her own limited education could scarcely have equipped her as teacher of a precocious and inquisitive child. Like many others before and after, she seems only to have existed as an adjunct to the men around her, her father, her brother Walter and her nephew. She was useful, so she was used, as farm helper, nurse, surrogate mother and general factotum. Her feelings are not expressed; her nephew recorded that she had a temper, but not what ignited it or at whom it was directed. That he was fond of her and retrospectively grateful is clear, but it is doubtful that he ever considered her emotional dependence on him, or the pain it must have caused her to have his company bestowed and withdrawn at will. All the anxiety and responsibility of the nurturing role were hers, but a very small share of the rewards.

For a year, however, she had the child to herself. At Bath they moved into lodgings where they lived quietly; Wattie continued to have lessons with Aunt Jenny, and for part of the time also attended a 'dame school', where a few young children were taught the rudiments of reading and arithmetic by a poor but genteel elderly woman. Interestingly, it is this unnamed teacher, not his aunt, whom Scott credited with teaching him to read. Each day, Wattie and Aunt Jenny walked from their lodgings to the Pump Room, where the boy bathed and drank the water. It was a lonely existence, though its tediousness was not unrelieved. Scott remembered the kindness of John Home, the Scottish dramatist most famous for his play *Douglas*. He was in Bath with his invalid wife, who would take Wattie for drives on the Downs in her carriage.

The highlight of the year, however, was a series of visits from his uncle, Captain Robert Scott, who was on leave from India. Robert took a liking to Wattie, and introduced him to 'all the little amusements which suited [his] age, and above all, to the theatre'. The play was *As You Like It*, and it was on this occasion that Wattie claimed to be so shocked by the spectacle of quarrelling brothers. It does seem, though, that he may have been conflating or rearranging his memories. By this time he had already spent several months at 25 George Square, and even if not involved himself, must have witnessed fights between his older brothers Robert and John. By all accounts, they were not a harmonious pair.

It was in Bath too that Wattie, who would be the subject of innumerable portrayals in later life, first had his portrait painted, probably by a fashionable miniaturist, Abraham Daniel. A profile in a small oval frame, it shows a pale little face, surrounded by curly brown hair, with a turned-up nose and eyes staring fixedly at some person or object unseen. The profile, Lockhart said, was 'wonderfully like what it was to the last', an opinion endorsed by some sketches of Scott in later life. But the Bath portrait is oddly disturbing; it shows the face of a child familiar with pain.

Wattie's other memories of Bath are fragmentary but vivid – the beauty of the Parade, the winding river Avon, a toy shop 'somewhere near the Orange Grove'. And he remembered being scared stiff by the stone angels climbing up and down ladders to heaven on the west wall of Bath Abbey, and being comforted by his uncle, who introduced him to a less alarming statue of Neptune beside the river. But sadly, in the summer of 1776, it had to be accepted that the Bath interlude had failed in its purpose. The 'water cure' had done nothing to alleviate Wattie's lameness. He returned home, speaking with a genteel English accent, to the rough and tumble of life at 25 George Square.

* * *

Once more unhappiness was the keynote of the visit. Yet again Wattie had been uprooted from a world where he was the centre of adult attention and deposited in another where he was not; the sense of being bounced from pillar to post, of having no 'fixed address', could only be stressful and upsetting. Although he was still allowed to sleep in his mother's dressing room, he could not avoid contact with his brothers, who took exception to his posh accent and made his life a misery because of it. They doubtless also objected to what they saw as his unfair position as his mother's favourite and the privileges it appeared to give him, a prejudice strengthened when Mrs Scott, impressed by Wattie's progress in reading, began to share her love of poetry with him. There is a famous anecdote, taken from Lockhart's biography, of a visit to George Square by Mrs Alison Cockburn, a friend and distant relation of Mrs Scott's and herself a minor poet. Describing the visit in a letter of which Lockhart claimed to have a copy, Mrs Cockburn wrote:

*I last night supped in Mr Walter Scott's. He has the most extraordinary genius of a boy I ever saw. He was reading a poem to his mother as I went in. I made him read on; it was a description of a shipwreck. His passion rose with the storm. He lifted his eyes and hands. 'There's the mast gone,' says he; 'crash it goes! They will all perish!' After his agitation, he turned to me. 'That is too melancholy,' says he: 'I had better read you something more amusing.' I preferred a little chat, and asked his opinion of Milton and the other books he was reading, which he gave wonderfully. One of his observations was, 'How strange it is that Adam, just new come into the world, should know everything – that must be the poet's fancy,' says he. But when he was told that he was created perfect by God, he instantly yielded .... Pray, how old do you suppose this child to be? Name it before I tell you. Why, twelve or fourteen. No such thing; he is not quite six years old.*

This is not an entirely convincing story. John Sutherland suggests in his *Life of Walter Scott* that Lockhart was adding embroidery to counteract Scott's consistently modest account of his scholarly achievements, and no doubt Lockhart was capable of doing so. But even if one can swallow the idea that a six year-old who, less than a year earlier, was learning phonics in an English dame school had so quickly progressed to reading and discoursing learnedly on Milton, the picture of the po-faced little performer is not particularly attractive. Later, Mrs Cockburn adds, Wattie remarked to Aunt Jenny that he liked Mrs Cockburn, 'for I think she is a virtuoso like myself'. 'Dear Walter, what is a virtuoso?' inquired Aunt Jenny, eliciting the smug reply: 'Don't ye know? Why, it is one who wishes and will know everything'. For once, one has a sneaking sympathy with the brothers.

The day when Wattie would have to come to terms with the fact that he was not the only star in the firmament was, however, still some way off. Mrs Scott had yet another baby to fret over and the limping six year-old was in everyone's way. Wattie was sent back to Sandyknowe, where once again he was granted the freedom and attention so lacking in George Square. Fancying himself the man of the house, he began to hang out with the shepherds and male farm servants, and developed imperious ways. His uncle, Thomas Scott, who was now managing the farm, gave him a Shetland pony named Marion, 'not so large as many a Newfoundland dog', on which, to the alarm of Aunt Jenny, he cantered among the crags of Smailholm and rode in and out of his grandmother's kitchen. Lockhart suggests that Walter Scott WS, somehow getting wind of Wattie's wild horsemanship and unruly behaviour, decided at this point that the boy needed the discipline of regular schooling. But before a final decision was taken, yet another desperate attempt to alleviate his lameness was made. In the summer of 1778, Aunt Jenny took her nephew to Prestonpans, on the Firth of Forth, to see whether sea bathing might prove the elusive cure.

*   *   *

Prestonpans had been briefly famous in 1745 as the site of Bonnie Prince Charlie's only victory in the second Jacobite Rising. When the pageant moved on, it had become again a quiet coastal village notable for nothing much, but frequented in the summer by a smaller and less colourful group of health-seekers than the Scotts had been used to in Bath. Aunt and nephew took lodgings in the cottage of a Mr Warroch, and socialised in a quiet way. His memory stimulated by another visit to Prestonpans fifty years later, Scott would recall in his *Journal* his seven-year-old self down by the shore, arranging shells on the turf and making little skiffs to float in the tidal pools. On a visit to Preston, he remembered, they had sheltered from a thunderstorm in the old tower, where he scared himself by imagining that the headless spectre of the knight Fawdon, slain by William Wallace in the thirteenth century, might appear at a window. He reminisced about stuffing himself with gooseberries in the garden, and playing with 'Miss Dalrymple', the ten-year-old daughter of a judge, Lord Westhall.

Being at ease with adults, Wattie also made two older friends. One was a retired military man who bore the courtesy title of 'Captain' Delgatty. He entertained the child with stories of his campaigns and discussed with him the ongoing American revolution against British rule. It was Delgatty who took Wattie to explore the nearby battlefield, which years later would feature in his first novel, *Waverley*. He would also give his name, slightly misspelt, to Dugald Dalgetty, the larger-than-life soldier of fortune in *The Legend of Montrose*.

Wattie's other companion was George Constable, a retired lawyer and friend of his father's, whom he would meet again later in Edinburgh. At Prestonpans, the child shrewdly observed, Constable was less interested in him than in Aunt Jenny. 'He was almost constantly philandering about my aunt, and of course, very kind to me.'

Miss Jenny, still handsome on the cusp of middle age, may have been flattered as well as amused, but nothing came of the seaside encounter.

Wattie, meanwhile, stored away Constable's stories of Falstaff and Hotspur, which further stimulated his interest in Shakespeare. He also noted some foibles and mannerisms which he would one day use in building the character of Jonathan Oldbuck, the Laird of Monkbarns, in *The Antiquary*.

It seems to have been a happy interlude, but dipping in the freezing salt water of the Forth estuary did nothing to help Wattie's leg. After Prestonpans, his parents seem to have realised that the problem was intractable, and although in the following years more attempts at therapy were probably made, at this point they accepted that their main effort had been in vain. The boy's general health now seemed good, and it was time for a change of regime. 'From Prestonpans,' Scott noted in *Memoirs*, 'I was transported back to my father's house in George's [*sic*] Square, which continued to be my most established place of residence, until my marriage in 1797.'

# CHAPTER 6

# High School Yards

*In October 1787 I was sent to the High School. Never having been at a public school before, and this one being notorious for its severity and riotousness, I approached its walls with trembling, and felt dizzy when I sat down amidst above 100 new faces .... The person to whose uncontrolled discipline I was now subjected was as bad a schoolmaster as it is possible to fancy. Out of the whole four years of my attendance, there were probably not ten days when I was not flogged, at least once.*

~ Henry Cockburn, *Memorials of His Time*, 1856 ~

THERE IS SOMETHING bleak but apt in Scott's use of the word 'transported' to describe his return to the family home in George Square. Later in life, he never attempted to disguise the trauma he experienced when obliged to put his happy existence at Sandyknowe behind him and learn to cope in a large household where the pecking order among the children was long-established. Although he described himself frankly as 'a single indulged brat' whose gentle grandmother and fond aunt had given him 'a degree of licence which could not be permitted in a large family', the pain of adjustment was severe. Although for a while he was still allowed a bed in his mother's dressing room, where he enjoyed reading by the fire when she was downstairs and he was supposed to be asleep, it was only a temporary refuge. All too soon he was accommodated upstairs with the rest of his brothers who, led by ten-year-old Robert, closed gleefully on the undersized, limping seven year-old whose quaint accent and country manners made him an easy target for cruel jibes. Robert, Scott remembered bitterly, 'kicked and cuffed without mercy'.

On his previous brief visits to George Square, Wattie had clung to his mother as his only friend in the house. Now, though she failed to stop the bullying tactics of her elder sons, of which she could hardly have been unaware, Mrs Scott's fondness for her disabled son developed into a deeper intimacy. 'I found much consolation during this period of mortification,' Scott recalled, 'in the partiality of my mother. She joined to a light and happy temper of mind a strong turn to study poetry and works of the imagination.' Anne Scott had lived for years with a work-absorbed husband whose education, his son remarked, 'had not been on an enlarged plan', four unruly boys and a peaky, accident-prone little daughter. The company of an intelligent, articulate child who understood her interests must have been a godsend to this book-loving woman. She had a small library which she shared with him; he read Shakespeare's plays and recited to his mother passages from Alexander Pope's translation of Homer's *Iliad*. His favourite scenes were of battle and uproar, the wonderful and the terrible. In this at least he was a normal small boy.

Unfortunately, in other ways he was regarded as a cissy, and probably not only by his brothers. Once his uncle Robert Scott, with whom he had enjoyed happy times in Bath, called in at George Square. Finding Wattie closeted with his mother, he asked whether he wouldn't rather be out of doors playing with other boys. 'No, uncle,' was the reply. 'You cannot think how ignorant these boys are. I am much happier here reading my book.' It is understandable if his mother, as Lockhart speculated, 'dreaded and deferred as long as she could, the day when he should be exposed to the rude collision of a crowd of boys'. The priggish reply to his uncle's question might have added to her alarm, since she knew full well that the 'rude collision' she feared could not be indefinitely postponed.

* * *

In the eighteenth century, when education was squeezed into a much shorter period than it is nowadays, his father at least was becoming impatient for Wattie's formal schooling to begin. Despite his phenomenal memory, immersion in oral culture and reading skill, there were still huge gaps in the boy's knowledge which needed to be filled. He had no Latin, then the *sine qua non* of Scottish education; nor did he know anything of mathematics beyond simple calculation. He was sent first to a small private school kept, according to Robert Chambers, by a Mr Leechman in Hamilton's Entry, Bristo Street; but when Walter Scott WS found his progress too slow he removed him. After that, a number of private tutors were employed to hurry him along to the standard required for entry to the High School. By the autumn of 1779 Mr Scott must have been satisfied that this intensive period of cramming had been successful. In October, aged eight years and two months, the young Walter was kitted out in the brown corduroy breeches, woollen stockings, reversible waist-coat and garishly coloured coat of a High School boy. With a round black hat on his head and, quaintly, heavy shoes that could be worn on either foot, the sheltered child was about to enter an unimaginably different world.

*   *   *

The High School of Edinburgh attended by Walter Scott was not the iconic building on Calton Hill that became its base from 1829 until 1968. The school he knew stood on the site of the old Blackfriars' Monastery, close by the old city wall in Infirmary Street. It was situated just south of the Cowgate and a stone's throw from his birthplace in College Wynd. In 1779 it was only two years old, having replaced a tumbledown, overcrowded school built during the Protestant Reformation in 1558. Scott's school still exists as the University's Department of Archaeology, its former use commemorated in the name of the surrounding area, the High School Yards. A plain, oblong, two-storied building with a classical portico and rows of windows formerly protected with iron netting, the new school had downstairs a large communal hall and upstairs five class-rooms, where classes of about a hundred boys were taught by men as famous for their inhumanity as for their erudition. The accommodation was already too cramped for a rapidly expanding roll; there were 500 pupils in 1780, and ten years later the High School of Edinburgh was the largest school in the United Kingdom.

The Scots have always been proud of the egalitarian ethos of their educational system; in country parish schools, before the fashion of educating aristocratic boys in England took hold, it was common for the laird's son to share a bench with the sons of ploughmen and shepherds. But greater glories were the creation of a literate population and the opening of a road to university for clever boys, regardless of class and background, at a time when these advantages were unknown elsewhere. The status of the High School in the 1770s was a source of great satisfaction to Edinburgh's citizens, but in reality there was less to be proud of than they imagined. Scott in his writings was critical of the school's organisation and narrow curriculum, but fairly downbeat about his own experience of classroom brutality.

It was left to his younger contemporary Henry Cockburn, a distin-guished judge and man of wide culture, to perform a hatchet job on his old school that must have resonated with hundreds of its former pupils. Terrified, at the age of ten, by the High School's reputation of 'severity and riotousness', Cockburn in *Memorials of his Time* (1851), said frankly of his first teacher, Mr Alexander Christison, that 'unacquainted with the nature of youth, ignorant even of the characters of his own boys, and with no conception of the art or duty of alluring them, he had nothing for it but to drive them, and this he did by constant and undiscriminating harshness'. Cockburn, one of the most eminent men of his day, confessed that during four years in Mr Christison's class, he 'never got a single prize, and once sat boobie at the annual public examination'. He did admit in fairness that the teaching of the Rector, Dr Adam, with whom he spent a further two years, was more humane. Still, his conclusion was devastating:

> As mere school years, these six were very fruitlessly spent. The hereditary evils of the system and the place were too great for correction even by Adam; and the general tone of the school was vulgar and harsh. Among the boys, coarseness of language and manners was the only fashion. An English boy was so rare that his accent was openly laughed at. No lady could be seen within its walls. Nothing evidently civilised was safe. Two of the masters, in particular, were so savage that any master doing now what they did every hour, would certainly be transported.

One at least of these charges was endorsed by the English writer George Borrow (1803–81) who spent two years at the High School a decade after Cockburn. He was beaten black and blue on his first morning by a 'bleareyed lad' who had picked on him solely on account of his accent, and thus, he recorded wryly, 'I first became aware of the difference of races and their antipathy to each other'.

The question that arises in the modern mind is, of course, why parents in what was called the Age of Enlightenment queued up to have their children admitted to such an appalling school. Above all, why were the Scotts prepared to send their undersized, limping eight year-old into such a hostile environment? They could not plead ignorance; they already had two sons being educated there. The principal reason was that in the eighteenth century, there was a universal belief that boys needed strong discipline; it was the only way to toughen them up and turn them into men. The words of the Bible, read and revered in the vast majority of

Scottish homes, gave authority to this view. Texts such as 'A father who spares the rod hates his son, but one who loves him punishes him' and 'The Lord disciplines those whom he loves; he lays the rod on every son whom he acknowledges' were used to justify brutality which would be unthinkable in modern schools and homes. That children survived into normal adulthood was a victory for young resilience; the sad thing is that, though according to Cockburn schools improved vastly during his lifetime, the belief that children could not be controlled without violence was passed down the generations until very recent times.

However much Mrs Scott had dreaded sending young Walter to school, she knew the day must come and, to be fair to Walter Scott WS, he seems to have been concerned that the boy should not be frightened out of his wits. Since the school's Rector, Dr Alexander Adam, was a friendly neighbour in George Square, he was certainly pressured to ensure that Wattie was placed with the least alarming of the four masters. In order to avoid Mr William Nicol, notorious for his sarcasm and savagery, it was agreed that young Scott would skip a year's schooling in order to be placed in the second class with Mr Luke Fraser. No doubt Fraser gave him a milder introduction to school life (though Cockburn reveals that he too was 'a flagellator'). The drawback of this arrangement was that Wattie, aged only eight and indifferently prepared, found himself in a class with ten year-olds (including his brother John) who had already spent two years in the school. It is clear that his lack of maturity told against him during the whole four years he spent there.

While it is difficult to imagine any eight year-old in a modern Primary 4 construing Latin authors such as Livy and Cicero, and translating Virgil into English verse, Scott was not being over-modest when he described his performance as undistinguished compared to that of the high-fliers in the class. Although he acquired enough Latin to read it easily in later life, he only occasionally rose higher than the middle of the class (a position he claimed to like because it was near the fire). The prizes went to older, steadier, more competitive boys, among whom was Robert Dundas, the son of Lord Melville, who was his companion on the walk to school from George Square, and who would in later life be his friend and patron. The relationship with Dundas illustrates a second reason for the popularity of the High School. It was there that acquaintances and connections were established that would, in the small world of Scotland's capital, improve career prospects and give advantages in later life.

Young Walter was fortunate that his father, like many middle-class parents, employed tutors privately to supplement the narrow, Latin-based curriculum offered by the school. French, Italian, history and geography were among the subjects available, so Walter acquired at least elementary knowledge that he could build upon in years to come. Unlike Henry Cockburn, who claimed never to have read a book for pleasure before he was 16, Walter also read insatiably: *The Arabian Nights Entertainments* and Edmund Spenser's *Booke of The Faerie Queene* were among his favourites at this time. For a while a live-in tutor named James Mitchell was also employed at 25 George Square, principally to teach writing and arithmetic and to help the boys with their homework. This young man, although a strict Presbyterian and Whig who 'thought it almost a sin to open a profane play or poem', was relaxed enough to discuss history and theology with his pupils. Walter would always remember the joy of winding him up by arguing against the Presbyterian Covenanters of the seventeenth century, and in defence of Episcopalian and Roman Catholic Jacobites and Cavaliers. The pious and earnest Mitchell rose to the bait every time.

'All work and no play makes Jack a dull boy.' This proverb was much quoted in days gone by, although probably few ambitious parents agreed with its sentiment. It would be easy to suppose that for young Walter Scott and his contemporaries, the relentless grind of learning must have squeezed out time for boyish amusements. Scott's reminiscences suggest that this was far from true.

# CHAPTER 7

# Wars and Peace

*Amongst the social features of a bygone age in Edinburgh were the
bickers in which the boys were wont to indulge – that is, street
conflicts, conducted chiefly with stones, though occasionally with
sticks also, and even more formidable weapons. One cannot but
wonder that, so lately as the period when elderly men now living were
boys, the powers for preserving peace in the city should have been so
weak as to allow of such battles taking place once or twice almost
every week. The practice was, however, only a piece with the general
rudeness of these old days.*

~ Robert Chambers, *Traditions of Old Edinburgh*, 1824 ~

A BRUTAL SCHOOL teaches brutality. It comes as no surprise that, in the
environment described by Henry Cockburn, Walter Scott was picked on
in the playground by tougher boys, or that his reminiscences are
concerned less with his classroom performance than how he coped with
the violence to which his frailty exposed him. We have in *Memoirs* and
in Lockhart's *Memoirs of the Life of Sir Walter Scott, Bart*, spirited
accounts of personal adversity overcome, by an author who as a child
loved heroic tales and whose mature work reflects his belief that heroism
is the greatest virtue of all.

Lockhart, writing after Scott was dead, recalled a walk with his
father-in-law through the High School Yards, during which the famous
author fell to reminiscing about his introduction to playground life. He
had scarcely arrived, said Scott, before he was threatened by a stronger
boy who then backed off with the offensive remark that 'there was no
use to argle-bargle with a cripple'. To this sneer Walter, perhaps remembering the jousts of story books, replied pluckily that 'if he might fight
*mounted*, he would try his hand with anyone of his inches'. By this time,

a crowd had gathered, and an older lad suggested that the 'two little tinklers' (a reference to their unbroken voices), should be placed facing each other on a wooden plank with their legs tied underneath. In this position a fist fight ensued in which Walter got a bloody nose but much credit among his peers.

This incident was, Lockhart indicates, a prelude to years of fighting to keep up with the rest. Refusing to let his lameness hold him back, Walter was to the fore in every act of daring. He scrambled up the Salisbury Crags and climbed the 'kittle nine stanes', a hideously dangerous ledge high up on the Castle Rock. He helped to man the Cowgate Port in snowball fights, knocking off the hats of passers-by. And, so recently contemptuous of rough boys playing out of doors, he now emerged as a participant in 'bickers', street battles fought, in his case, between the High School boys and gangs of children from the tenements of the Old Town, armed chiefly with sticks and stones.

As early as 1529 the Town Council of Edinburgh had issued a solemn injunction against '*bickeringis betwix barnis*', but, despite the stern command '*in our Suerane Lord the King's name the prouest and ballies of this burgh that na sic bykkeringis be usit in tymes to cum*' and the all too modern threat that '*faderis ane moderis sall ansuer ande be accused for that deidis*', the encounters proved impossible for the Town Guard to police. (Indeed it was not until this decrepit and absurd militia was replaced, in 1805, by an unarmed police force that the 'general rudeness' noted by Robert Chambers as characteristic of Enlightenment Edinburgh was gradually brought under control.) In the 1780s, when Walter Scott and his brothers took to the streets, the expansion of the city meant that the bickers were no longer confined to the Old Town, and the 'company' to which the Scott boys belonged was made up of mainly middle-class children from George Square. Their enemies were the less privileged lads from the tenements of nearby Bristo Street, Potterrow and Causewayside.

Often beginning on a Saturday afternoon and extending late into the evening, these running battles were always dangerous, and sometimes blood was spilled. On the most famous occasion, described at length by Scott in an appendix to *The General Preface to the Waverley Novels* (1829), the leader of the Bristo Street faction, unnamed and distinguished only by a pair of green breeches, was struck down by an over-excited opponent armed with a hangar, or short sword. The injury was so serious that the 'young Goth' had to spend several days in hospital, while his

frightened adversaries sweated and guiltily contributed to a compensation fund. Once he had recovered, however, the nameless lad took the
moral high ground, refusing to name his assailant to the authorities, and
spurning the money offered, apart from a coin or two to buy snuff for his
grandmother. Such noble behaviour was unexpected, but certainly appre-
ciated by the juvenile toffs of George Square.

In the same account, the adult Scott was to claim that the bickers
were untainted by 'feelings of democracy or aristocracy, or indeed by
malice or ill will towards the opposite party'. This is surely disingenuous.
Robert Chambers in 1824 admitted that 'the animosity assumed a darker
tinge if there was any discrepancy of rank or condition between the
parties'; and one does not have to go all the way with Douglas Dunn,
who in 1983 excoriated Scott in a memorable poem in defence of 'Green
Breeks' to feel uneasy about the element of class warfare which Scott was
so anxious to disown. The account of the incident on which Dunn draws
is, as he acknowledges, by Lockhart, who can be insufferably snobbish,
but to a modern reader Scott's own account is every bit as complacent.
The tone is unmistakably *de haut en bas*, and he does not scruple to use
words now regarded as inflammatory, such as 'plebeian'. This points to
a great difficulty for some modern Scots with an egalitarian perspective
in understanding Scott, yet in a society where class was more generally
accepted as a fact of life, he was universally popular. It should also be
remembered that at the time of the bickers he was only eleven, and
reading was his major influence. Bred on tales of fighting forebears and
steeped in the knights-and-giants world of *The Faerie Queene*, it would
have been surprising if he had not identified with the knightly side.

The aspect of the bickering in Edinburgh most foreign to the modern
mind is surely the attitude of adults to the lawless behaviour of children.
For many, it seems to have been a spectator sport. In 1530, only a year
after the Town Council issued its decree, and according to the contemporary historian David Calderwood, 'the Lord Herries departed this life
suddonlie [sic], going to an upper chamber in William Fowllar's *to see the
boys bicker*'. In the same year the Earl of Haddington, a former High
School boy, was so excited to see from a window in the Cowgate a gang
from his old school brawling with street urchins, that he put up his fists
and ran outside to join in.

A century and a half later, apparently little had changed. The bickers
in which the Scott boys were involved took place not only on the cobbles
outside the tenements in Bristo Street, but actually in George Square,

home to lawyers, judges and the Rector of the High School. If the fist fighting and stone throwing were as noisy and violent as they sound, what were these genteel, law-abiding adults doing to stop the rioting? Were they watching from the windows, or simply turning a blind eye? Some certainly were openly partisan. The Scotts' aristocratic neighbour, the Countess of Sutherland' displayed the same spirit as Lord Herries and the Earl of Haddington, becoming so excited that she actually presented the George Square contingent with a 'handsome set of colours' to carry into war against their social inferiors. As for Mrs Scott, it is just possible she was unaware that Walter had been scaling the Salisbury Crags and hanging by his fingernails from the Castle Rock, but she could scarcely have failed to notice that he was in the thick of battle outside her front door. One can only imagine what the modern media would have made of these events.

It is evident that, at this period of his life, Walter's overwhelming desire was to be strong and popular, and always to be on the winning side. In the tales of wild exploits with which he regaled his son-in-law, as well as in his autobiography, he was establishing the story of himself that he wanted to be told. He did not deny that he used charm as a weapon, writing in *Memoirs*:

> *Amongst my companions, my good nature and a flow of ready imagi-nation made me very popular. Boys are uncommonly just in their feelings, and at least equally generous. My lameness and the efforts which I made to supply that disadvantage, by making up in address what I wanted in activity, engaged the latter principle in my favour; and in the winter play hour, when hard exercise was impossible, my tales used to assemble an admiring audience round Lucky Brown's fireside, and happy was he who could sit beside the inexhaustible narrator. I was also, though often negligent of my own task, always ready to assist my friends; and thus I had a little party of partisans and adherents, stout of hand and heart, though somewhat dull in the head – the very tools for raising a hero to eminence. So, on the whole, I made a brighter figure in the yards than in the class.*

Man of action, charmer and teller of exciting tales around the tavern fire – this is the image of himself that Scott chose to present in public for the rest of his life. The precocious infant, the 'little virtuoso' whose brilliance had impressed Mrs Cockburn, the mother's boy who refused to play with rough lads in the street – all were repressed in the struggle to be an ordinary, intellectually average schoolboy. What was lost was the emotional openness of his early years, replaced by a suppression of intimate feelings that fifty years later would harden into a desperate stoicism. In the short term too there was a price to be paid. During his last year at school, when he was eleven and in Dr Adam's class, Walter became ill. 'My health,' he records, 'had become rather delicate from rapid growth.' It is more likely that it had never been as robust as he had claimed, and that his strength, mental and physical, was exhausted by constant battling to keep up with older, stronger boys.

*   *   *

Whatever was really wrong with Walter in the spring of 1783, his anxious parents took fright. Once again he was despatched to stay with Aunt Jenny, now, according to her nephew, 'an ancient maiden lady' of 46. She had moved, following the death of her mother, to a house in Kelso, on a small estate then belonging to Walter Scott WS, but earmarked for the retirement of his brother, Captain Robert Scott. Known then as 'The Garden', the house was not large but distinctly grander than the farmstead at Sandyknowe, with several acres laid out in the 'Dutch style', with mazes, labyrinths and bowers. There were fruit and ornamental trees, and flowing below the house the shining river Tweed.

Walter was not ill enough to be confined indoors, and was able to spend four hours each day at Kelso Grammar School. The Rector of this small establishment was the felicitously named Mr Lancelot Whale, 'an excellent classical scholar' who was almost seven feet tall and not unnaturally 'had a supreme antipathy to puns which his very uncommon name frequently gave rise to …. The least allusion to Jonah, or the terming of him an odd fish, or any similar quibble, was sure to put him beside himself.' Walter found the school undemanding compared to the High School, although he credits Mr Whale with helping him to make the important transition from wrestling with Latin syntax to fluency in reading the text. But he was so far ahead of his classmates that Mr Whale used him (when not yet twelve) as an usher, or pupil teacher of even younger children. It was at this school that he met James (1772–1833) and John Ballantyne (1774–1821), sons of a local draper, whose later careers would be closely bound to his. Now, he entertained them, as he had his High School friends; years later James Ballantyne recalled the allure of the invitation, 'Slink over beside me, Jamie, and I'll tell you a story'.

A break from the violence of the classroom and playground strife was what Walter needed at this time. The affectionate company of Aunt Jenny, the gentler discipline of Mr Whale's school and the fresh county air relaxed him, and gave him freedom to go on educating himself. He took out books from local libraries and borrowed others from a neighbour; sitting out of doors, he immersed himself in the novels of Henry Fielding, Samuel Richardson and Tobias Smollett, whose works would one day be regarded as forerunners of his own. He made his first acquaintance with the writing of Henry Mackenzie (1745–1831), the Edinburgh author of *The Man of Feeling*, who would later become his friend, and read in translation the Italian poet Tasso's *Jerusalem Delivered*, a tale of conflict between Christians and Muslims at the time of the First Crusade.

Most importantly, during this visit Walter got his hands on a copy of Bishop Thomas Percy's *Reliques of Ancient English Poetry*. This famous work, first published in 1765 and a major influence on the poets of the Romantic generation, he remembered reading 'under a huge platanus tree in the ruins of what had been intended for an old-fashioned arbour' in his aunt's garden. The *Reliques*, a collection of songs, folk ballads and more modern poems compiled and annotated by Bishop Percy from a seventeenth-century folio manuscript, fascinated Walter and rekindled his interest in the ballads so loved in his early childhood at Sandyknowe. He memorised them at a first reading, and once again Aunt Jenny's house resounded with his delighted recitations.

In 1808, Scott wrote in the first draft of his *Memoirs* a passage that is worth quoting at length:

> *To this period also I can trace distinctly the awakening of that delightful feeling for the beauties of natural objects which has never since deserted me. The neighbourhood of Kelso, the most beautiful if not the most romantic village in Scotland, is eminently calculated to awaken these ideas. It presents objects, not only grand in themselves, but venerable from their association. The meeting of two superb rivers, the Tweed and the Teviot, both renowned in song – the ruins of an ancient abbey – the more distant vestiges of Roxburgh Castle, the modern mansion of Fleurs [sic], which is so situated as to combine the ideas of ancient baronial grandeur with those of more modern taste – are themselves objects of the first class; yet so mixed, united and melted among a thousand other beauties of a less prominent description that they harmonize into one general picture and please by unison rather than by concord …. The romantic feelings which I have*

*described as predominating in my mind naturally rested upon and*
*associated themselves with those grand features of the landscape*
*around me, and the historical incidents, or traditional legends*
*connected with many of them, gave to my imagination a sort of intense*
*impression of reverence, which at times made my heart feel too big for*
*my bosom. From this time my love of natural beauty, more especially*
*when combined with ancient ruins or remains of our fathers' piety or*
*splendour, became with me an insatiable passion.*

Few people, whether natives or visitors, fail to be entranced by the landscape and atmosphere of the Borders. From the red cliffs and pale beaches of the North Sea coast in the east to the eerie quicksands and deep-running tides of the Solway Firth in the west, it is a land strangely self-contained, its contrasts more dramatic because its area is relatively small. Border towns have grown in size but kept their integrity, and beyond them are the same sweeps of hillside and moist green valleys that Scott knew, rivers of chuckling shallows and deep, sinister pools, the same changeable skies. The ravaged abbeys and deserted towers are both material and ghostly, standing witness to the congruence of human history and countryside, the sense of generations leaving their footprints in places they loved.

That the grown-up Scott did experience the feelings expressed is not in question. The quoted passage is a statement of his artistic *credo*, as well as a précis of a wider Romantic philosophy. Yet as modern scholars have noted, however precocious and well read the child, the sentiments described by Scott in this passage are more adult than childlike. Since this would not be his only extended visit to Kelso, it really seems more likely that they belong to a later period of his adolescence. If so, in 1808, either Scott's memory of exact dates was at fault or, more probably, he was deliberately rearranging events to give a particular shape to his own story.

It is a revealing account, nonetheless. Some critics, notably the Scottish poet Edwin Muir (1887–1959), have complained of Scott that although he understood the movements of history and could describe the surface of life, he was little concerned with complexity of character and had no 'inner life' of his own. This passage surely gives the lie to such a perception. Scott did have an inner life, based on his affinity with the natural world and his sense of its unseen, almost supernatural connections to human history. Yet it is also true that there was a duality in his personality which inevitably coloured his work. From the time of his entry to the High School in 1779, the stony streets of Edinburgh may be seen as representing the class conscious, socially ambitious and emotionally repressed side of Scott. Country places, with their haunting sense of human continuity, provided a gentler counterpart, a space in which he could quietly develop his more imaginative, introspective side.

# CHAPTER 8

# A College Boy

*If it should ever fall to the lot of youth to peruse these pages – let such a reader remember, that it is with the deepest regret that I recollect in my manhood the opportunities of learning which I neglected in my youth; that through every part of my literary career I have felt pinched and hampered by my own ignorance; and that I would at this moment give half the reputation I have had the good fortune to acquire, if by doing so I could rest the remaining part upon a sound foundation of learning and science.*

~ *Memoirs, 1837* ~

WALTER SCOTT DID not return to the High School. In November 1783, with his head full of books but with only three and a half years of formal education behind him, he was enrolled as a student at the University of Edinburgh. It was not unusual in eighteenth- and early nineteenth-century Scotland for boys to transfer from school to university at such an early age: Henry Mackenzie was only 11, Scott 12 and Thomas Carlyle (1795–1881) 13 when he first walked fifty miles from Ecclefechan to study in Edinburgh. Henry Cockburn, who had spent six years at the High School, was still only 14 when he moved across the road to 'The College'.

The age of entrance was only one of the significant differences between Scottish and English universities at this time. In England, a university education was the preserve of the Anglican upper classes; students had either been privately educated by tutors or, more commonly, had attended one of the great public schools such as Eton, Harrow, Charterhouse or Winchester. Aged 18 or 19, they came to Oxford or Cambridge already educated, almost exclusively, in Latin and Greek, to a very high standard. School provision for the lower classes was haphazard and few underprivileged boys had the opportunity of extended education. The bar was social as well as educational; you could rarely be a scholar in England unless you were born a gentleman.

Some historians are now sceptical of claims to vastly superior literary skills among the post-Reformation Scottish population, and the number of 'lads o' pairts' who broke through the glass ceiling to join the learned professions. Class, however, was not a barrier to their doing so. It was the humane policy of the universities to keep fees low, so that all intelligent boys might have an opportunity to learn; entry was at a young age because life was short and the need to start earning often urgent. It stands to reason that the standard of entry was lower than at Oxford and Cambridge, but few concessions were made once studies were underway. Scottish universities were not glorified secondary schools. The scholarship of the professors in mathematics, science, philosophy, classics and law was formidable, and many of Scott's classmates went on to occupy high positions in public life.

None of this is to deny that there was a problem in accepting such immature young people and expecting them to behave like grown-ups. At the High School, discipline had been maintained by ruthless corporal punishment, but at least it had been maintained. At the College, there was no discipline at all; theoretically, the students were expected to attend lectures and behave well without coercion, but with young teenagers this was an unlikely outcome. These were the same boys who a year ago had been horsing around in the High School Yards and bickering with gangs in the street. The idea that they would suddenly transform themselves into mature young gentlemen, listening politely to lectures and studying diligently at home was far-fetched. The amazing thing is that anyone learned anything at all.

At the College, in keeping with the Scottish ideal of a broad curriculum, the choice of subjects was wide but not prescribed. The options depended, for such young students, on parental rather than personal preference, and by no means all proceeded to take a degree. Walter's father had decided that initially he should study Humanity (Latin), of which he knew more than enough to cope, and Greek, of which he knew nothing – rather mysteriously, since the rudiments had been taught in Dr Adam's class at the High School. Perhaps he had had more absences through illness than the one that took him to Kelso during his last months at the High School. By his own account his Latin class, taught by a Mr Hill, was so riotous that he quickly forgot much that he

47

had learned from Dr Adam and Mr Whale, while the Greek class was a disaster. Humiliated by finding himself so far behind others, Walter's response was to sulk, state loudly his contempt for the Greek language and refuse point-blank to learn it.

A well-intentioned attempt to help him out made things worse, and left him with lasting regrets. One day a fellow student surnamed Archibald came to call on Walter in George Square, told him candidly that his behaviour was stupid and informed him that he was becoming known in the College as the 'Greek Blockhead'. Not surprisingly this intervention did not go down well. Archibald might be a gifted Greek scholar but he was, like 'Green Breeks', of a lower class than Scott. The mortified Walter turned down a generous offer of tuition with 'sulky civility', and the innkeeper's brilliant son departed, never to be spoken to again. Scott's conscience troubled him afterwards, especially since Archibald died young, but this incident says much about his enduring social attitude. Robert Chambers said approvingly of the grown-up Scott that 'Sir Walter speaks to every man as if they were blood relations'. But for all his bonhomie, that did not mean he expected every man to address him in the same way.

Inevitably Walter's inglorious career as a Grecian ended in tears – and a row with his teacher, Dr Andrew Dalzell, a man who made fireworks in the kitchen to entertain his own children and was described by Cockburn as 'a great favourite with all boys, and with all good men'. Only Walter, apparently, was immune to his charm. The tipping point came with an essay in which Walter, in an act of adolescent defiance, decided to compare Greek Homer with Italian Ariosto, and absurdly to denigrate Homer. The 'mild and affectionate' Dalzell lost his temper and pronounced the student a dunce, but 'at the same time' Walter did not resist remarking smugly, 'he could not suppress his surprise at the quantity of out-of-the-way knowledge which I displayed'.

* * *

Arriving at university after six months away, Walter was reunited with many of his classmates from the High School, among them the future Sir Archibald Campbell, the Hon. Robert Dundas, George 'Lordie' Ramsay, heir to the earldom of Dalhousie, and others who were lawyers' sons like himself. Despite the social diversity of the College intake, he showed no inclination to enlarge his circle of friends. (A century later Robert Louis Stevenson, who was as adept as Scott in writing sympathetically about a wide range of human society, showed the same contempt for students not distinguished as 'gentlemen', dismissing them as 'lads fresh from the heather [hanging] around the stove in cloddish embarrassment'.)

Walter's particular friend around this time was a former schoolmate John Irving, with whom he spent Saturday afternoons and holidays on Arthur's Seat and Blackford Hill. High above the city they lay on the grass, made up stories for each other and shared library books. Among those which most delighted them were 'romances of knight errantry', including Walter's old favourite *The Faerie Queene*, and translations from Italian of *Orlando Innamorato* (1495) by Matteo Maria Boiardo and *Orlando Furioso* (1532) by Luigi Ariosto – which last provided the material for Walter's ill-judged attack on Homer. So spellbound were the two boys by these highly coloured and fantastical romances that they took Italian lessons together. Writing to Lockhart after Scott's death, Irving remembered that 'the number of books [they] devoured was very great'. He also mentioned his companion's beginning to collect ballads. 'As my mother could repeat a great many, he used to come and learn those she could recite to him. He used to get copies of all the ballads he could, and select the best.'

Set against these enthusiasms, it is clear that, despite later self-reproaching and doubtless some reproaching at home, Scott had no interest in learning Greek, or any of the other subjects he encountered during this stage of his university career. As late as 1830 he confessed in his *Journal* that 'whatever was forced on me as a task, I would have detested'. His study of Greek was terminated by another spell of illness and recuperation at Kelso with Aunt Jenny, during which he 'continued for a long time reading what and how [he] pleased, and of course reading nothing but what afforded [him] immediate entertainment'. He thus missed most of the classes in Logic and Metaphysics taught in the second year. Returning briefly to College, his subjects once again chosen by his father, he studied Mathematics, Ethics and Moral Philosophy, all before he was 14. It is small wonder that he suffered from academic overload.

Forty years later, at the lowest point in his life, Scott would write in his *Journal*:

> *What a life mine has been. Half educated, almost wholly neglected and left to myself – stuffing my head with the most nonsensical trash and undervalued for a time in society by most of my companions – getting forward and held as a bold and clever fellow, contrary to the opinions of all who thought me a mere dreamer ....*

At one level, Scott certainly believed all of this to be true. His failure to do himself justice at school and university troubled him. He had been called the Greek Blockhead by other boys and a dunce by Dr Dalzell, public humiliations which must have been hard to bear. Seen in this light, the modesty which his contemporaries found so endearing was a coping strategy; to deflect criticism, he criticised himself. Scott must have known long before 1825, when the words above were written, that his private reading, far from being 'nonsensical trash', had been the wellspring of his creative life. Indeed, in more positive mood he wrote to Lockhart that 'all men who have turned out anything have had a hand in their own education'. Yet it never ceased to matter that academic success eluded him. He blamed himself, but not everyone has agreed with him.

John Sutherland, in *The Life of Walter Scott,* lays the responsibility for the son's patchy education squarely at the door of the father. The elder Scott, in this hostile version, took little interest in his physically frail third son, boarding him out for most of his childhood then rushing him through school and university, concerned only for appearances sake to provide the veneer of a gentlemanly education. Walter Scott WS, according to Sutherland, had always planned to apprentice young Walter in his own office, refusing him any choice in the matter.

This is unduly harsh. From the perspective of twenty-first-century Scotland, with its child-centred, comparatively undemanding educational system, the idea of a sickly, often-absent pupil being pushed through school and university in little more than five years seems bizarre and even cruel. Yet there is no evidence that Walter Scott WS, according to the customs of his time, was an uncaring parent. Indeed, his early fretfulness over Walter's health, the increasingly desperate attempts to find a cure for his lameness, his willingness to fund a year in Bath and a summer at Prestonpans, give a different impression. It is more probable that, seeing his son constantly reading, hearing his wife's proud repetition of the boy's precocious remarks and gratified by the praise of visitors like Mrs Cockburn, he believed him bright enough to cope with anything.

Walter's father has also been accused of binding him to an apprenticeship against his will. There is no evidence of this either. It was an age when primogeniture loaded family privilege, in law as well as in accepted practice, in favour of the eldest son. The bully Robert, despite some nervous resistance by his mother, had been allowed to join the Royal Navy, and in 1780, when Walter was still at the High School, fought under Admiral Rodney at the Battle of Martinique in the West Indies. The wish of the second son, John, for a military career was also gratified, at some financial cost to his father, and it is easy to imagine the chagrin of Walter, who dreamed constantly of battles and heroic deeds, when letters arrived home describing adventures he could never have. Exasperated by his third son's poor results at university, Walter Scott WS could be forgiven, as young Walter turned 15, for giving serious thought to his future. Realistically, the only professions open to a lame, bookish boy were law and the Church. Authorship might be regarded as an elegant accomplishment, but middle-class people with a living to make, including Walter himself, would never have considered it a 'proper job'. Anne Scott touchingly preserved her son's early verses in her writing desk, but the very Scottish attitude of both father and mother to his talent is amusingly summed up by Robert Chambers:

> *His sober-minded parents and other friends regarded his literary leanings, poetical recitations and retentive memory with satisfaction; they marvelled at the thirst for reading and powers of memory, but thought it all to little good purpose, and only excused it in consideration of the infirm health of the little prodigy.*

A respectable profession was the key to future prosperity. The Church was easily dismissed; the father who had for years observed his son yawning through Sabbath morning sermons and fidgeting at evening devotions would scarcely have thought him cut out to be a clergyman. Necessity and preference happened to be the same for Walter Scott WS. His wish to have a son succeed him in the business he had so painstakingly built up was natural; he was immensely proud of his profession. Nor is there anything to suggest that young Walter, so far having failed to shine at university, resisted the prospect of a legal apprenticeship. He would not be the only teenager to like the prospect of earning money. On 15 May 1786, father and son appeared together before the Society of Writers to the Signet, to sign a contract of indenture lasting five years, 'under a mutual penalty of £40 sterling' should either renege on the agreement.

# CHAPTER 9

# The Writer's Apprentice

*I cannot reproach myself with being entirely an idle apprentice – far less than the reader might have expected, 'A clerk foredoomed his father's soul to cross'.*

*~ Memoirs, 1837 ~*

MANY YEARS WOULD pass before Scott could bring himself to confess in his *Journal* that he had really been unhappy at the High School, blaming the 'confinement' he had experienced there. He complained too of the confinement of life in his father's office, speaking of it as a 'dry and barren wilderness of forms and conveyancing' – naturally enough for a 15 year-old with chivalric dreams and a passion for the Border hills. There is evidence, however, that this was not an unhappy period of his life. In the first years of his apprenticeship Edinburgh was providing new pleasures, and a degree of independence contingent on having some money of his own.

In 1784 a 'Disannexing Act' was passed in the British parliament in London, which allowed the heirs of Jacobites whose estates had been forfeited after the Rising of 1745 to claim them back from the Crown. This piece of legislation provided a bonanza for Edinburgh's Writers to the Signet. Because most of the Jacobite landowners had been Scots, the transfer of property had to be done according to Scots law. Work came flooding into the office of Walter Scott WS and the transcription of legal deeds kept several clerks busy, as well as the son of the house. At this time young Scott developed the clear, swift, copperplate handwriting that would distinguish the manuscripts of his early novels, and till the end of his days he would sign off every page with the legal flourish (intended to prevent later insertions) taught to him by his father.

According to Lockhart, the Writer's apprentice was paid an allowance of three pence for every page he transcribed, and since Scott could, on a busy day, copy 120 pages, the addition to his regular wage might amount to thirty shillings – an enormous sum which absurdly would have put his earnings on a par with his father's. Although it seems that Lockhart got the story from Scott himself, it must have been an exaggeration. It is impossible to believe that the canny Writer to the Signet would shell out so much cash to an apprentice, even if the apprentice was his own son. It can be believed, though, that young Mr Scott's diligence was earning good wages which, he wrote in his *Memoirs,* 'reconciled me in some measure to the confinement'. Scott's natural affability and willingness to fit in endeared him, at least in the early days, to the clerks who might otherwise have resented working with their master's son; and since Scott was crafty enough to read novels and propose games of chess only when the Writer to the Signet was out of the room, the old gentleman had reason to be pleased with his son's conduct. Indeed, one senses at this period a harmony between them that would not forever characterise their relationship.

In his spare time – evenings and Saturdays, since the Sabbath observances of his father's house left no time for Sunday leisure – Scott found many diversions. One of the uses to which he put his new-found wealth was to subscribe to the lending library founded by Allan Ramsay (1684–1758) in the 1720s. In Scott's lifetime it was run by James Sibbald, a bookseller whom Scott described as 'a man of rough manners but some taste and judgment'. From the shelves of Sibbald's bookshop in Parliament Square he was able to borrow books in French and Italian, and 'fastened also, like a tiger, on every collection of songs and romances which chance threw in [his] way'. It was here too that he first glimpsed Robert Burns (1759–96), who was enjoying a short-lived social success in Edinburgh following the publication of his first book of poetry. A closer encounter was to follow in early 1787, when both Burns and Scott were guests in the house at Sciennes belonging to Professor Adam Ferguson, whose son, also Adam, was among Scott's closest friends. Scott's account of this meeting is moving, recalling his teenage awe in the presence of an idol:

*Of course we youngsters sate silent, looked and listened. The only thing I remember which was remarkable in Burns' manner, was the effect produced on him by a print of Bunbury's, representing a soldier lying dead in the snow, his dog sitting in misery on one side of him, on the other his widow with a child in her arms. These lines were written beneath, –*

*Cold on Canadian hills, on Minden's plain,*
*Perhaps that parent wept her soldier slain:*
*Bent o'er her babe, her eyes dissolved in dew:*
*The big drops, mingling with the milk he drew,*
*Gave the sad presage of his future years,*
*The child of misery, baptized in tears.*

*Burns seemed much affected by the print, or rather the idea of what it represented. He actually shed tears. He asked whose lines they were, and it chanced that nobody but myself remembered that they occur on a half-forgotten poem of Langhorne's, called by the unpromising title of 'The Justice of the Peace'. I whispered my information to a friend present, who mentioned it to Burns, who rewarded me with a look and a word which, though of mere civility, I then received, and still recollect, with very great pleasure.*

Recent critics have pointed out that Langhorne's name is clearly printed beneath the verse on Bunbury's print, suggesting that Scott invented the encounter to display his own brilliance. If he did so, it was unlike him; no one can accuse Scott of exaggerating his academic credentials. There is also a tone of modesty in the account which rings true; if it had been an invention, surely he would have given himself a more confident role. Perhaps Burns, through his sentimental tears, simply didn't notice. What is really impressive is that Scott actually knew the poetry of John Langhorne (1735–79) and indeed of Burns, Robert Fergusson (1750–74), and also James MacPherson (1736–96), remembered as the literary hoaxer 'Ossian'. This shows that among his vast reading of the literature of the past – Italian, French, Spanish and English authors, as well as the ballads which he was forever collecting and memorising – he had some knowledge of what was then modern poetry.

However delightful Scott found the pursuits of Edinburgh (which included lolling in taverns with his friends and developing a lifelong passion for the theatre), he must have been frustrated that he had so little experience of the world beyond it. Apart from his spells at Sandyknowe and Kelso, where poor health had curtailed his roaming, and at Bath as a five year-old, he had reached the age of 15 without ever travelling more than thirty miles or so from the city's southern boundary. He speaks in his *Memoirs* of walking to Prestonpans with one of his father's clerks, and of fishing expeditions to Howgate in the Moorfoot hills with a rather grander coterie of friends. It is doubtful whether at this period Scott knew or cared much about the other Scotland to the west, where the green Lowlands were being encroached upon by massive industrial development. Deep coal-mining was throwing up enormous black bings of sludge and dross, disfiguring the landscape in West Lothian. The Carron Ironworks at Falkirk, founded in 1760 and shortly to become the largest smelting works in Europe, were already producing for the Royal Navy the famous carronades used at the Battle of Trafalgar. The Forth and Clyde Canal, completed in 1790, carried coal and iron goods to the port of Glasgow, then becoming a mercantile hub to rival Liverpool and Manchester. The erosion of the pastoral by the industrial, with its loss of traditional ways of life, would in later years impinge upon Scott's consciousness, fuelling his increasingly entrenched political conservatism, but in the 1780s his passion was for the romantic scenery and the past of his country. The past was unconcerned with heavy industry.

So it was that when in 1786 Walter Scott WS, who had numerous clients in the Highlands, decided to send young Walter on an errand to Alexander Stewart of Invernahyle, an old Jacobite who had seen action in the Risings of both 1715 and 1745, and even provided him with a pony for the journey into Argyllshire, excitement was boundless. Writing the introductory chapter to *The Fair Maid of Perth* in 1828, Scott recalled through his narrator Chrystal Croftangry his feelings of 'childish wonder' when he reached the Wicks of Baiglie and saw before him the city and the Highlands beyond:

> *The valley of the Tay, traversed by its ample and lordly stream; the town of Perth with its two large meadows or Inches, its steeples and its towers; the hills of Moncrieff and Kinnoul faintly rising into picturesque rocks, partly clothed with woods; the rich margins of the river studded with elegant mansions; and the distant view of the huge Grampian mountains ... I recollect pulling up the reins without meaning to do so, and gazing on the scene before me as if I had been afraid that it would shift like those in a theatre before I could distinctly observe its different parts, or convince myself that what I saw was real.*

The wild grandeur of the Highland landscape thrilled Scott as he rode further and deeper into the mountains, fording streams and gazing on dizzying heights and tumbling waterfalls. Arriving at Invernahyle, he was entranced by the conversation of the old Jacobite; Alexander Stewart had fought a duel with Rob Roy and enjoyed regaling his admiring young visitor with tales of his exploits at the Battles of Prestonpans and Culloden, where he had been close to the Prince. It was the kind of living history most appealing to the romantic 15 year-old, reinforcing the pro-Jacobite sentiments he had first felt during his infancy at Sandyknowe. This visit and another the following year were the catalyst of the mature Scott's Highland novels, *Waverley*, *Rob Roy* and *The Fair Maid of Perth*. Its influence on his imagination and adult mindset can be discerned in many more.

\*   \*   \*

Sadly, it was not long before young Scott's jovial life was unpleasantly interrupted. It is difficult to be certain exactly when his critical episodes of illness occurred; he admitted himself that he sometimes confused dates. But he did place his most serious breakdown 'about the second year of my apprenticeship', and attributed it to the 'rapid growth' usually associated with adolescence. According to his own account, he suffered a broken blood vessel in his lower bowel, although the real cause of what was patently a serious malady remains a mystery. Suggestions of ulcerative colitis, diverticulitis and polyps have been made, but modern medical opinion suggests that none of these ailments could have been confidently identified using the diagnostic tools available at the time. If blood was apparent in his stools, it is possible that Scott was suffering from piles, but that would not account for the complete collapse he suffered.

Once again, it is hard not to suspect that the treatment made bad much, much worse. The unfortunate patient was put to bed in a room in his parents' house, with the window open to the snell draughts of an Edinburgh spring and with only a single blanket to cover him. He was bled and blistered, he says, 'till I scarcely had a pulse left' and forbidden to eat anything except tiny portions of vegetables and boiled rice. He was not allowed to talk; if he even so much as opened his mouth he was pounced upon by one of the old ladies who kept him company. With his faithful friend John Irving he played chess in silence, but otherwise he had nothing to do but read military history – he mentions the Abbé de Vertot's *Knights of Malta* and Robert Orme's *History of Indostan* – and lay out battle formations on the blanket with shells, pebbles and seeds. Later, 'with the assistance of a friendly carpenter', he contrived to build a model fortress. Poignantly, with a combination of mirrors arranged so that he could see out of the window, he lay in bed watching troops garrisoned in Edinburgh Castle marching out to exercise in the Meadows beyond the house.

By the time Scott rose from his bed he was six feet tall, an unusual height for a man in the eighteenth century. And unsurprisingly, after months of such punishing treatment, he experienced 'a disposition to start up upon slight alarms – a want of decision in feeling and action, which has not usually been my failing – an acute sensibility to trifling inconveniences – and an unnecessary apprehension of contingent misfortunes', for which he blamed his vegetable diet. As usual, he was packed off to Kelso for another protracted convalescence, though not this time to Aunt Jenny at The Garden. Since his last long visit, his uncle, Captain Robert Scott, had retired from the Royal Navy and now owned and occupied the main house named, like the estate, Rosebank. Although Aunt Jenny and her nephew must have met frequently, since he picked up his mail from her house, he was no longer her companion as in the past. Masculine company and pursuits – fishing, hare coursing and shooting – were no doubt considered more suitable for an adolescent boy. Although she lived until 1806, from this time Jenny Scott fades as a presence in her nephew's life. Whether she felt hurt or slighted by the new arrangement is, like so much else about her, impossible to know.

At Rosebank, a strong friendship developed between Scott and his uncle, whose cheerful, relaxed personality made him more fun than the anxious, pernickety Writer to the Signet. Besides an interest in field sports they found literary and antiquarian interests in common, enjoyed discussing their reading and visiting castles together. They paid, Scott wrote to his mother, a nostalgic visit to Smailholm and Sandyknowe. It seems that Captain Scott's original intention had been to make Walter's eldest brother his heir; a namesake often enjoyed such privilege. Robert's choice of a naval career may have been made in the hope that his uncle would promote his interest, and Captain Scott probably paid his nephew's initial expenses.

This impediment to Walter's prospects was, however, unexpectedly removed. The childhood bully had not prospered in the Navy. After the Peace of Paris ended the American Revolutionary War in 1783, promotion had become hard to achieve for officers like Robert who had no grand patrons to speak for them. His haughty spirit also counted against him, and there were rumours that he had quarrelled with his superiors. Probably angry and certainly frustrated, Robert switched from the Royal Navy to the service of the East India Company; he was serving as third mate on the Company's vessel *Rodney* when, on a voyage from Madeira to Bengal in 1787, he died and was buried at sea aged only 23. Whatever the cause of his death – malaria and heavy drinking have been suggested – the blow to his parents, who had already buried six children, must have been a bitter one. Walter, who never had reason to love his brother, presumably felt the loss less keenly. Certainly he can be said to have profited. Robert's death occurred in the same year as his first visit to Rosebank. As the eldest son, John Scott could now expect to be provided for by his father, and Walter was quickly established as his uncle's heir.

Although Walter would spend happy summer holidays at Rosebank in the next few years, his convalescent visit could not be spun out indefinitely. By the autumn of 1788 he was again in residence at 25 George Square, restored in health and obliged, rather than keen, to resume his apprenticeship in his father's office. Sadly, the days of concord between father and son were over; Scott was 17, six feet tall and, in his own eyes at least, a man. Lockhart, following the reminiscence of the Scotts' neighbour, the Countess of Sutherland, describes him gushingly at this period as having 'outgrown the sallowness of early ill health and [having] a fresh, brilliant complexion. His figure, excepting the blemish in one limb, was eminently handsome, tall, much above the usual standard, it was cast in the very mode of a young Hercules ....'

Others differed, and indeed eyewitness descriptions of Scott throughout his life are wildly contradictory. His friend James Hogg, the 'Ettrick Shepherd' (1770–1835), was much in awe of his shaggy eyebrows and elongated lower lip. A later acquaintance, Lady Shelley, wrote unenthusiastically of his 'club foot, white eyelashes and clumsy figure. He has not any expression when his face is in repose' – although she did admit that 'upon an instant some remark will light up his countenance and you will discover a man of genius.' The Lichfield poet Anna Seward opined that neither the face nor the features of 'the proudest boast of the Caledonian muse' were elegant. Scott's admiring correspondent Joanna Baillie (1762–1851), a dramatist popular at the time who had been born in Bothwell and now lived in London, was comically dismayed on meeting him in the flesh: 'I was fresh from *The Lay* [*of the*

*Last Minstrel*],' she lamented, 'and had pictured to myself an ideal elegance and refinement of feature.'

It was Scott's friend, the journalist R. P. Gillies, who provided the explanation: 'Through life he possessed that mutability of countenance which occasioned much discrepancy in the productions of his portrait painters. It was possible that half a dozen pictures might resemble the original and yet be very unlike one another.' This is borne out by even a casual perusal of Scott's many likenesses. What is not in doubt is the good humour and affability of his manner, which made him much loved even by those disappointed by his appearance, and those who found his political opinions unpalatable.

Back in the office, the Writer to the Signet must have been disappointed to find his son less pliant and diligent than of yore. For some months, young Scott continued his apprenticeship, but increasingly his father noted irritably his loss of interest in transcribing documents, his absences without leave, and no doubt his too frequent hangovers in the morning. Perhaps young Walter, weary of the 'dry and barren wilderness of forms and conveyancing', had already decided that a solicitor's life was not for him. Perhaps his equally weary father thought that a further spell of study might settle him and at least give them a break from each other. A decision was taken to combine the apprenticeship, which still had two years to run, with a further period of study. In the winter term of 1789, the young man returned to the University of Edinburgh to attend classes in Civil Law.

# CHAPTER 10

# A Man of Law

*I have all my life delighted in travelling, though I have never enjoyed that pleasure upon a grand scale. It was a propensity which I sometimes indulged so unduly as to alarm and vex my parents.*

~ *Memoirs*, 1837 ~

WHEN WALTER SCOTT returned to the Old College of Edinburgh University after three years' absence, he was a very different being from the one who had fooled around, sulked and refused to learn Greek. The range of his adolescent reading had been wide but chaotic and, on his own admission, self-indulgent. Now he was on the threshold of manhood, and ready to benefit from the discipline of rational thinking and the stimulus of abstract ideas. It was his good fortune to be at the University of Edinburgh between 1789 and 1792, when Enlightenment influences were still strong, and to be taught by three men whose ideas would later inform his greatest work.

Perhaps the most remarkable thing about the professors at Edinburgh at this time was their youth. Two of the men whose classes Scott attended were less than twenty years older than he was, their accolades won by sheer merit. David Hume (1757–1838), nephew and namesake of the great Enlightenment polymath, had become an advocate and, in 1786, Professor of Scots Law. He was the author of *Commentaries on the Law of Scotland: Respecting Crimes*, and his lectures on criminal law so impressed Scott that he made two copies, one for himself and one as a present for his father. Around the same time, he was attending the classes of Dugald Stewart (1753–1828), a phenomenally gifted young man who had been teaching mathematics at the University when he was 19, and was appointed to the Chair of Moral Philosophy when he was only 32. A Whig who sympathised with the aims of the French Revolution, Stewart was unlikely to find a ready acolyte in the already conservative Scott. Nonetheless his lectures in political economy and his work in defining 'theoretical history', a new discipline which speculated on the causes rather than the mere recording of historical events, encouraged his student to define his own position.

A third, slightly older teacher whose ideas influenced Scott's thinking was Alexander Fraser Tytler (1747–1813), a trained advocate and later a judge with the title Lord Woodhouselee. Tytler, the Professor of History who was remembered by Henry Cockburn for his 'elegant and judicious' style, argued that a true democracy was unattainable; equal representation was an impossible ideal because there must always be rulers and ruled. He pointed out that however high their ideals, democracies such as those of Greece and Rome faded, as they grew richer and more powerful, into corruption and moral decline. This pessimistic view was probably congenial to the Scott who later would bitterly oppose electoral reform, and whose romantic attachment to feudalism informed his dream of an ideal community at Abbotsford. Tytler's argument seemed to support his anti-democratic view that feudalism was not really outdated, but an essential condition of progress – which in Scott's mind was social, mercantile and intellectual rather than political. Scott emerged from this period with an idea of 'living history', the life of a nation modified and altered as ideas, habits and manners matured and altered, under the rule of law. As David Daiches summed up in *Scott and his World*, 'changes and their causes: here lay Scott's definition of history in a nutshell'. Unfortunately, Scott was to prove less amenable to change and the causes of change in his own lifetime, when his opposition to progress and reform famously defined his political position.

Back in the world outside the classroom and the Writer to the Signet's office, of course, the convivial Scott did not allow his newly found seriousness to interfere with his social life. Old friends, particularly Adam Ferguson, in whose company he had met Burns, and John Irving, remained part of his circle, but it was a time for making new alliances. No more inclined than he had been five years earlier to extend friendship to the less affluent and influential among his fellow students, Scott chose carefully. George Cranstoun (afterwards Lord Corehouse), Patrick Murray of Simprim, George Abercromby (later Baron Abercromby of Aboukir and Tullibody), John Edmonstone of Newton and William Erskine (afterward Lord Kinneder) were all drawn into Scott's ambit at this time.

Apart from Erskine's, these were not literary friendships. Even after he became famous, Scott remained pleasingly indifferent to the bookish coteries that existed then as now. His intimates were the fellow lawyers with whom he hung out when young, whose country houses he visited and in whose Edinburgh dining rooms he was entertained, as they in his. His closest companion as his legal studies progressed was Will Clerk, younger son of Sir John Clerk of Eldin. It was he who noted with amusement that around the time when Scott began seriously to cultivate upper-class friends, he decided to smarten up. He had his hair cut, and where previously he had dressed badly and carelessly – probably in reaction to his brothers in their smart uniforms – he now began to appear in well-cut coats, tasteful waistcoats, silk stockings and neatly fitting breeches.

The meaning of this transformation was not lost on the clerks in the elder Scott's office, cruelly disabused of the notion that their master's son was 'one of them', but it was the intimacy with Will Clerk that brought their resentment into the open. With unfortunate timing, they chose the occasion of the firm's annual dinner to accuse Scott of discarding them in favour of 'dons like William Clerk'. In Lockhart's version, this provoked Scott into making a hilariously hoity-toity speech which could only confirm their opinion:

> Gentlemen, I will never cut any man unless I detect in him scoundrelism; but I know not what right any of you have to interfere with my choice of company. If anyone thought I had injured him, he would have done well to ask an explanation in a more private manner. As it is, I fairly own, that though I like many of you very much, I think William Clerk is worth all of you put together.

It is not hard to imagine the angry huff pervading the rest of the dinner, or the annoyance of the Writer to the Signet who was picking up the bill. But the incident underlines young Scott's determination to get on and up in the world, and the ruthlessness he could always show when it came to his own interest.

In other ways too, harmony between father and son was becoming ever more strained. Although still nominally an apprentice, Scott now spent little time in the office. When not attending lectures, or meetings of the Speculative Society at which would-be advocates and orators honed their debating skills, he was out in the countryside with his friends, rambling and fishing, drinking at village inns and staying in grand mansions. He was a guest at Tullibody House, seat of the Abercrombys, at Penicuik House, home to Will Clerk's family, and on the estate at Meigle in Angus belonging to the father of Patrick Murray of Simprim. It was all a far cry from the austere terraced house in George Square. The friends made expeditions through the Borders, to the coast of Fife and into the Highlands. Sometimes Scott was away for several days, worrying his mother and exasperating his father, who famously expostulated on one such occasion, 'I doubt, I greatly doubt, sir, you were born for nae better than a gangrel scrape-gut'.

When he was not behaving like a tramp with a fiddle, Scott was acting in a manner commonplace among students but bound to arouse the ire of earnest, puritan Walter Scott WS. Fuel was added to the flames of paternal discontent when young Scott made a friend of whom he disapproved. Charles Kerr of Abbotsrule, four years older and already a qualified Writer to the Signet, had by this time embarked on a career of idleness and debauchery which would eventually lead to the loss of his patrimony and exile in the West Indies. He now became Scott's principal drinking companion, and set out with him on what a pained Lockhart, on the cusp of the Victorian age, described as 'juvenile Bacchanalia ... indulged among the young men of Edinburgh, whether students of the law, solicitors or barristers, to an extent that is now unknown'.

That his father's concern was justified is not in doubt. Kerr was a roaring boy who involved his new friend in street brawls and drunken sprees. The public attitude to drink in the eighteenth century was relaxed. Although Scott had been frequenting taverns since he was a ten year-old telling stories to his companions round 'Lucky Brown's fireside', and his tolerance of alcohol was legendary, at this time his intake was dangerous. Forty years later he noted in his *Journal* that with a friend he could drink three bottles of claret at a sitting. He was having blackouts, and the wonder is that he was fit to go to College at all. Nor was drink the only temptation in an Old Town teeming with brothels as well as public houses. Lockhart, anxious to present his father-in-law as a paragon of virtue (he was married to Scott's daughter, after all), did his prim best to refute any suggestion that Scott regularly used prostitutes. But even he had to admit through clenched teeth that Scott 'in this season of hot and impetuous blood may not have escaped quite blameless'.

Throughout his life, Scott managed to pack an astonishing variety of activity into every day. Now, in the midst of study and revelry, he found time for a new enthusiasm, German literature. The craze for

German Romanticism hit Edinburgh in 1788, when Henry Mackenzie gave a lecture to the Royal Society of Edinburgh on German theatre, and for a while translations from German sold like hot cakes. Never behind the fashion, Scott and his friends hired a German tutor and soon, without much heed for accuracy, were devouring the plays of Schiller and Goethe. Their zeal was given a further boost by the then well-known English poet Anna Laetitia Barbould (1743–1825) who gave in Dugald Stewart's house a reading of Gottfried August Bürger's romantic ballad 'Lenore'. Scott – who was not present but heard it repeated by a friend who was there – was enthralled and managed to track down a copy through the German wife of his cousin Hugh Scott of Harden. The work rekindled his interest in the ballad form, and his own translation of 'Lenore', titled 'William and Helen', was his first printed work. A shared passion for German books was the vital link of Scott's relationship with Will Erskine, a small, gentle, delicate young man who qualified as an advocate in 1790 and was to be Scott's best-loved friend for almost thirty years.

* * *

Around 1790, the Writer to the Signet offered young Walter a partnership in the family firm. In his *Memoirs*, Scott gave his own version:

> It became necessary that I should seriously consider to which department of the law I was to attach myself. My father behaved with most parental kindness. He offered, if I preferred his own profession, immediately to take me into partnership with him, which, though his business was much diminished, still afforded me an immediate prospect of a handsome independence. But he did not disguise his wish that I should relinquish this situation to my younger brother, and embrace the more ambitious prospect of the Bar. I had little hesitation in making my choice – for I was never very fond of money ....

It is worth keeping in mind that the *Memoirs* were written to give the public 'what they [were] entitled to know', for this bland statement fails completely to explain the more complicated reasons behind the father's offer and the son's refusal. In 1790 Walter Scott WS was 61, a greater age in the eighteenth century than it seems today. His health was failing and although business had indeed declined since the good years following the Disannexing Act, there was still enough work to provide a viable career for young Walter. The older Scott was genuinely worried about his son's lifestyle, and may have thought to do them both a good turn; himself by acquiring a trustworthy partner to share the burden of the business, and young Walter by imposing some discipline on his unruly behaviour and giving him an incentive to work. He may also have hoped wistfully to restore the good relationship they had enjoyed in the early days of the apprenticeship. There is no way of knowing whether he really told Walter that he would prefer him to become an advocate and leave the partnership open for Tom, then only 16 and apparently undistinguished, but on balance it seems unlikely. And if Walter was 'never very fond of money', he was very fond of the things money could buy. In turning down the partnership he must have calculated that long-term, a better living could be made elsewhere.

It is likely that long before the partnership was offered, young Scott had made up his mind to aim for a career at the Bar. He had social as well as professional ambitions and knew from observation that as a Writer to the Signet he might be comfortable enough financially, but would never be perceived in society as better than second class. It was not for this that he was choosing his friends so carefully, and keeping an eye on the possibility of patronage. More than any dislike of 'confinement', it was ambition that governed his choice. He refused his father's offer, no doubt causing more disappointment than he admits. Nonetheless Scott WS went on patiently supporting Walter and financing his legal studies until 1792 when, in the company of his friend Will Clerk, he was admitted to the Faculty of Advocates and 'put on the gown' of a member of the Scottish Bar.

For all their frivolity, Scott and Clerk had prepared for this day with great earnestness. They had risen at dawn, meeting at seven o'clock every weekday morning for two years to quiz each other on the texts they had to master for the 'trials' which would decide their fitness to enter the Faculty of Advocates. But when the great day came, and for the first time they appeared in wig and gown, nothing could subdue their high spirits. Clerk remembered standing in the Outer Court after the ceremony, and Scott remarking in a high, falsetto voice, 'we've stood here an hour by the Tron, hinny, and de'il a ane has speered our price'. According to the genteel Lockhart, he was mimicking a Highland servant waiting at the Cross to be hired for harvest work. It is more likely that he had less respectable young women in mind. A kindly solicitor gave Scott a guinea as a fee in advance of his first case. As he and Clerk swaggered down the High Street en route to the tavern, he went into a draper's shop and spent it on a new nightcap. 'This is a sort of wedding-day, Willie,' he remarked obscurely.

\* \* \*

As things turned out, Walter Scott, Advocate, was not a great success at the Bar. A fluent storyteller and brilliant conversationalist, he seems to have lacked the cut-and-thrust debating skills required to make an impression in a court of law. Perhaps a slight speech impediment spoiled his oratory; James Hogg wrote of his 'Northumbrian burr', and gave as an example of his speech a remark to his daughter: 'You are a veghy good gighle, Sophia.' Whatever the reason, despite his father's networking on his behalf, Scott failed to find the easy access to patronage he had hoped for, and had to settle for unrewarding pleadings *in forma pauperis*, on behalf of clients who qualified for what is nowadays called legal aid. It was the memory of this work which inspired the grotesque figure of Poor Peter Peebles, who provided the comic subplot of *Redgauntlet*.

One patron the young advocate did have in a small way. This was the Lord Justice Clerk, Robert MacQueen, Lord Braxfield (1722–99), who was the Scotts' neighbour in George Square. To him the student Scott (it seems on the advice of his father) had dedicated the thesis that was part of his study for the Bar, causing raised eyebrows at the time and attracting opprobrium ever since. Braxfield was a judge notorious for his cruelty, being callous and brutally sarcastic to the prisoners brought before him; his relish in taunting and humiliating the condemned made him distasteful even to those who shared his zeal for severe punishment. Frequently compared with the infamous English 'hanging judge' Jeffreys, Braxfield's legend was still powerful enough, a century after his death, to inspire the bitter, domineering character of the fictional Lord Justice Clerk in Robert Louis Stevenson's last novel, *Weir of Hermiston*. But it is not helpful to see Scott's dedication as an act of solidarity; it was calculated flattery, and produced a meagre reward.

The best Braxfield seemed willing to offer Scott was some work on the provincial circuit. This involved travelling round the countryside in the wake of judges appointed to try crimes too trivial to be heard in the High Court. Most of Scott's employment was in the Borders (where he collected ballads when not in court defending poachers and sheep-stealers), appearances no more rewarding than those he could pick up in the Parliament Hall in Edinburgh. Otherwise, as Will Clerk put it, he 'by and by crept into a tolerable share of such business as may be expected from a writer's connexion' – meaning that he was dependent on his father and his father's colleagues to find him work. Much of this involved writing court papers, and was not at all what the young man had in mind when he decided to assume the advocate's gown.

The case most often cited as proving Scott's unsuitability for his chosen profession took place not in the Court of Session, but before the General Assembly of the Church of Scotland in 1793. He had been engaged in the defence of a delinquent minister, the Rev. Mr McNaught of Girthon in Galloway, who was accused of 'habitual drunkenness, singing of lewd and profane songs, dancing and toying with a sweetie-wife at a penny wedding'. At a fee of five guineas, this was the most remunerative of his commissions so far; it was also farcical, since the client's misdemeanours were much the same as his counsel committed every night of the week. Nonetheless, Scott was anxious to make a good impression, and had prepared a rather ingenious defence based on the different meanings of the Latin word *ebrius*, being occasionally, and *ebriosus*, being habitually drunk. Meanwhile, word of the case had got round and his legal chums, anticipating entertainment, piled into the public gallery of the Assembly hall to 'support' him. Lockhart, not entirely devoid of humour, takes up the tale:

> *He began in a low voice, but by degrees gathered more confidence; and when it became necessary for him to analyse the evidence for the penny wedding, repeated some coarse specimens of his client's alleged conversation in a tone so bold and free that he was called to order with great austerity by one of the leading members of the Venerable Court.*

This unexpected intervention rattled Scott and killed his 'bold and free' delivery on the spot. He became confused, and when he had to read out a verse from one of the minister's lewd songs, panic seized him. Up above, the chums had so far managed so far to choke back laughter, but when Scott 'breathed out [the verse] in a faint and hesitating style', they could contain their glee no longer. To the horror of the assembled ministers and elders, they erupted into thunderous applause, and the hall resounded with shouts of, 'Hear! Hear!' and 'Encore! Encore!'

Immediately the raucous 'supporters' were collared by indignant Presbyterians and manhandled out into the street, leaving the hapless advocate to stumble through the rest of his plea 'not much to his own satisfaction'. Nor indeed to his client's, since Mr McNaught was dismissed from his ministry. When Scott issued from the hall 'in melancholy mood', however, he was met by an unrepentant Adam Ferguson and dragged off to a nearby tavern, where the rogues in the gallery had reassembled. Scott's dejection lasted until he had a few drinks, after which the evening passed as usual in laughter and 'high jinks' of the kind that had cost the reprobate Mr McNaught his living.

Scott's earnings tell his story. In his first year as an advocate he earned 23 guineas. In his second, this had risen to 55 guineas, and in the third year to 84 guineas. A guinea was worth £1.05, and even allowing for the vast inflation of three centuries – in the region of 70% – these figures were unspectacular. Scott remained almost as dependent as ever on his father's increasingly reluctant bounty, which was not a state of affairs to be long tolerable to either of them. As his hope of cutting a dash at the Bar crumbled, Scott was forced to think again. By the end of his third year of advocacy, he seems to have concluded that the best way forward professionally lay in acquiring one of the salaried positions available to clever young men within the legal system. The snag was that these posts were in the gift of powerful, well-connected men; it would take time to find patrons more influential than any who had shown interest in him to date. Meanwhile, there was an alternative, or complementary road to financial independence, and by 1795 Scott had embarked enthusiastically upon it.

## CHAPTER 11

# First Loves

*Scarce one man in twenty marries his first love, and scarce one out of twenty of the remainder has cause to rejoice in having done so. What we love in those early days is generally a fanciful creation of our own, rather than a reality. We build statues of snow, and weep when they melt.*

~ Letter to G. H. Gordon, 1820 ~

THE LOVE LIFE of Sir Walter Scott is often presented as two radically contrasting episodes. First came the passionate wooing of a beautiful teenage heiress whose rejection of his love left 'a crack in my heart that will remain till my dying day'. Then, on the rebound, came marriage to a 'smart-looking little girl with dark brown hair' with whom he lived in lukewarm contentment for nearly thirty years. In fact Scott, whose flirtatiousness at parties in the early 1790s earned him the teasing soubriquet 'the squire of dames', had probably been quite seriously smitten at least once before then.

The evidence for Scott's earliest prolonged love affair is sparse, relying chiefly on passages of an unpublished biography which found its way into the manuscript collection of the Victoria and Albert Museum in London. The provokingly anonymous author claims to have the permission of the lady concerned to include four letters from Scott which she had kept and allegedly allowed him (or her) to copy. It has been suggested, in the absence of the originals, that these are forgeries, but they convinced Sir Herbert Grierson, who published them as authentic in *Letters of Sir Walter Scott 1788–1807* (1932). The subject was also mentioned by George Allan, an early and unauthorised biographer of Scott in 1834. But Lockhart was silent, and no amount of academic sleuthing over almost two centuries has revealed more than the girl's forename, 'Jessie'. Still the story has persisted, the four letters fleshed out like many tales of Scott in the telling, yet plausible enough despite its sketchy source material.

The letters reveal that around 1787–88, while convalescing at his uncle's house in Kelso, the 17-year-old Scott met and fell in love with the daughter of a local shopkeeper. 'I cannot sufficiently express the impression which your lovely features have made in my heart ... your gentleness, your goodness, your kindness have filled me with the sweetest feelings I have ever known,' he gushed. A common interest in poetry is suggested as the reason for their intimacy. Scott sent Jessie ballads and poems of his own, and was delighted with her warm response. They moaned about their awful parents, and Scott assured Jessie that he had burned her notes to him 'from fear that they might be discovered by some curious person and the course of our true love made to run less smooth even than it does at present'. This is standard adolescent stuff. Jessie was probably no more than 15 when she first encountered Scott – 'old enough', as John Sutherland tartly remarks, 'to lose her virginity, but still under the age of consent'. Certainly it is hard to believe that poetry was the sole attraction in a teenage affair said to have lasted, on and off, for four years.

Whatever the basis of the relationship, however, from Scott's point of view it must have been a dalliance. He asked Jessie to burn his letters and his fear of discovery, either by his family or hers, was real. He was too young to think seriously of marriage, and even in 1787 had social ambitions that could not be assisted by an alliance with a shopkeeper's daughter. Jessie was more vulnerable; aware that Walter Scott was likely to become a Writer to the Signet and heir to Rosebank, she no doubt dreamed of 'upward mobility'. The relationship is thought to have floundered when Jessie moved to Edinburgh to look after a sick aunt. Clearly she did not fit into Scott's upper-class circle, and by then he had another, more elevated romance to pursue. According to Edgar Johnson, the most exhaustive but also most gossipy of Scott's biographers, Jessie's aunt died, leaving her a small property. Rebuffed by her lover, she married a medical student, went off to London and harboured 'a resentment that never subsided' against Walter Scott.

\* \* \*

Meanwhile, away from Kelso for most of the year, it seems that Scott had been two-timing Jessie. As early as 1790, Will Clerk remembered, he had fallen seriously in love with someone else. Although again there is a dearth of personal correspondence, this second relationship is better documented than the first and matters more to Scott's development, both as a man and a writer. The object of his passion was Williamina Belsches (1776–1810), the only child of Lady Jane Leslie, daughter of the Earl of Leven and Melville and John Belsches, an advocate, land-owner and member of Parliament. In 1797 Belsches inherited the barony of Stuart of Castlemilk and, already established on an estate in Kincardineshire, changed his name to Sir John Stuart of Fettercairn. Without mentioning Williamina by name, Lockhart writes coyly of her first meeting with Walter Scott:

> *I have been told that their acquaintance began in Greyfriars church-yard, when rain beginning to fall one Sunday as the congregation was dispersing, Scott happened to offer his umbrella, and the tender being accepted, so escorted her to her residence, which proved to be at no great distance from his own.*

Tradition has it that Williamina was wearing a green cloak on this occasion, hence her association with the mysterious 'Lady Green Mantle' beloved of the two young heroes in *Redgauntlet*. Lockhart dates the churchyard encounter as 1790, guided by Will Clerk, who confirmed Scott's early passion in a letter written to Sophia Lockhart in 1835. If this is correct, Williamina was no more than 14, which would explain why, despite escorting her home regularly on Sundays and making himself agreeable to her parents, it was not until 1795 that Scott began to court her seriously.

By this time, life in the house in George Square was becoming well-nigh intolerable to Scott. Although he had his own 'parlour', furnished with books and the antiquarian bric-a-brac on which he spent most of his money, he was still obliged to eat *en famille* with his parents, younger brothers Tom and Daniel, and sister Anne – a sad, shadowy figure with a history of illness and terrible accidents, who lived on the fringes of her brothers' lives and was doomed to wait hand and foot on her increasingly irascible father. Walter Scott WS must have realised that in Tom he had acquired more of a liability than a partner, and blamed Walter for his disappointment. As his strength failed, he became ever more critical of young Walter's drinking and stravaiging round the country with wild companions – habits to which he bitterly ascribed his son's failure to shine at the Bar.

For his part, the gloom of family dinners and the unrelenting rituals of the Sabbath were becoming ever more painful to Scott, assailed now by doubts about his own professional skills. The patronage he coveted had so far eluded him, and in his mid-twenties it was not unnatural to turn his mind to the possibility of marriage. That he was attractive to women was obvious; the 'squire of dames' was an assiduous attender of the soirées and balls which were an important feature of upper and upper-middle-class Edinburgh social life, and always managed to attract an admiring circle despite his inability to dance. Scott was too much a romantic to marry without affection, but, in an age when the property of the bride automatically became that of the husband, the endowment of a future wife mattered to him.

Williamina Belsches was an obvious first choice. He had long been in love with her; as early as 1792 he described her to Will Clerk as '*ma chère adorable*', and the following year, in passionate mood, he cut her name into the turf at the Castle gate in St Andrews. By 1794, when she was 18 and beginning to attend the same social events as Scott, she did not discourage his attentions. Besides, although there was considerable social disparity between them – Williamina was the daughter of a baronet, an earl's granddaughter and heiress to a fortune – Scott felt secure in his status as a gentleman. It seems not to have occurred to him that Williamina's parents might have a more ambitious plan for their only daughter than marriage to an impecunious lawyer.

In the summer of 1795, egged on by Will Clerk, Scott decided to propose. Neither his letter nor Williamina's reply survived, but Scott must have sent the reply to Will Clerk, and a further letter to Clerk dated 25 August, shows his belief that his proposal had been accepted:

*It gave me the highest satisfaction to find, by the receipt of your letter of the 14th current, that you have formed precisely the same opinion with me, both with regard to the interpretation of* [Miss Belsches's] *letter as highly flattering and favourable, and to the mode of conduct I ought to pursue for, after all, what she has pointed out is the most prudent line of conduct for us both, at least till better days, which I think myself now entitled to suppose, she, as well as myself will look forward to with pleasure. If you were surprised at reading the important billet, you may suppose how agreeably I was on receiving it; for I had, to anticipate disappointment, – struggled to suppress every gleam of hope, and it would be very difficult to describe the mixed feelings her letter occasioned, which,* entre nous, *terminated in a very hearty fit of crying.*

Since that 'prudent line of conduct' recommended by Williamina presumably meant keeping their relationship secret from their parents, her unwillingness to commit openly seems, with hindsight, ominous. So does the fact that for months afterwards Scott neither saw nor heard from her. By the turn of the year he was becoming despondent and irritable, but his hopes were raised again in the spring of 1796. After a visit to Aberdeen to attend the Circuit Court he was, after some apparent hesitation on the part of Williamina's parents, invited to stay with the family at Fettercairn. The visit seemed to go well – Scott was even invited to stay on for an extra couple of days. He returned to Edinburgh in high spirits and with no inkling of the thunderbolt shortly to fall. In fact, the Belsches family had deceived Scott. Between his proposal and his visit, Williamina had met William Forbes of Pitsligo (1773–1828), member of a rich Edinburgh banking family and heir to a baronetcy. In the summer Forbes succeeded Scott as house guest at Fettercairn, and on 12 October his engagement to Williamina was announced.

Now Scott's stoic reserve deserted him. His reaction to the news was so explosive that close friends feared for his reason. 'I shudder for the violence of his ungovernable mind,' wrote one to another. Consumed with chagrin, yet gallantly unwilling to find Williamina at fault, Scott – to some degree correctly, as it turned out – blamed her mother for his discomfiture. Fortunately only much later did he discover that Walter Scott WS had visited Williamina's father to warn him that an unsuitable relationship was developing between his heiress daughter and the unsuccessful advocate who was his own son. Scott poured bitter scorn on Forbes, referring to him absurdly as 'dot and carry one', meaning a mere ledger-bound office clerk. Stridently he insisted that the marriage could only be one of convenience, entered into for yet more money and the prospect of a title. The idea that Williamina might really love William Forbes was too much for Scott to bear.

\* \* \*

It is impossible, after more than two centuries, to understand what it was about Williamina that inspired such violent passion in Scott. A preliminary sketch for a portrait shows a conventionally fair-skinned, brown-haired young woman with hazel eyes, a straight nose, small mouth and round chin. In the finished work, 'Williamina Belsches, Lady Forbes' by the society miniaturist Richard Cosway, she appears older, her coiffure more elaborate and her features and dress more emphatically drawn. We know that in her youth she was taught by James Mill, the utilitarian philosopher and father of John Stuart Mill, that he praised her intelligence and was probably also in love with her. We do not know what she and Scott talked about privately or whether, after the umbrella-sharing days, she really encouraged him to believe that his love was reciprocated. Perhaps all the time she was amusing herself by teasing the poetic young man, and clearly he and Will Clerk were over-optimistic in their reading of her reply to his proposal. All that is really known of Williamina is that she married William, later Sir William Forbes in January 1797, gave birth to six children and died of tuberculosis, outlived by both her parents, at the age of 32. There is evidence that she had a happy marriage, but historically she only matters because she figured so dramatically in the life of Walter Scott.

Despite romantic claims that she was the model of every heroine he ever created, it is not clear either how much of Scott's love for Williamina was transmuted into his writing. He was abetted in his wooing by Jane Cranstoun, sister of his friend George, and it was at her suggestion that, when his mania for German literature was at its height, he translated two ballads by Gottfried Bürger as 'The Chase' and 'William and Helen' and had them printed primarily so that he could send a copy to Williamina. It may thus be said that she was the inspiration for his first published work, though what a genteel young woman would have made of such ghoulish, death-laden verses is hard to imagine. In 1797, in the bitterness of disappointment, he wrote 'The Violet', twelve simple lines that anticipate the beautiful lyrics embedded in his novels; and in the narrative poem *Rokeby*, Scott himself remarked, the character of Matilda was infused with his memory of Williamina. It also seems likely that in *Redgauntlet*, written a quarter of a century later, the figure of 'Green Mantle' owes something to the author's long-dead but unforgotten love.

Whether Williamina's memory inspired other characters is harder to know. It is misleading to suppose that a character in a novel is a 'picture' of someone the writer has plucked either from history or his or her acquaintance. It is more probably a fusion of physical and mental characteristics drawn from different people and formed into a new being; the greatest writers are those who can inhabit the minds of their creations as well as describe their outer selves. Intriguingly Scott, despite his social background, achieved this greatness most often in his humble characters who live on the rough margins of history, but stay for ever in the reader's mind.

Edwin Muir, whose poor opinion of Scott's 'inner life' has already been noted, believed that his thwarted passion for Williamina stunted his development as a writer; Muir (1936) attempted to explain Scott's perceived failure to write convincingly about upper-class romantic relationships by suggesting that 'his resolute burial of Williamina probably crippled his imagination on one side and made him incapable of portraying love in his novels .... It may be that he could not afford to resurrect her, or perhaps the ghost of his father forbade him.' This is ingenious, but dubious. Scott's immersion in high-flown chivalric literature had long since formed his ideas of how noble heroes and heroines ought to behave.

Scott was 27 when William Forbes married Williamina, and during the next three decades he would keep her memory green, writing her into his life story by dropping hints in letters and journal entries that his heart had never recovered from her loss. Yet the less dramatic truth may be read in a few lines from *Peveril of the Peak*, written when he was over fifty:

> *There are few men who do not look back in secret to some period of their youth, at which a sincere and early affection was repulsed, or betrayed, or became abortive from opposing circumstances. It is these little passages of secret history which leave a tinge of romance in every bosom.*

# CHAPTER 12

# The Lieutenant of Horse

*After the war broke out again in 1803, Edinburgh, like every other place, became a camp, and continued so till the peace of 1814. We were all soldiers, one way or other. Professors wheeled in the college area; the side arms and the uniform peeped from behind the gown at the Bar, and even on the Bench; and the parade and the review formed the staple of men's talk and thoughts.*

~ Henry Cockburn, *Memorials of his Time*, 1856 ~

HIS FRIENDS' ANXIETY about Scott's mental state after his jilting by Williamina proved misplaced. Some natural sour grapes digested, his long-practised stoicism led him to control his 'ungovernable and irritable' feelings and move on. And paradoxically, the time of his great disappointment also saw the fulfilment of a lifelong dream.

It is sometimes hard, when reading of the legal careers and jolly social life of Walter Scott and his friends in the 1790s, to remember that they were living through a period of social turmoil and subsequently war. In fact, the years following the cataclysmic 1789 revolution in France had been nervy, not only in Edinburgh, but throughout Britain. Underlying tension was periodically ratcheted up not only by fear of invasion by the French, but also by an alarming rise in subversiveness among previously quiescent working men. Emboldened by events in France, groups were formed where the inflammatory *The Rights of Man* by Thomas Paine (1737–1809) and the delinquency of the ruling class were openly discussed. As the victory of the French populace deteriorated rapidly into terror and regicide, the reaction of the ruling class in Britain turned from disapproval to panic, while intellectuals who had initially sympathised withdrew their approval in horror. Scott's friend

William Wordsworth, who had said of Paris in 1789 that there it was bliss to be alive, 'but to be young was very heaven', hastily changed his mind and became a fervent reactionary. In 1790 Scott had thought it cool to belong to a group of friends who adopted the French ultra-revolutionary nickname 'Montagnards' or 'Mountain Men'. Three years later, when the French guillotined their king and declared war on Britain, he could not scramble away fast enough. It was in the light of these bloodthirsty and alarming events that the sentimental Jacobitism of Scott's adolescence turned to a more hardline conservatism, which he demonstrated on more than one occasion.

Edinburgh's response to the national crisis of 1793 was to form a military volunteer force, partly to deal with possible civil disorder, and partly to defend the city in the event of a French invasion. Scott, with his high-flown notions of martial glory, was wild with excitement, and at once wrote to his uncle Robert, asking him for a strong horse and offering to sell his coin collection to pay for it. His disappointment when his services were refused on account of his lameness was crushing and his response, according to an unnamed member of his family who confided in Robert Chambers, extreme:

> He left the room in an agony of mortified feeling, and was found some time afterwards suspended by the wrists from his bedroom window. On being asked the cause of this strange proceeding, he said he wished to prove that, however unfitted by his lower limbs for the profession of a soldier, he was at least strong enough in the arms. He had actually remained in that uneasy and trying posture for upwards of an hour.

It would be difficult not to pity the young man, or to imagine the distress of the parents who had tried so hard to find a cure that would save him from such a humiliation. Although the remarks of Henry Cockburn about Edinburgh as a camp belong to a later phase of the war, they might equally describe the atmosphere in 1793. Scott had to endure the sight of his brothers John, Tom and Daniel in uniform, listen to the sound of trumpets, drums and marching feet, and feel left out while everyone else dressed up and enjoyed the thrill of playing soldiers. It was probably to prove that despite his rejection he was capable of tough, patriotic action that he took part in an incident more wisely avoided.

Scott and his friends were all ardent theatre-goers. So were a party of Irish medical students who had for some time, according to Lockhart, been disrupting performances by 'calling for revolutionary tunes, applauding every speech that could bear a seditious meaning, and drowning the national anthem in howls and hootings'. There had been minor skirmishes with indignant young loyalists of the legal profession, but one night in April 1794 resentment boiled over into a real disturbance. Scott and his chums had somehow got wind of the Irishmen's intention to provoke a confrontation, and after a hasty conference they turned up at the theatre armed with cudgels. A fracas ensued, and Scott later boasted that he had broken three Irish heads before being arrested by the Town Guard. Worse still, he was detained in a cell overnight and next morning bound over before a magistrate to keep the peace. What the Writer to the Signet had to say about this escapade is not recorded, and it was left to Scott's uncle Robert to point out sternly that a criminal record, however trivial, would not do his reputation as an advocate any good.

Later in the same year, events in Edinburgh took a dramatic turn. For some time a workers' club, a branch affiliated to the 'Society of the Friends of the People', had been meeting in the Grassmarket to talk of revolution. As long as they stuck to words, the authorities had turned a blind eye, but when a cache of weapons was found in the house of one of their ringleaders, a firebrand named Robert Watt, panic ran through the town. Rumours flew of plans to seize the Castle and the banks and, horror of horrors, to arrest and imprison the judges. Unsurprisingly, the judges came off unscathed; Watt and his chief associate David Downie were arrested and, after a trial of sickening ferocity before Lord Braxfield, Downie was sentenced to transportation to Australia and Watt to be hanged at the Tolbooth. After the execution, Watt's head was cut off and held aloft to the vengeful crowd, among whom was Walter Scott.

'It was a very solemn scene,' he wrote to his aunt Christian Rutherford, 'but the pusillanimity of the unfortunate victim was astonishing considering the boldness of his nefarious plans.' He went on to express regret that Downie had not been hanged as well, and to denounce the affair as 'the most atrocious and deliberate plan of villainy which has occurred perhaps in the annals of G. Britain'. This reaction to a pathetic and squalid conspiracy is absurdly over the top, but the trial and execution of Watt (which was not the only one during these jittery years) fuelled Scott's growing illiberalism. All his life he would freak out at the whisper of a public uprising.

* * *

Between 1794 and 1797, against a background of growling urban unrest, occasional riots over the scarcity and price of bread and low-key fear of invasion, Scott was busy wooing and losing Williamina. But although the early enthusiasm for volunteering waned somewhat in the city, he did not abandon his dream of being a soldier. Opportunity at last presented itself in 1796, when there was a serious invasion scare, inflamed by a French attempt to gain a foothold in Ireland. This was too close for comfort and voluntary service again becoming fashionable, Scott was determined that this time he was not going to be left out. During the past few years he had discovered that although he could not march, he was a more than competent rider, and when the formation of a cavalry force to defend the city was proposed he managed to convince those in authority of his ability to serve. A suitable horse was bought and named Lenore. Scott's indulgent uncle paid for his uniform, and in April 1797 the King gave his consent to the formation of the Edinburgh Volunteer Light Dragoons.

Scott was appointed quartermaster and, his training in his father's office proving useful at last, secretary and paymaster of a troop of a hundred men. Excitedly he penned a fairly awful 'War Song':

> To horse! to horse! The standard flies,
> The bugle sounds the call;
> The Gallic navy stems the seas,
> The voice of battle's on the breeze,
> Arouse ye, one and all!

He was nicknamed 'Earl Walter' and hugely entertained, by his military bearing and devotion to protocol, his more laid-back companions in the officers' mess. Up at the crack of dawn to don his colourful uniform and drill on Portobello sands, thundering about on horseback, practising sabre thrusts by aiming at turnips stuck on poles, barking out orders and singing flamboyant songs at company dinners, Lieutenant Scott was in his element. His translations of German ballads at this time are full of galloping rhythms and frantic rides:

> And hurry! hurry! off they rode,
> As fast as fast might be;
> Spurn'd from the courser's thundering heels
> The flashing pebbles flee.

For the first time in his life, he felt equal to everyone else.

\* \* \*

It was not all about patriotism and martial fever, of course. Scott had always sought and enjoyed the company of aristocratic folk; it was the characteristic singled out by the less gentlemanly James Hogg as both incomprehensible and laughable, and he was probably not alone. Among the dragoons with whom Scott was now rubbing shoulders were the young Earl of Dalkeith, heir to the Duke of Buccleuch, and his old classmate Robert Dundas, son of Henry Dundas, Lord Melville. Through soldierly comradeship with their sons, he was for the first time within reach of the two most powerful patrons in Scotland – connections which, he wrote quite openly, he would use to his advantage. Intriguingly, another of Scott's fellow volunteers was William Forbes, so recently fulminated against as 'dot and carry one', the rival in whose favour Williamina Belsches had rejected him.

In the circumstances, coolness at least might have been expected between the two young men, but there is no evidence that their relationship was anything but relaxed and cordial. And although Scott gives the impression of a dramatic parting of the ways, it is not possible that he and Williamina never again met after her marriage. William Forbes and his new wife set up house at 39 George Street in the New Town of Edinburgh. Within a year, Scott had moved into number 50, just across the road. They could not avoid running into one another on the pavement, at the theatre, suppers and balls. If there was embarrassment, it must have been heroically covered up, and when Sir William Forbes died in 1828 Scott paid tribute to him in a letter to a mutual friend: 'In the whole course of life our friendship has been uninterrupted, as his kindness has been unwearied.' By then, of course, the story of Scott's lost love was thirty years old, told through his letters and the memorials of his friends as he wanted it to be. The passion itself had dwindled into wistful remembrance.

\* \* \*

Scott's fixation on the idea of glorious warfare can become wearisome to modern people sated with the blood-stained narrative of the twentieth century, and contemporary conflicts which show no sign of abating soon. But at the turn of the nineteenth century, Scott the soldier was only acting out his own fantasies of knights jousting, flags flying, battles in which the noble and virtuous always won. He had never experienced at first hand the heat of battle and the carnage inflicted by steel on human flesh.

Scott's love affair with the colour, pomp and panoply of war continued unchecked until 1815, when the war which had dragged on through most of his adult life ended with the crushing defeat of Napoleon and his French army on the field of Waterloo. Scott, who at 44 had never travelled further than London and Bath, was avid to see the battlefield where his countrymen and their allies had fought and died. The battle was fought on 18 June, and by 27 July Scott was on his way to Belgium. He had written poetic accounts of war, and in recently published *Waverley* had given a lively account of the Battle of Prestonpans. But nothing prepared him for the impact of the field at Waterloo, the bloodied weapons, bullet-shot standards, inadequately covered graves and dead horses putrefying in the summer sun. Aware of the incongruity of his position as a tourist, a genuinely shocked Scott picked his way among them, shuddering at the sight of corpses exhibiting 'heads cloven to the chine [backbone], severed from the shoulders'.

Being Scott, he naturally did not leave Brussels without acquiring a few souvenirs for his collection at home, including three standards and a piece of wood, later made into a quaich, from the tree beneath which the Duke of Wellington had directed his troops. His account of his tour, published as *Paul's Letters to his Kinsfolk*, tends to grate in its glorification of the British and its denigration of allies and enemy alike, but that Scott was shaken by what he had witnessed is not in doubt. What happened next, however, is not without a tincture of farce.

Making the most of his first visit abroad, Scott moved on from Brussels to Paris, where post-war euphoria among the victors was in full swing. Parades and banquets, music and dancing occupied the glitterati of Europe. Scott, by then a famous author, was taken under the wing of the Earl of Cathcart, a former British ambassador in St Petersburg. He was introduced to Wellington, and invited to dinner with Czar Alexander I of Russia, an awesome ruler who had led his army bravely in many battles. Presumably to be prepared for any sartorial eventuality, Scott had packed a splendid red and blue dress uniform and so attired he sallied forth to meet the Czar. The conversation was in French, which Scott spoke with little variation of his native accent; the Czar, who had probably never heard of him, made the customary polite royal remarks. Lockhart recounts the incident:

> *The Czar's first question, glancing at his lameness, was 'In what affair were you wounded?' Scott signified that he suffered from a natural*

*infirmity; upon which the Emperor said, 'I thought Lord Cathcart mentioned that you had served.' Scott observed that the Earl looked a little embarrassed at this, and promptly answered, 'Oh yes; in a certain sense I have served – that is, in the yeoman cavalry; a home force resembling the Landwehr of Landsturm.' – 'Under what commander?' – 'Sous M. le Chevalier Rae.' – 'Were you ever engaged?' – 'In some slight actions – such as the Battle of the Cross Causeway and the affair of Moredun Mill.'*

Scott was skating on thin ice. Jesting with emperors was not diplomatic and Lord Cathcart hastily intervened. Yet the joke must have covered awkwardness in Scott, as he stood uniformed in the presence of so many renowned and battle-hardened soldiers. Cross Causeway was where he had bickered with 'Green Breeks' and his cohort as a child. The 'affair of Moredun Mill' was an even nastier encounter, but one more to Scott's credit. On one of the few occasions when the Light Dragoons were actually called into action, it had been to control an angry crowd of starving men who had broken into a mill in search of meal to feed their families. Nearly killed by a well-aimed brick that startled his horse, Scott had lost his temper, drawn his sword, and was spurring forward to cut down his attacker when he saw the man's thin, terrified face and heard him scream, 'Upon my soul, I did not mean it for you'. With a stab of compassion, Scott held his hand, giving the man no more than a light stroke with the flat of his sword. 'Truth to say,' he confessed later, 'it was a dreadful feeling to use violence against a people in real and absolute want of food.'

Scott's belief in soldiering as a noble profession was not snuffed out by his experience at Waterloo. Warriors go striding and riding through novels he was yet to write – *Old Mortality, Woodstock, Ivanhoe, The Legend of Montrose* – and despite disclaimers, he was as pleased as punch when his elder son, also Walter, became a professional soldier. Scott never lacked personal courage either, whether he was getting a bloody nose at the High School, breaking Irish heads at the theatre or facing the agonies of his old age. But the wasteland of Waterloo forced him to acknowledge the terrible price of war, as his failure to strike at Moredun Mill had raised questions about his capacity to kill. For all his songs of death and glory, it was really the role-playing of the Edinburgh Light Dragoons that Scott loved, the fellowship, snazzy uniforms, weapons, bugles, pipes and drums.

# CHAPTER 13

# Charlotte

*O, young Lochinvar is come out of the west,*
*Through all the wide border his steed was the best;*
*And save his good broadsword, he weapons had none,*
*He rode all unarm'd, and he rode all alone.*
*So faithful in love, and so dauntless in war,*
*There never was knight like the young Lochinvar.*

~ 'Lady Heron's Song', *Marmion*, 1808 ~

ALTHOUGH HIS LEGAL work and military duties gave him excuses for shunning their company, at the age of 27 Walter Scott was still living at home with his parents. With Williamina and her fortune lost and a salaried post still proving elusive, his need for funds to facilitate his escape was as pressing as ever. It was probably mainly to get a break from stress at home that, when the Court of Session rose for the summer recess in July 1797, he joined his brother John and friend Adam Ferguson on a riding holiday into the English Lake District. But when, at the spa resort of Gilsland in Cumbria, he met a dark-haired, dark-eyed young woman with lively manners and a charming French accent, Scott was ready to charm in return. Wearing his Light Dragoons uniform, which he had packed in case he was called back suddenly to duty but was not averse to wearing to impress, he ceremoniously handed her in to dinner, where they charmed mutually with strange accents and found out quite a lot about each other's lives. The lady had the more dramatic story to tell, and Scott was intrigued to discover that her attractions were financial as well as physical. Margaret Charlotte Carpenter, or Marguerite Charpentier as she had been born, was a year older than Scott, not as young as most brides at the time, but she was attractive and fashionable and, to Scott's delight, gratifyingly well-connected. There was also some mystery about her.

Lockhart, the ever dutiful son-in-law, draws a family-friendly picture of Charlotte's background. In this version she was the daughter of Jean-François Charpentier, director of the Royal Military Academy in Lyons, who had married a Protestant wife and was a friend of Viscount Fairford, heir of the Marquess of Downshire. Fearful of revolution in France, Charpentier prudently decided to invest £4000 in English securities, partly in a mortgage on one of Lord Downshire's estates, then promptly died just as the Revolution was kicking off in 1789. His widow, left alone with her two children Charlotte and Jean-David, fled to Paris and then to England. There 'they found a warm friend and protector in Arthur, the second Marquess of Downshire who, in the course of his travels, had formed an intimate acquaintance with the family, and indeed, spent some time under their roof'.

Soon after her arrival in England, Madame Charpentier also died, and Lord Fairford (who did not actually inherit his father's title until 1793) became guardian of the two 'children', by then in their late teens. Jean-David Charpentier, his French name diplomatically anglicised as Charles Carpenter, was despatched to service in the East India Company where, through Lord Fairford's lobbying on his behalf, he rose quite rapidly to 'the lucrative position of commercial resident in Salem'. Charlotte, who had been brought up as a Protestant, was placed in the care of a Miss Jane Nicholson who, Lockhart was at pains to point out, was a daughter of the Dean of Exeter and granddaughter of the Bishop of Carlisle. On her visit to Gilsland, Charlotte was accompanied by Miss Nicholson and also by an Anglican clergyman, the Rev. John Bird, and his wife.

So far, so respectable, but other versions of the story soon began to circulate. An impudent Edinburgh acquaintance of the Scotts also happened to be a friend of Mrs Bird, to whom she wrote to inquire, 'what sort of a young lady was it who was going to take Watty Scott?' – proving that in his home town the 'busy whisper' was already going round, its uncharitable nature assured. In his serial biography published in *Chambers's Edinburgh Journal* when Scott was barely cold in his grave, Robert Chambers was drawing on gossip already thirty years old when he stated that Fairford had repaid Charpentier's hospitality by eloping with his wife, thus casting a doubt on Charlotte's paternity which has never been dissipated. Chambers went on to claim that Charlotte had been educated in a convent, contradicting the claim that she had been brought up Protestant, and further damaged Lord Downshire's posthumous reputation by suggesting that Charles Carpenter's promotion in India had been dependent on his promise to remit £200 annually for the support of his sister. Lockhart, already at work on his sanitised version, must have been furious.

Scott stayed at Gilsland for three weeks, appearing in his uniform to dine with Charlotte and accompany her on rides into the countryside. On an excursion to Hadrian's Wall, he was moved to write a poem, titled 'To a Lady, with Flowers from a Roman Wall', which neatly manages to combine a romantic gesture with his other infatuation:

> Take these flowers which, purple waving,
>   On the ruin'd rampart grew,
> Where, the sons of freedom braving,
>   Rome's imperial standards flew.
>
> Warriors from the reach of danger
>   Pluck no longer laurels there,
> They but yield the passing stranger
>   Wild flower wreaths for Beauty's hair.

By the time Scott left to return to Edinburgh, he and Charlotte were informally engaged. There was much still to do; Lord Downshire's consent must be obtained and his parents' blessing (and hopefully financial contribution) sought. Although Scott's letters to Charlotte struck the right note of fervour, money matters were never far from his mind. Some sacrifices to household economy were of course not to be thought of:

> I do not like to leave the Cavalry tho' attended with some expence [sic] because my situation gives me access to the Duke of Buccleuch & several other persons who may be useful to me – besides all my dress and accoutrements have been long bought so that the chief Expence is already incurr'd – add to all this, the Service is a little stylish which I don't think you will dislike it for.

Scott had read his fiancée well. In the end, the Marquess proved amenable, the Writer to the Signet less so. The careful emphasis on Charlotte's Anglican connections failed to impress the old Presbyterian, nor did her undeniable Frenchness at a time when Britain and France were at war. Diminished by a number of strokes and probably regarding

Walter's love affair as another example of his fecklessness, he pleaded poverty and the need to provide for John's career in the army. It seems he finally agreed to give Walter a paltry allowance, but still Scott could not count on enough 'to hold', as he wrote to his mother, 'the rank in Society which my family and situation entitle me to fulfil'. At one point, caught between his father's girning and Charlotte's peevishness over intrusive questions about her background, he threatened to leave Edinburgh for the West Indies. When he urged Charlotte to 'think how much happier you will find yourself surrounded by friends who will love you, than by those who will only ever regard my beloved Charlotte while she possesses the power of interesting and entertaining them', it is hard to know which of them he was trying to convince.

In the end, it was Charles Carpenter who settled the matter, by increasing Charlotte's allowance to £500 a year. This sum, combined with Scott's earnings from the Bar and expectation of a legal appointment as Sheriff of Selkirkshire – a reward at last for his tireless social networking – would finally enable him to marry. On 21 December 1797 Scott wrote to his friend Patrick Murray of Simprim from Carlisle, announcing his imminent nuptials. Well aware of the interest his private affairs had provoked in his native city, he added only half-facetiously:

> As the public curiosity has been so much excited about Miss Carpenter, it may be proper to say that this fortunate young lady is, in the opinion of the whole world, the delight of the male sex, and the envy of her own.

Walter Scott married the fortunate Miss Carpenter in St Mary's Church, Carlisle on Christmas Eve. Neither Lord Downshire nor any member of Scott's family attended. On the evening of their wedding day, the couple returned to Edinburgh, first to 50 George Street, then a year later to another rented house at 10 South Castle Street. In 1801, they moved again to 39 North Castle Street, which would be their home until 1826.

Charlotte was, in the early years, a good kind of wife for a young lawyer with a reputation to make. Scott found occasion to chide her for extravagance, but she loved entertaining his friends and colleagues, who found her French speech and spritely manner amusing, and she shared her husband's enthusiasm for the theatre. They dined in the houses of Scott's friends and their wives, but one has no impression that Charlotte made any close women friends of her own. Nor was she, as Scott had hoped, 'surrounded by loving friends' in the sense of 'friends' meaning 'family'. Walter Scott WS had opposed the marriage, and although Anne Scott exchanged pleasantries with her daughter-in-law there is no suggestion that they became close. Scott is reported as saying that Charlotte 'would bring him bairns and not interfere with his work, and that was all he cared for'.

This was a fairly bleak assessment of the wifely role, but one for which Charlotte had to settle. She had four children with Scott who treated her with respect and wrote her affectionate letters over the years, but she was incapable of sharing his intellectual life and there was none of the wild passion he professed for Williamina. Charlotte's sphere comprised the household and the children while, true to his intention, Scott continued his association with the Edinburgh Light Dragoons, promoted his legal career, paid visits on his own – Scott especially liked to forge friendships with local gentry and nobility – and became increasingly absorbed in his secondary career as poet and novelist. Treading a fine line between formality and intimacy, respectfulness and flirtation, he also conducted ostensibly literary correspondences with aristocratic women, such as Lady Louisa Stuart, the Marchioness of Abercorn, and the Countess of Dalkeith, soon to be Duchess of Buccleuch. Charlotte had to settle for the honour of being Mrs Walter Scott.

In 1810, when Williamina Forbes lay dying at Lympstone in Devon and he was already a famous poet, Scott summed up his marriage in a letter to Lady Abercorn, again hinting at the pain of greater love lost:

> *Mrs Scott's match & mine was of our own making & proceeded from the most sincere affection on both sides which has rather increased than diminished during twelve years of marriage. It was something rather short of Love in all its forms which I suspect people only feel once in their lives, folks who have been nearly drownd* [sic] *in bathing rarely venturing a second time out of their depth.*

Whether Charlotte shared her husband's feelings, or whether she would have been hurt by these remarks, is not of course recorded. Like his mother and sister, aunt Jenny and Williamina herself, she only figures in history as a character in the story of Walter Scott.

# CHAPTER 14

# Getting Forward

*Till towards the age of thirty, Scott's life has nothing in it decisively pointing towards Literature, or indeed towards distinction of any kind; he is wedded, settled, and has gone through all his preliminary steps, without symptom of renown as yet. It is the life of every other Edinburgh youth of his station and time.*

~ Thomas Carlyle, *The London and Westminster Review*, 1838 ~

AFTER SCOTT, THOMAS Carlyle was the most famous and influential Scottish writer of the nineteenth century. Born in Ecclefechan, Dumfriesshire in 1795, he spent most of his life in London, becoming famous as 'The Sage of Chelsea', journalist, biographer, historian, controversialist and prophet of doom. A profoundly serious and painstaking writer, Carlyle was generally sour about Scott's work, dismissing his apparently effortless prose as mere 'ready-writing'. Yet his remarks about his predecessor's early life are accurate. Scott had written ballads and poems for private circulation, but by the time of his marriage in 1797 his only published work had been the two translations from German with which he hoped in vain to impress Williamina Belsches. That situation was now about to change.

In the spring of 1798, through his friend Will Erskine, Scott made the acquaintance of the short-lived celebrity Matthew Gregory Lewis (1775–1818), better known, since the 1795 publication of his gruesome and scandalous novel *Ambrosio, or the Monk*, as 'Monk Lewis'. Still only 24 when he visited Edinburgh, the tiny but urbane and handsome Lewis, whose Gothic play 'The Castle Spectre' had run for sixty performances at Drury Lane, was all the rage in London. Initially, Scott was immensely gratified by his interest. Lewis was putting together material for a ballad collection to be titled 'Tales of Wonder', and over dinner Scott agreed to contribute some of the old Scots ballads he had collected, along with a few originals of his own, among them 'Glenfinglas, or Lord Ronald's Coronach', 'The Eve of St John' and 'The Fire-King'. In return, Lewis helped Scott to find a London publisher, Joseph Bell, for his translation from German of Goethe's tragedy *Goetz von Berlichingen*, though Scott's gratification at receiving fifty guineas in payment was spoiled by an error on the title page, announcing the author as 'William Scott'. He could not have been pleased either by the well-publicised sniggering of German scholars over howlers in his translation, but at least it sold enough copies to justify a second printing with the correct author's name.

It seems that at this time, Scott was so elated by his meeting with Matt Lewis and buoyed up the publication of *Goetz* that he seriously believed that he might have a future as a dramatist. He set to work on a Gothic play of his own, 'The House of Aspen', hoping that through Lewis's influence the actor-manager John Philip Kemble (1757–1823), who had presented 'The Castle Spectre' at Drury Lane, might be persuaded to stage it. With this in mind, he and Charlotte set off for London in March 1799. It was Scott's first visit since he and Aunt Jenny passed through on their way to Bath more than twenty years earlier, and in many ways he thoroughly enjoyed himself. Lewis introduced him to his literary friends, and he relished poking around the antiquities in Westminster Abbey and the Tower of London. Then problems arose: Charlotte became pregnant, 'The House of Aspen' failed to find favour with Kemble, and in the middle of April Scott's father died.

Much has been made of the supposed frigidity of the letter Scott sent to his mother on 19 April, in which he said that 'the removal of my regretted parent from this earthly scene, is to him, doubtless, the happiest change, if the firmest integrity and the best spent life can entitle us to judge of the state of our departed friends'. He went on to tell her that 'the affection and attention which you have a right to expect from your children, and which I consider the best tribute we can pay to the memory of a parent we have lost, will … contribute its full share to the alleviation of your distress'.

The sentiments are conventional and the eighteenth-century prose formal, but there is really nothing to suggest the father-hatred which has sometimes been ascribed to it. Scott was probably not the only member of the family to have a sense of a burden lifted; the Writer to the Signet had been irascible and unreasonable in his long decline, and his daughter

Anne's life is thought to have been shortened by the stress of nursing him. Scott was concerned about Charlotte's pregnancy, particularly since they had lost their first child the previous year, and they did not get home in time for the funeral. The Writer to the Signet had not chosen to exercise his right to burial in Dryburgh Abbey, and was interred in the churchyard of Greyfriars in Edinburgh, where he had worshipped for over forty years.

*　*　*

The early years of the nineteenth century brought great happiness to Scott. Apart from the death in 1801 of his younger sister Anne, which he described briefly as 'a heavy family misfortune, the loss of an only sister in the prime of life', no sorrow touched him. In the last days of 1779, he had at last received the salaried legal post he had yearned for; through the influence of the Duke of Buccleuch and Henry Dundas he was appointed Sheriff-Depute of Selkirkshire at an annual salary of £250, later raised to £300. Scott was rising in the world; as Lockhart recorded, the Duke and Dundas 'had both seen [him] frequently under their roofs, and been pleased with his manners and conversation'. Devotion to his comrades in the Edinburgh Light Horse had clearly opened doors. The duties of Sheriff were not onerous, as most of the work was done by a Sheriff-Substitute who lived locally – in Scott's case Charles Erskine, a Melrose solicitor, and later his cousin, the delightfully named William Scott of Maxpoffle. The district was quiet, and few cases brought to court required Scott's presence on the Bench. Erskine presided over the rest, sending details to Scott who returned written judgements. Scott continued with his career at the Bar, but since the courts in Edinburgh only did business for less than half the year and he was not continuously employed, that did not take up too much time either.

Scott now felt secure enough financially to rent from the Clerks of Penicuik a 'cottage' at Lasswade, near Dalkeith. It was actually a small country house with a large garden and, though far from spacious, it provided a retreat where he could take up the country sports he had loved at Rosebank; shooting, fishing and riding. He walked his dogs along the river Esk, and did some gardening during the long summer vacation. Nearby was Dalkeith Palace, the main residence of the Buccleuchs and home to the Earl of Dalkeith, Scott's messmate in the Dragoons. The Scotts were often invited to dine, and it was there that Scott first met the young Countess of Dalkeith and Lady Louisa Stuart, a daughter of the Earl of Bute, who would later be a trusted and discerning critic of his work.

Scott had other, less exalted friends in the neighbourhood; the novelist Henry Mackenzie and his former university teacher Alexander Fraser Tytler had country houses in Midlothian, and Will Clerk was often nearby. Visits were arranged, and occasionally people turned up uninvited. One morning, when the Scotts came downstairs, they found waiting in the drawing room the Lakeland poet William Wordsworth and his sister Dorothy, who were touring Scotland with a horse and two-wheeled Irish 'jaunting car'. One wonders what Charlotte made of these windblown, sunburnt people with their unkempt clothes and plain manners, although she must have got used, as the years went by, to the procession of eccentrics who trooped through her house: outspoken James Hogg, the 'Ettrick Shepherd', who stretched out on her drawing room sofa and made the gaffe of calling her 'Charlotte'; Scott's unconventional assistant John Leyden (1775–1811), who ate a raw steak in her dining room to rebuke a pernickety vegetarian; twitchy Henry [Heinrich] Weber, a half-German student who in 1812 acted as Scott's amanuensis, until one evening in North Castle Street he had a sensational mental breakdown and came within an inch of killing his employer.

Scott, who admired the *Lyrical Ballads* published by William Wordsworth and Samuel Taylor Coleridge in 1798, was delighted with the Wordsworths. At two o'clock he walked back with them to the inn at Roslin, and arranged to meet them again in the Borders. He spent three days showing them his beloved haunts of Yarrow, Gala, Teviot and Tweed, regaling them with anecdotes and ballads and proving himself to Dorothy 'a man of very sweet manners, mild, cordial and cheerful'. On their last day together, Scott had to attend the Circuit Court in Jedburgh; although Scott had discouraged them from attending, the Wordsworths managed to get themselves into the courtroom to hear the judge's summing-up. 'A most curious specimen of old woman's oratory and newspaper-paragraph loyalty that was ever heard,' wrote Dorothy tartly in her travel diary. Afterwards they witnessed Sheriff Scott leaving the court in procession, 'to the sound of a trumpet, the Judge first, in his robes of red, the Sheriffs next, in large cocked hats, and the inferior officers following'. It was 'a show not much calculated to awe the beholders', snapped English Dorothy.

Charlotte had not accompanied them on their excursion; the Wordsworths belonged to the area of Scott's life she did not expect to share. But this was a happy time for her too, when she was in good health and the novelty of married life had not worn off. She was proud to be the wife of a rising young man, pleased with her aristocratic neighbours, content to immerse herself in running two households – though not, it seems, very efficiently. Although the Scotts' first child had been stillborn in 1798, later pregnancies were successful and there were children to look after. Sophia was born in 1799, Walter in 1801, Anne in 1803 and Charles in 1805.

\* \* \*

Meanwhile Scott, no longer fretting about money and with plenty of leisure, was pondering a new literary venture. Recently he had made two new friends, George Ellis, a retired diplomat with Tory political friends and antiquarian interests which included ballads, and Richard Heber, an immensely wealthy Oxford graduate, antiquarian and above all, biblio-phile. Scott was greatly impressed by Heber, who supposedly spent £100,000 on his collection of 150,000 rare books. Correspondence with these literary men would become a regular feature of his life in years to come.

Around the same time, with the failure of his attempt to write for the stage came the cooling of Scott's friendship with Matt Lewis. This was due partly to his annoyance over delay in the appearance of *Tales of Wonder*, partly to warnings from his friends that association with the 'bad boy' Lewis was not good for his reputation. But perhaps the deciding factor was his unease that his new friend Ellis and his right-wing associates detested German-Gothic literature, regarding it as danger-ously radical. But to be fair, Scott's severing of his link with the 'Monk' was caused principally by disillusionment with Lewis' editorial tampering with the Scottish ballads he had provided for the yet unpub-lished book. He found Lewis' emendations too English and too Gothic and, as his self-confessed 'German madness' faded, he regretted the loss of the unadorned simplicity that made them specifically Scottish.

By the autumn of 1779, Scott had extricated himself from 'Tales of Wonder', but the project was still, in a sense, unfinished business. On a visit to Rosebank, he learned that his old Kelso school friend James Ballantyne, after a failed attempt become a solicitor, had set up in business as a printer and editor of a newspaper, the *Kelso Mail*. A cordial meeting followed, at which Scott arranged for James to print privately a small anthology, entitled *An Apology for Tales of Terror* ('apology' here used in the sense of 'vindication'), in which he included ballads by Robert Southey, John Aikin and, perhaps as a farewell gesture, Matthew 'Monk' Lewis, alongside his own. The edition sold reasonably well and Scott's delight in the quality of Ballantyne's printing led him to offer his old friend the much greater challenge of publishing the work which would establish Scott's reputation as one of the great literary figures of his age. This was the *Minstrelsy of the Scottish Border.*

Scott had been collecting ballads since his childhood, and in his introduction to the *Minstrelsy* he states that these were the foundation of the work. But since ballads were kept alive by word of mouth, different versions existed; verses had been lost, others added and, when finally they were written down, forged. Since the early 1790s, Scott had been making regular summer raids into the remote parts of Ettrick Forest and Liddesdale in search of new versions of ballads; his work now would involve collation, explanatory notes and the production of a 'definitive' printed text. His original intention had been to confine his researches to what he called 'historical' ballads, but as the project ballooned, it became clear that if he was to combine his research and writing with his other responsibilities, he was going to need help. Although Wordsworth had the impression that by 1802 he had all but abandoned hope of profes-sional advancement, and talked of the easy money he might make from publishers, Scott never intended to abandon the legal profession. Although he occasionally claimed to dislike the Law, even at the height of his success he stayed within its circle, vowing that literature should be his 'staff but not his crutch'.

One of Scott's greatest talents was his ability to enthuse. Soon he was writing tactful letters to Bishop Percy, whose *Reliques* he had read in Aunt Jenny's garden as a young teenager, and to the famously irascible antiquarian Joseph Ritson, whose obsession with the accuracy of texts was ahead of his time. Other collaborators and assistants were roped in and kept onside; some were well educated men like Ellis and Charles Kirkpatrick Sharpe (1781–1851), a notoriously difficult and reclusive Edinburgh antiquarian charmed into helpfulness by Scott. Others were less grand but closer to the Border tradition of balladry, such as James Ballantyne, Scott's Sheriff-Substitute Charles Erskine, and the Ettrick countrymen William Laidlaw and James Hogg. Scott was perhaps most indebted to his new friend Heber, who not only gave him advice drawn from his vast knowledge of early literature, but introduced him to John Leyden who would do most of the legwork required on Scott's behalf.

Leyden is an unjustly neglected figure. Born in a shepherd's cottage in the Border village of Denholm, he was taught to read by his grand-mother and by the age of eight had memorised large parts of the Bible,

John Barbour's *The Bruce* and Blind Harry's *Wallace*. He also knew the work of Homer and Milton. The perhaps apocryphal story is that when his father bought a donkey for him to ride to school three miles away, the previous owner casually gave young Leyden an unwanted book titled *Calepini Dictionarium Octolingue*. This was a dictionary of eight languages – Latin, Greek, Hebrew, Italian, French, German, Spanish and Dutch. By the time he entered the University of Edinburgh, Leyden was said to have mastered the lot. However he acquired his knowledge, there is no doubt that he was a phenomenal linguist, who, by the time he died in 1811, knew forty languages including Urdu, Persian and Malay.

It seems that Leyden's parents hoped, like many of their class, that their son would become a minister. But although he sailed through the divinity examinations, while attending classes in almost every subject offered by the University of Edinburgh, young Leyden's attempts to find a parish were unrewarded. Apparently the only language he refused to use was English; and although speaking Scots was not a bar to the ministry, it is thought that his unkempt appearance, strong Teviotdale accent and spectacularly uncouth manners were held against him. By the time he met Richard Heber in an Edinburgh bookshop in 1800, this gifted eccentric was unemployed, apart from occasional editing jobs put his way by Dr Robert Anderson, the editor of the *Edinburgh Literary Magazine*. Heber, seeing an opportunity to do both Scott and Leyden a good turn, arranged a meeting, at which Scott discovered that the young man had two passions, the Border ballads and the exploits of the Selkirkshire explorer Mungo Park (1771–1806), which had inspired in him a yearning to travel. Scott saw that he could use Leyden's knowledge and expertise immediately, and reckoned that he might later be able, through his Dundas connections, to help him to a position abroad. Thus Scott in his turn became a patron; a modest salary was arranged and Leyden went to work for Scott. Sometimes he travelled alone, ferreting out and bringing back copies of ballads to Scott at North Castle Street or Lasswade. At other times Scott accompanied his assistant, which was why Leyden was present at one of the most famous meetings in the history of the *Minstrelsy*, between Walter Scott, Sheriff of Selkirkshire and an elderly peasant named Margaret Hogg.

# CHAPTER 15

# A Modern Bard

*The way was long, the wind was cold,*
*The Minstrel was infirm and old;*
*His wither'd cheek, and tresses grey,*
*Seem'd to have known a better day ...*
*The last of all the bards was he,*
*Who sang of Border chivalry.*

~ *The Lay of the Last Minstrel*, opening lines, 1805 ~

IT WAS LEYDEN, with his knowledge of ballads and enthusiasm for his new job, who knocked Scott's plan for a modest five-shilling volume on the head. 'Does Mr Scott mean another thin thing like *Goerz of Berlichinen*?' he asked incredulously. 'I have more than that in my head myself. We shall turn out three or four volumes at least.' Scott accepted the challenge, but there were problems which had to be circumvented one way or another. Although his work is the most comprehensive and best remembered, at the turn of the nineteenth century Scott was by no means the only collector in the field. In Scotland alone, a minister's wife named Anna Gordon, 'Mrs Brown of Falkland', was busy collecting 'romantic' ballads; she seems to have proved amenable to Scott's use of her material, but Robert Jamieson, a Morayshire-born school teacher and collector, proved stickier. With him Scott was obliged to make a pact, promising to confine himself to the Border 'riding' ballads and leave the 'romantic' ones to Jamieson. Leyden, who had been away on holiday when this agreement was made, was furious, and persuaded Scott to renege and incorporate Jamieson's work into the *Minstrelsy*. Jamieson was bought off by Scott in his new role of patron; a government post was obtained for him in

Edinburgh and he faded from the scene. It is a distasteful episode, just the same.

Scott and Leyden were out and about a great deal in 1801, riding through the hills of Teviotdale and Liddesdale, following leads, knocking on doors, transcribing the ballad recitations of old men and women who had learned them from their parents and grandparents and were doubtless puzzled to meet people interested in writing them down. The first two volumes of the *Minstrelsy* were published in London in 1802 and printed by James Ballantyne in Kelso. The first contained Scott's annotated versions of 'historical' ballads such as 'Sir Patrick Spens' and 'Kinmont Willie', the second 'romantic' specimens encompassing ballads of love and the supernatural. These included 'Young Tamlane', 'The Lament of the Border Widow', 'The Wife of Usher's Well and 'The Twa Corbies'. It goes without saying that Scott liked the warlike ballads best. The third volume, which was to include a number of modern imitations as well as originals, was scheduled for 1803, and during the remaining months of 1802 Scott was again on the hunt.

One of his most fruitful leads came from Sheriff-Substitute Charles Erskine, who had introduced Scott to his cousin William Laidlaw, the well-educated son of an Ettrick farmer who would become one of Scott's most trusted and best-loved friends. Laidlaw was interested in ballads, and in turn introduced Scott to *his* cousin James Hogg, another impoverished autodidact, but one with the seeds of literary genius within him. Hogg had been fortunate in that, being employed by the Laidlaws as a shepherd, they had taken the trouble to advance his education, introducing him to a range of poetry including Blind Harry's *Wallace* in the modernised version of Hamilton of Gilbertfield (1772) and Allan Ramsay's pastoral *The Gentle Shepherd* (1725). It was through these connections that Scott and Leyden arrived one afternoon at the cottage 'in Ettrick's bleakest, loneliest sheil', not to call on James Hogg specifically (although he was present and anxious to make a good impression on Scott), but on his mother. Margaret Hogg, Laidlaw had told them, knew many ballads by heart, notably the 65-stanza 'Auld Maitland' which Scott was eager to have in his third volume. Leyden was suspicious of forgery and Scott shared his concern, but after hearing her recitation he accepted the ballad's authenticity and published it. His meeting with Mrs Hogg, which took place after the publication of Volumes I and II, is most memorable for her trenchant criticism of his work:

*There war never ane o' my sangs prentit till you prentit them yoursel',
an' you hae spoilt them awthegither. They were made for singing an'
no for reading, but ye hae broken the charm now, an' they'll never be
sung mair. An' the worst thing of a', they're nouther right spell'd nor
right setten down.*

There have been many scholarly criticisms over the past two
centuries of Scott's method, his confident 'improvements' of 'orally
corrupted' versions, interpolations of his own verses, rewritings and
general tidyings-up. His belief that the ballads had originally been
composed by a single 'bard' attached to a king or chieftain, and had
been passed down through similar channels to the common folk of his
own time has also been scorned by the greater number who hold that
the ballads originated among the folk themselves. It is true that the oral
ballads were fluid – stanzas were omitted, forgotten, altered and invented by reciters down the years. It was only when literate collectors like
Percy, Ritson, Mrs Brown of Falkland and Scott were able to transcribe
them that their form was fixed and, as the astute Mrs Hogg recognised,
a charm was broken. But Scott was right too when he spoke of the
superstitions and legends of Scotland which 'if not now collected, must
soon have been totally forgotten'. The same is true of the ballads
themselves.

\*    \*    \*

When the final volume of the *Minstrelsy* – assorted ballads padded out
with modern imitations by Scott himself, John Leyden, Charles
Kirkpatrick Sharpe and other friends, was published – Leyden was out
of a job again. It has been said with justice that his contribution entitled
him to be named as Scott's co-author, but only 'Walter Scott, Esq.,
Advocate' appeared on the title page. The devoted Leyden, however, did
not complain. Scott repaid him in the usual fashion of the time by
putting a word in the right ear, this time of his politically connected
friend George Ellis. A position abroad was found for the eccentric young
man – not in Africa like his hero Mungo Park, but in India, as a surgeon's
assistant. Instead of the usual four years, Leyden needed only six months
to achieve a degree in medicine, and in the seven years of life left to him,
he practised and abandoned that profession to become Professor of
Hindustani at Calcutta University and a district judge. He died of fever
while exploring Java in 1811.

\*    \*    \*

In 1804, two things happened almost simultaneously. The first was that Sir Francis Napier, the Lord Lieutenant of Selkirkshire, became uneasy about the amount of time Scott was spending on the *Minstrelsy* and the Edinburgh Light Dragoons. The Sheriff-Depute was reminded fairly sharply that his position required him to spend four months each year in Ettrick Forest. Scott, who had so far got away with using the inn at Clovenfords as a base when he had to go to court in Selkirk, grumbled, but accepted that he must think again. Then on 10 June, his uncle Robert died, leaving his favourite nephew the estate of Rosebank and £600 in cash. Rather surprisingly, given his fondness for the place and the fact that his aunt Jenny Scott was still living, Scott chose not to move to Kelso; Lockhart suggests that Rosebank was too close to the town to count as a proper country residence. Whatever the reason, Scott did not swither. On 11 July he wrote to William Smith, a Kelso solicitor, instructing him to place advertisements for the sale of the estate. The cottage at Lasswade was given up, and later in the summer the family moved to Ashiestiel, a large country house six miles from Selkirk. High above the river Tweed, the situation of the house was beautiful, with views overlooking 'a wild pastoral country'. For the time being, Scott reserved the £5000 he had received from the sale of Rosebank, and rented from a cousin who was absent in India. Ashiestiel became the family's country base for eight years; there Scott wrote the memoir of his early years, and he afterwards remembered this as the happiest period of his life.

Scott was already a lawyer and a literary man. At Ashiestiel, he found that he also liked the lifestyle of a landowner, even though he did not actually own the land. He planted trees and kept sheep, and requiring a shepherd, hired a local man named Tom Purdie.

Lockhart claimed that Purdie first met Scott in the Sheriff Court, where Scott was on the Bench and Purdie was in the dock on a charge of poaching. In this version, Scott was so distressed by the prisoner's pitiful tale of domestic misfortune which had driven him to crime that he dismissed the case and gave the culprit a job.

This story has been dismissed by later biographers as unlikely. The case seems too trivial to have required Scott's presence in court. But it must have been part of the story Scott told Lockhart about himself, and was in turn incorporated into Lockhart's story of Scott. Not only the ballads were transmitted orally, and Scott's story never lost anything in the telling. Yet, however they first met, Tom Purdie was to attain great importance in Scott's life, the friendship proving, as did Leyden's, that his obsession with pedigree was only one aspect of Scott's social personality. Tom Purdie was devoted to 'The Shirra' as his master was known in Selkirkshire, and as well as shepherd became farm foreman, gillie, estate manager, fearless critic and, in Scott's last years, his support and right-hand man.

It was also at Ashiestiel that Scott got into the habit of rising at five o'clock in the morning, so that he could be dressed and at his desk by six. He wrote until breakfast between nine and ten, then returned to his desk until noon. After that, he claimed to be 'his own man' for the rest of the day. Only if the weather was bad would he work in the afternoon, otherwise by one o'clock he was out on horseback with his dogs running alongside. Scott maintained this routine both in the country and in Edinburgh almost to the end of his life.

With the *Minstrelsy* glowingly reviewed and selling well, Scott had a success to build on. At Lasswade, in the summer of 1802, he had written the first draft of *The Lay of the Last Minstrel*. At that time he had intended it for the third edition of the *Minstrelsy*, but its length excluded it. For the first time, he was writing something really original, rather than tweaking, arranging and expanding the work of others. His friends Will Erskine and George Cranstoun were enthusiastic, and Scott began to see *The Lay* as a stand-alone work. Influenced, although unwilling to admit it, by Coleridge's unfinished ballad 'Christabel', he composed it in the 'galloping rhythm' which was fresh and novel to readers accustomed to the measured formality of eighteenth-century couplets.

Scott's much later claim that the poem was written at the 'command' of the young Countess of Dalkeith is best understood as another of Scott's stories of himself; it seems more likely that Lady Dalkeith's suggestion of a poem featuring the local legend of the goblin Gilpin Horner was incorporated into a text already well underway. *The Lay*, nonetheless, is the tribute of the modern 'bard' to the half-legendary past of the Scott family, and was dedicated to his friend the Earl of Dalkeith. Essentially, it is a tale of love, murder, child abduction, sorcery and ghosts, told by an ancient minstrel of the kind Scott believed to be the source of the ballads he had been working on. Its distance from the spare, ambiguous, teasing poems in favour today makes it look formidable, but from its famous opening couplet to its lyrical closing description of 'the Minstrel's lowly bower', it is vastly entertaining and fun to read.

Published in 1805, the success of *The Lay* was phenomenal. It sold out six editions in three years, bringing its author fame and in the first two years, royalties amounting to around £770. Scott had chosen a London publisher, and the work was published by Longman, Hurst, Rees & Orme in London, but also, significantly, by Archibald Constable in Edinburgh. Constable had identified Scott as an author to watch, and had shrewdly negotiated a quarter share in *The Lay* from Longman before its publication. The printer was James Ballantyne who, at Scott's urging, had recently moved from Kelso to Edinburgh, leaving the management of the *Kelso Mail* to his younger brother Sandy. Thus the names of Constable and Ballantyne, the most important figures in Scott's publishing life, both appeared on the title page of his first successful work.

Archibald Constable had been born in Fife in 1774 and apprenticed to an Edinburgh bookseller when he was twelve. By 1800, when Heber met Leyden in his shop, this confident, personable man had established himself in the High Street as a dealer in rare books. But he had larger ambitions; in 1801 he bought the *Scots Magazine*, and the following year became the commercial manager of a new quarterly magazine, the *Edinburgh Review*. Founded by the Whig lawyers Francis Jeffrey (1773–1850), Henry Brougham and Francis Horner, *The Review* was a huge success and launched Constable on a stellar publishing career. Cockburn summed up his achievement:

> *Abandoning the old timid and grudging system, Constable stood out as the general patron of all promising publications, and confounded not merely his rivals in trade, but his very authors, by his unheard-of prices. Ten, even twenty guineas a sheet for a review, £2000 or £3000 for a single poem ... drew authors from dens where they would otherwise have starved, and made Edinburgh a literary mart, famous with strangers, and the pride of its own citizens.*

Walter Scott was far from starvation, but Constable's eye-watering advances (every £1000 the equivalent of £70,000 today) appealed as much to him as to his needier fellow authors. He was on good terms with the first editor of the *Edinburgh Review*, Francis Jeffrey, and despite their political differences, was soon writing articles and reviews for the magazine. It is painful for admirers of Scott to admit flaws in their hero but, despite his charmingly modest manner, ready hospitality and a genuine warmth in his praise of the work of others, there is no denying an element of avarice in Scott's character. Financial ambition had mattered in his search for a wife, he was frustrated by his failure to make pots of money at the Bar, and it is hardly surprising that, with the success of the *Minstrelsy* and *The Lay of the Last Minstrel*, his resolve not to make literature his crutch began to weaken.

It was suggested by Eric Quayle in *The Ruin of Sir Walter Scott* (1968), a generally hostile study, that Scott's greed might be traced to a sense of insecurity induced by his physical disability, but that is not the whole story. Scott had always been ambitious socially. Although deferential to his aristocratic friends, he was proud of them and wanted to impress. Setting such store by his condition as a 'gentleman', it is probable that he had always coveted a lifestyle to which his upbringing had hardly accustomed him. In 1805, through literary fame and Constable's liberality, the wealth he had dreamed of suddenly seemed within his grasp, and Scott began to make plans. The first step he took was fateful, but must have seemed like a splendid idea at the time.

# CHAPTER 16

# Friends and Family

*I have imagined a very superb work. What think you of a complete edition of the British Poets, ancient and modern? There is a scheme for you! At least a hundred volumes, published at the rate of ten a-year ... . If the booksellers will give me a decent allowance per volume, say thirty guineas, I shall hold myself well paid on the writing hand. This is a dead secret.*
~ Letter to James Ballantyne, 12 April 1805 ~

WHEN JAMES BALLANTYNE brought his printing business to Edinburgh in 1802, Scott had lent him £500 to help with his set-up costs. His much-admired production of the *Minstrelsy* brought him so many orders that by 1805 Ballantyne had to bear twice the cost of moving to larger premises. The success of *The Lay of the Last Minstrel* stretched his resources to breaking point; to cope with the demand for copies he had to invest in new machinery, employ more printsetters and hold up the printing of other orders. Naturally he turned to his old friend to bail him out and Scott, who still had the money he had saved from the sale of Rosebank, agreed to advance him a further £1500.

Throughout his life, Scott often helped friends in need, but on this occasion his generosity was not completely altruistic. For all that he had decided against making literature his main profession, the warm reception of the *Minstrelsy* and the roaring success of *The Lay* had shown him how profitable it could be. His mind was swarming with schemes for writing poems and editing reissues of other authors, and the notion of having a controlling interest in Ballantyne's business appealed to him. The outcome was that, in return for his investment, in May 1805 he signed a partnership agreement with his old school friend, which effec-tively ensured that he would receive half of the printer's profits. This arrangement was to be kept 'a dead secret', as Scott reminded Ballantyne in the letter proposing a one hundred-volume edition of British Poets – just one of the money-making wheezes he was dreaming up at the time.

There are two plausible explanations for Scott's determination to hide his – in the event, calamitous – business connection with his printer. He may have felt it incompatible with his position as an officer of the Law, although that did not prevent his pushing, rather dubiously, legal printing jobs in Ballantyne's direction. More pressing still was surely his social unease at the role he was adopting. Scott was, in his own and others' eyes, a gentleman. Trade was not a gentlemanly occupation. He was afraid that if he were unmasked as a tradesman's partner, he would become *persona non grata* among the grand folk he had worked so hard since his schooldays to cultivate.

Nor was he mistaken. When, twenty years later, his financial affairs became spectacularly and publicly unstuck, his old acquaintance Dorothy Wordsworth gave voice to an almost universal indignation. 'How *could* it happen,' she demanded in a letter to a friend written in March 1826, 'that [Scott] should have so entered into *trade* as to be involved in this Way – he a Baronet! A literary Man! A lawyer!' Pausing only for a catty remark about Lady Scott's being 'unfortified' for such a calamity, being 'a person fond of distinction and expence [*sic*]', Dorothy returned with relish to the main point: 'No doubt Sir Walter, having retained his offices, will still have a sufficient income for a plain gentleman; but does he retain his *Estates*?' Even the granddaughter of a Cumberland shopkeeper was affronted.

Perhaps Scott's secret was never quite as absolute as he imagined; his insistence that every work he wrote must be printed by Ballantyne could hardly fail to arouse suspicion, among his publishers at least. But they had their reasons for keeping quiet, and for many years Scott's commercial activities went undetected by his friends. Lockhart points out that at this point Scott had enough money to sustain his position as what Dorothy Wordsworth called 'a plain gentleman', but with a growing distaste for advocacy, four children and a hankering after 'Estates', more substantial income was important. At this stage of his life he probably saw his profit from the Ballantyne partnership, like his Sheriff's office, as a financial cushion, should literature fail him. Fortunately Scott had an aptitude for multi-tasking.

The one hundred-volume edition of the British Poets proved a non-starter. Archibald Constable liked the idea but could not find a London publisher ready to share the cost. Scott's plan for an 18-volume edition of the works of the English poet John Dryden (1631–1700) fared better; it was undertaken by London publisher William Miller, providing work for both its editor, Scott, and its printer, Ballantyne. Lesser projects also found favour, and in the mid-1800s Scott was constantly busy editing miscellaneous, often obscure antiquarian texts. None greatly enriched the publishers, but since all were printed by Ballantyne, Scott made money anyway. He was also at work on a new long poem, but events conspired to hold it up. Scott had family problems, and he was seriously considering quitting the Bar – though only for another salaried legal position.

*  *  *

At this time, Scott had three surviving brothers. For the eldest, John, who had been an accomplice in the childhood bullying in George Square and who had left home while Walter was still a student, he had little affection but some family feeling. John had initially prospered in the Army, but his later career seems to have been ruined by alcoholism – the same weakness rumoured to have killed his brother Robert. By 1808 he had retired and returned to Edinburgh to live with his mother, his pension inflated by Walter's lobbying among his political friends in London. But there was no warmth between them, and when John died, aged 47, in 1816, the only person who really grieved was his mother.

The youngest of the family, Daniel, had also started well enough. He was a lieutenant in the Edinburgh Volunteers while still in his teens, and appears to have been educated, like many younger sons, in the 'mercantile line' – a Lockhartian euphemism for the ungentlemanly 'trade'. Daniel probably worked for some time in London and Walter described him as 'a very good natured young man, who writes and figures very decently' – stock phrasing when writing a reference. When Daniel returned to Edinburgh, Walter used his influence to obtain for him a post in the Customs House, and it was there that he first went off the rails. It seems he was involved in some financial wrongdoing, leading to his being hustled off to Liverpool and then, through the string-pulling of George Ellis, to the West Indies.

What followed was painful for all concerned. Ellis, who had Jamaican connections, had secured a place for the young man on a sugar plantation worked by African slaves. The owner, kept in the dark about Daniel's relationship to his more famous brother, soon wearied of his new employee, accusing him of idleness and addiction to rum. In 1805 a rebellion broke out. Lockhart, at his most pious and poisonous when describing such events, states that 'being employed in some service against a refractory or insurgent body of negroes, Daniel exhibited a lamentable deficiency of spirit and conduct. He returned to Edinburgh a dishonoured man'.

It is known that there were slave risings in Jamaica and Haiti in 1805, and that there was public criticism of the feeble British response. It is possible that Daniel, among others, simply had no taste for flogging and executing defenceless slaves, but his fate as the Scott family's black sheep was sealed. He caused further scandal by fathering an illegitimate son (allegedly with the housekeeper of Walter's upper-crust friend the Marquess of Abercorn) and, lacking funds to marry, moved back in with his long-suffering mother. Walter Scott was understandably embarrassed, but even so, his conduct towards his brother was markedly at odds with the kindliness to which so many of his contemporaries attested.

Scott agreed to maintain Daniel's son William, writing in May 1806 to his Sheriff-Substitute in Selkirk, 'My mother is anxious to have Daniel's business finishd [sic] .... The money is ready in Sir William Forbes's [Bank]. In short, you must just close on the best terms you can & write (if you please to my mother on the subject) as I do not care to be seen in it myself'. He did not care either to have anything further to do with Daniel, cutting his brother in the street and, when the young man died in his mother's house aged only thirty, refused to attend his funeral or wear mourning for him. Whatever Daniel had done, this seems uncommonly vindictive, and one can only conjecture that Scott felt his brother's behaviour as a stain, not only on Daniel's honour, but on his own. There may also have been a private score to settle. Daniel was too young to have joined Robert and John in the physical bullying of their disabled brother, but as he grew up he may have developed his own line in slighting remarks. Meanwhile, another of the Scott brothers was foolishly courting disaster.

Thomas Scott, known in his family as Tom, was three years younger than Walter, and the only sibling for whom the latter seemed to feel much affection. Scott persistently overrated this very ordinary man, holding, against much evidence to the contrary, that Tom was a gifted writer who lacked nothing but opportunity. In an appendix to the *General Preface to the Waverley Novels*, written as late as 1829, Scott titled his account of the 'Green Breeks' story 'Anecdote of Schooldays upon which Mr Thomas Scott proposed to found a Tale of Fiction'. The proposition was more probably Walter's.

Tom Scott had accepted a partnership with his father when Walter refused it, at a period when the business was still reasonably profitable. Even after the good times following the Disannexing Act were over, Walter Scott WS retained such plum contracts as the agency for the city of Aberdeen and – more pertinently – the factorship of the Duddingston estates of the Marquess of Abercorn. By 1807 Tom, who had married in the year of his father's death, had five children to support and, as his financial ineptitude drove clients from the firm, was very short of money. One of his responsibilities was rent collecting on behalf of the absentee Lord Abercorn and – committing a professional misdemeanour vastly more heinous than any transgression of Daniel's at the Custom House – Tom embezzled his employer's rents to pay his own bills.

When this crime came to light, Tom Scott scarpered, leaving his unfortunate wife to face public opprobrium. In his absence, he was debarred from practising Law again in Edinburgh, and was only saved from being hunted down and sent to prison by the intervention of his brother. In marked contrast to his unforgiving treatment of Daniel, Walter Scott volunteered to pay back £3000 which Tom had stolen; for the first time he was displaying the capacity for appearing high-minded in questionable circumstances that would resurface when financial imprudence left him insolvent in 1825. His efforts to help his favourite brother were not, however, without cost; to raise money he was forced to undertake for Constable the heavy task of editing the works of Jonathan Swift (1667–1745) and to rush his new poem *Marmion* into print before it was quite ready. Constable's huge advances – he paid £1500 for Swift and 1000 guineas for *Marmion* – made these contracts irresistible, but the whole affair took a heavy toll on Scott, who suffered blinding headaches brought on by stress and humiliation. The unexpected civility of the Marquess (guided no doubt by the pleading of his wife) was a comfort in bleak times, but Scott lost no time in banishing Tom and his family to the debtors' haven of the Isle of Man. Later, after yet more string-pulling by Scott's friends Heber and Ellis, Tom was commissioned into the British Army. Piquantly, considering his earlier exploits, he was appointed Paymaster of the 70th (Glasgow Lowland) Regiment of Foot.

\* \* \*

Despite advocacy's being Scott's chosen profession, he soon realised that he was never going to shine at the Bar and thereafter lost taste for it. Even the web of powerful patronage he had built up, largely through his contacts in the Edinburgh Light Dragoons, had been indifferently rewarding, and by 1805 he was minded to cut his losses and look for other work. His post as Sheriff of Selkirkshire had given him a modest but secure income of £300 a year for very little labour, and he now had his eye on another, more profitable part-time job. This was a Clerkship of the Court of Session, a position which would only require him to attend for a few hours on four or five mornings a week, during the six months of the year when the court was sitting. The work, which involved the arrangement of papers connected to a case and making a *précis* of each judgement delivered from the bench, was not onerous. Tenure was for life and the salary £800 a year.

Now Scott was assured of the patronage he needed to secure a Clerkship. The Duke of Buccleuch and Lord Melville were disposed to help him, and the nationwide success of *The Lay of the Last Minstrel* had brought his name to the attention of the Tory government in London. Even the Prime Minister, William Pitt the Younger (1759–1806), had read the poem and approved. Since Clerkships were political appointments, the post he coveted should have been Scott's for the asking, but there was a snag. None of the four Clerks was ever obliged to retire, and there was no vacancy. Scott endured some sleepless nights before a compromise was found; it was arranged that he should take over the duties of the aged, stone-deaf George Home of Wedderburn and perform them without pay until the old man's death – an event optimistically assumed to be imminent.

Even now, however, Scott's position was not safe. Pitt, who had been Prime Minister almost continuously since 1783, was dying, and a change of government seemed almost certain. The Whigs in opposition had made no secret of their desire to reform the Scottish legal system by abolishing sinecures. Scott's Tory sympathies were well known, and it was all too likely that his appointment would be blocked. The inevitable happened; Pitt died in January 1806, the government fell, and Lord Melville, 'the Uncrowned King of Scotland', was impeached for 'gross malversation and breach of duty' in his former role as Treasurer of the Navy. (He was acquitted, much to the disappointment of his many enemies in Edinburgh.) In February Scott was obliged to go to London to plead in person for his own position to be ratified, and his relief may be imagined when the new government under Lord Grenville generously agreed that the arrangement with Home, though irregular, should be allowed to stand.

Unfortunately for Scott, the notion that Home was at death's door was wide of the mark. The old man was still alive six years later, by which time Scott, heartily disgruntled, had spent more than a year firing off letters to his influential friends, grousing about the amount of work he was doing for nothing. To Lady Abercorn, who had remarked on his bad mood, he replied stuffily:

> On the whole if your ladyship expects any more harmony from me, you must take into your kind consideration recollecting always that I am only craving to be promoted to the emoluments of [the] situation of which I have held rank & discharged the duty gratis for five years compleat [sic] & which I believe no one will say is much disproportioned to my birth expectations or standing in society.

It took until 1812 for a compromise was reached. Home was persuaded to give up his income in exchange for a generous pension, to which Scott, no doubt with gritted teeth, contributed. Scott, between his Sheriff's office and his Clerkship, was now assured of £1100 for the rest of his days – for all that within a year of taking the job in 1806 he had been wishing that he had held his nerve and hung on for a better appointment. 'Nobody to be sure could have foreseen that in a year's time my friends [the Tories] were all to be in again,' he wrote ruefully to his brother-in-law Charles Carpenter. The feared Whig government of Lord Grenville had fallen within a year and, for a while at least, the Tory hegemony in Scotland remained secure.

There were other compensations. On court days a lumbering conveyance known as 'the Clerks' Coach' picked up Scott and his fellow Clerks after breakfast, giving time for mirth and gossip on the slow trundle up the Mound and, since the cases were shared among three Clerks, there was usually time to write letters during the working day. Scott enjoyed the company at the Clerks' table, and was on friendly terms with the Judges, many of whom he had known since boyhood. This was his milieu, and it is hard not to suppose that he would have lost something vital had he ever completely abandoned the circle of the Law. Usually the court rose at one o'clock, leaving him free for the rest of the day, and in the vacations there were long ribbons of time at Ashiestiel for writing, planting, farming and having fun with his children. With the problems of the past few years behind him, Scott was ready to publish his much-delayed second narrative poem, *Marmion*.

# CHAPTER 17

# Rivals

*Let such forego the poet's sacred name,*
*Who rack their brains for lucre, not for fame.*

~ George Gordon, Lord Byron,
*English Bards and Scotch Reviewers*, 1809 ~

PUBLISHED IN 1808, *Marmion* was subtitled *A Tale of Flodden Field*, its background is the battle between Scottish and English armies in Northumberland in 1513 in which the Scots sustained disastrous losses, including their king, James IV. It was a defeat seared into the Scots' collective memory, and is commemorated in legend and song to this day. Asked by his Lichfield correspondent, Anna Seward, whether such a subject might not be wounding to Scottish pride, Scott replied loftily that 'all was lost but our honour', a sentiment with which Scots generally agree. As in *The Lay of the Last Minstrel*, the core narrative is melodramatic, concerning lust, false accusations, a duel, the walling up of a sinful nun in a convent, and a wronged lover bent on revenge. The finale is set at Flodden where the English Lord Marmion – a strange hybrid of honourable knight and unspeakable rat – dies, leaving the way clear for star-crossed lovers to marry.

For the most part, the story rattles along with pace and vigour and is studded, particularly in the introductory epistles and earlier cantos, with songs and descriptive passages of great beauty. It also contains the story of 'Young Lochinvar' memorised by generations of Scottish children unaware that it was part of *Marmion*. But the uninspired and easily parodied late verses do suggest the pressure to finish that Scott was under:

*Young Blount his armour did unlace*
*And gazing on his ghastly face,*

*Said, 'By Saint George, he's gone!*
*That spear-wound has our master sped, –*
*And see the deep cut on his head!*
*Good night to Marmion!'*

'Ready-writing', as Carlyle called it, and easy reading, but not Scott at his best.

Even so, commercially *Marmion* was a success. Archibald Constable had sold 25 per cent of the rights each to John Murray and William Miller, so that the poem was published in February 1808 simultaneously in Edinburgh and London. The very pricey first edition of 2000 copies sold out in April; by the end of May the poem was in its third edition and remained popular through most of the nineteenth century. Its critical reception, however, was markedly less enthusiastic. Reviewers objected to the dedicatory 'epistles in verse' to his friends which Scott inserted as introductions to each of the six cantos, pointing out correctly that they spoiled the narrative's flow. The plot was found obscure, and the mixture of evil intent and noble posturing in the central character puzzling in the days before Lord Byron suddenly made anti-heroes fashionable. The most comprehensive hatchet job was performed by Scott's Whig friend Francis Jeffrey in the *Edinburgh Review*. One of the most eloquent and incisive critics of his time, Jeffrey filleted *Marmion*, pointing out the improbability of the plot, dismissing the verse as 'flat and tedious' and, most woundingly, accusing Scott of lack of patriotism.

Socially, his own frankness put Jeffrey in a tight corner. He stood by his opinion but, in a small town like Edinburgh, he did not want a public falling-out. Invited to dine at 39 North Castle Street just before his article was to be published, he decided to send Scott an advance proof, giving time for the invitation to be withdrawn. It was not, and Scott proved an exemplary host, cheerful and solicitous for his guests' comfort, talking animatedly about everything except *Marmion*. At the end of the visit, Jeffrey must have breathed a sigh of relief, but he was not to get off so lightly. Charlotte knew what had happened and was not amused. 'Well, good-night, Mr Jeffrey,' she said haughtily, brushing aside the critic's farewell compliments. 'Dey tell me you have abused Scott in de *Review*, and I hope Mr Constable has paid you well for writing it.' Constable was of course in the crazy position of having paid Scott 1000 guineas for writing *Marmion*, and Jeffrey 25 guineas a sheet for trashing it – not that this was a unique shooting-in-the-foot. In 1859 Scott's other publisher,

John Murray, would publish Charles Darwin's *The Origin of Species by Means of Natural Selection*, and a year later pay Samuel Wilberforce handsomely to attack it in the *Quarterly Review*.

Scott, himself a most amiable and generous critic, sensibly affected indifference to bad reviews. In private he was hurt and offended. He wrote occasionally for the *Edinburgh Review* after Jeffrey's panning of his poem, but his easy relationship with the magazine and its publisher was over. When John Murray (the second of that name in the long history of London publishing) decided that it was time for a new magazine to challenge the Whiggish bias of the *Edinburgh*, Scott was foremost among its enablers. The *Quarterly Review* was first published in March 1809 under the editorship of minor poet and satirist William Gifford (1756–1826), and ran until 1967. The *Quarterly*'s Conservative bias, its opposition to major political reform and emphasis on the gradual elimination of abuses like the slave trade were congenial to Scott, who was among its first and most faithful contributors.

Unfortunately Scott's resentment against Constable went further than this one act of disassociation. Scott seems to have disapproved of Constable's politics without disliking him personally, but when the publisher acquired a business partner, an estrangement became inevitable. Alexander Gibson Hunter was everything Scott loathed, a rough-mannered, outspoken Whig with no notion of his place in society. Meritocracy is a modern concept of which Scott had no inkling; his letters to those he regarded as his social superiors show him as almost floridly deferential, while with those he saw as equals, such as Clerk, Heber and Jeffrey, he was comfortable. To everyone else he was so pleasant that even educated men like John Leyden, Charles Erskine and Will Laidlaw barely noticed his condescension. But there was a line it was unwise to cross. Hunter was highly intelligent and financially shrewd, but he was not in awe of Walter Scott.

By 1808, when Constable and Hunter heard rumours that their money-making author was cosying up to John Murray and his *Quarterly Review*, their relationship with him rapidly cooled. The breaking point came when Hunter, quite reasonably for a man of business, questioned not only the vast amount of money the firm had invested in Scott's edition of Swift's *Works*, much of which had found its way into the editor's pocket, but also the time it was taking to deliver – six years, when the initial agreement had been for two. Uncivil words were exchanged and Scott took umbrage. Partly to spite Constable and punish Hunter for his lack of deference, but more because he saw a way to accrue to himself the huge profits from his poems which he was currently obliged to share with the publishers, he made a fateful decision. He would take everything – writing, printing and publishing – under one umbrella, and set up a publishing house of his own. Of course he could not be seen publicly to do so; a manager must be appointed and his name put above the door. Scott's choice was John Ballantyne, his old Kelso acquaintance and brother of his printer James.

No doubt this 'keeping things in the family' seemed like a good idea at the time, but John Ballantyne did not have a good track record. As a youth he had served an apprenticeship at a London bank, returning to Kelso to become a partner in the family business. As early as 1797 he had fallen out with his father and set up a rival store, which might have prospered had he not lived so rashly beyond his means. By 1806 he had estranged his wife and brought himself to the verge of ruin. To save the situation he accepted a clerical post in his brother's printing office in Edinburgh where he once again met Walter Scott, who was greatly amused by John's spritely manner, talent for mimicry and clear singing voice. Scott nicknamed thin, vivacious John 'Rigdumfunnidos', and fat, serious James 'Aldiborontiphoscophornio'. They were entertaining and loyal, and happily had no aversion to being patronised. None of John's accomplishments qualified him as a publisher, but he no doubt talked up his experience of banking and retail, and in July 1809, the new firm of John Ballantyne & Co., Publishers opened in Hanover Street in the New Town. Scott provided half of the capital, and lent John the equivalent of another quarter. This was clearly dangerous because, if the venture failed, Scott would be by far the greatest loser. But optimistic Scott dismissed the risk; he regretted that he could not afford to take back his unfinished edition of Swift from Constable, but he could make sure that his money-making poetry would in future be published by the firm he practically owned.

\* \* \*

Scott's first inspiration for a new story-poem had come on a holiday to the Trossachs with Charlotte, his daughter Sophia and a Welsh friend, Lydia White. Miss White, whom Scott described to Lady Abercorn as 'lively and clever and absurd to the uttermost degree', was a woman of wild enthusiasms; in the summer of 1808 she was keen to share her current passion for landscape painting with Charlotte and nine-year-old Sophia. Scott, who had taken painting lessons as a schoolboy and knew his limitations, declined to join in. Leaving the women to their pastime he went walking along the shore of Loch Katrine, falling again under the spell of sunlit peaks, turbulent streams and dappled, darkly lapping water. He had been considering a poem with a Highland setting for some time, and had decided to make it less dependent on location than on the exploration of character. Yet the wild beauty of Loch Katrine lingered in his mind, and the new poem, when it came to be written, would be as heavy with imagery as any of his works. But once again other concerns ate into his writing time; he had his court work to attend to, all four of his children were seriously ill with measles, and the business of setting up John Ballantyne & Co. consumed much energy. It was late in the following year before he felt free to concentrate on turning his idea into verse.

The Lady of the Lake (which should, according to quibblers, be The Lady of the Loch) was finally ready for publication by John Ballantyne & Co. in May 1810. The first of Scott's works to feature the native Gaels of the Highlands and set against the magnificent scenery of the Trossachs, it tells of the personal enmity of King James V and James Douglas, Earl of Bothwell, and the complications that arise from the feelings aroused in three men, Malcolm Graeme, Rhoderick Dhu and the King himself disguised as 'Fitz-James', for Douglas's daughter Ellen, who loves only Malcolm. Divided into six cantos, each describing the events of a single day, the action-packed narrative encompasses a magnificent stag hunt, a threatened attack on Roderick's island fortress in Loch Katrine by a royal army, and a counter attack by a force of tartan-clad Highlanders. A key figure in the story is the King, who in real life was reputed to wander about the countryside disguised as a vagrant or 'Gaberlunzie Man'; it is he who gives Ellen a ring as a pledge for her safety and presides over the magnificent finale at Stirling Castle, where Douglas is forgiven and the lovers united by the clemency of the King. That the King in question was in fact vindictive to the end in his treatment of the Douglases, not to mention already married, matters little in a storyline containing so many elements of romance and fairy tale.

The Lady of the Lake was another roaring success. The Gaels, who after the Jacobite Rising of 1745 had dwindled into an economically and culturally depressed remnant of the Scottish population, were suddenly romantic again. Tartan and bagpipes became all the rage, and within a decade the story had become a Rossini opera, 'La Donna del Lago', and was about to open as a stage play at Edinburgh's Theatre Royal with Henry Siddons in the role of Fitz-James. The critics were almost all enthusiastic; even the lofty Jeffrey wrote that *The Lady of the Lake* contained 'a profusion of incident, and a shifting brilliancy of colouring, that reminds us of the witchery of Ariosto and a constant elasticity, and occasional energy, which seem to belong more peculiarly to the author now before us'.

Published under the imprint of John Ballantyne & Co. in Edinburgh and Longman & Co. in London, the poem sold 25,000 copies in eight months and remained popular well into the twentieth century. Even nowadays it still influences the perception of Scotland by those who are not Scots. When *The Lay of the Last Minstrel* was published, there had been a modest increase in the number of visitors to Melrose Abbey, but nothing to match the avalanche of tourists descending on the Trossachs in the wake of *The Lady of the Lake*. The banks of Loch Katrine were thronged with English holidaymakers; then as now, there were complaints about the shattering of peace and spoiling of landscape, but the local population cheerfully cashed in. A hotel was hastily built in Callander, shops selling souvenirs and lengths of tartan opened, and boatmen took to their oars, ferrying enthusiasts eager to visit 'Ellen's Isle'. The area's popularity as a tourist destination is strong to this day.

Few people could have foreseen in 1810 that *The Lady of the Lake* would be the high point of Scott's career as a poet. Yet even as the author celebrated and the Ballantynes shared out the profits, there were straws in the wind suggesting that Scott's reign as Britain's premier bard might not last for ever.

\* \* \*

In June 1807, a collection titled *Hours of Idleness* was published in London at the author's own expense. The poems were the work of George Gordon, Lord Byron (1788–1824), the son of a dissolute army officer and an impoverished gentlewoman from Aberdeenshire. At the age of ten, George Gordon had succeeded, on the death of his great-uncle, to the estate of Newstead Abbey in Nottinghamshire, and to the Barony of Rochdale. Educated at Aberdeen Grammar School and at Harrow, he had entered the University of Cambridge in 1805. There, despite a congenital deformity of one foot, he soon became famous for his academic brilliance, sporting prowess and exotic good looks – and notorious for his extravagance and dissipation. *Hours of Idleness*, from which young Byron's most explicitly erotic poems had been omitted on the advice of a friendly clergyman, received mixed reviews, but by far the most mortifying to the young author's feelings appeared anonymously in the *Edinburgh Review*. The poems were mawkish and derivative, but it is questionable whether any collection of juvenilia deserved such a lengthy, destructive and personally offensive notice. Byron, who admired the *Review*, affected indifference but, according to a close friend, 'he was very near destroying himself'. Unfortunately, when a year later he took revenge, he hit the wrong targets.

*English Bards and Scotch Reviewers* appeared under Byron's name in 1809 and made him known as *Hours of Idleness* never could. An indignant and hard-hitting satire modelled on *The Dunciad* by Alexander Pope (1688–1774) and William Gifford's *Baviad* of 1791, it vented its chief spleen on Francis Jeffrey, whom Byron erroneously supposed had written the offending review; it was actually by Henry Brougham. But it also took potshots at poets whose only sin was to deviate from the eighteenth-century style which Byron professed to admire. Southey, Wordsworth and Coleridge were savaged, as was Walter Scott. *Marmion* in particular was sneered at, and Scott accused of writing for money:

> *And thinks't thou, Scott! By vain conceit perchance,*
> *On public taste to foist thy stale romance?*
> *Though Murray with his Miller may combine*
> *To yield thy muse but half-a-crown per line? ...*
> *For this we spurn Apollo's venal son,*
> *And bid a long good-night to Marmion.*

It was the word 'venal' that got Scott's dander up. To his fellow victim Robert Southey he wrote peevishly:

> *In the meantime, it is funny enough to see a whelp of a young Lord Byron abusing me, of whose circumstances he knows nothing, for endeavouring to scratch a living with my pen. God help the bear, if having little else to eat, he must not even suck his own paws. I can assure the noble imp of fame it is not my fault I was not born to a park and 5000 a-year, it is not his lordship's merit, though it may be his great good fortune, that he was not born to live by his literary talents or success.*

\* \* \*

This seems a tad hypocritical, coming from someone who had taken such pains to ensure that he would always have a decent income independent of literature, but the provocation had been great. Three years would pass before, with the publication of *Childe Harold's Pilgrimage*, Byron could say, 'I awoke one morning and found myself famous', but the sensational success of *English Bards and Scotch Reviewers* gave a strong hint that Scott's status as the most fashionable poet of the age was not secure. It would be surprising if Scott himself were unaware of this.

# CHAPTER 18

# The Leeside of Prudence

*I do not intend to proceed upon this great adventure for a while as yet; the little farm-house has five tolerable rooms in it, kitchen included, and if all come to all we can adopt your suggestion and make a bed in the barn; so you see I keep the leeside of prudence in my proceedings.*

~ Letter to Joanna Baillie, 1812 ~

THE LADY OF *the Lake* made a great deal of money, most of which went into Scott's pocket. But just as the publication of *The Lay of the Last Minstrel* had strained the finances of James Ballantyne's printing business, so did this latest runaway success. Again the number of presses had to be increased, and there were huge costs for paper and other outsourced materials. In quarrelling with Archibald Constable, Scott had brought publishing rights to John Ballantyne, but lost work for the printing office as Constable took his business elsewhere.

It also transpired that Scott was a better writer than he was a publisher; he seemed to have little instinct for what, apart from his own work, was likely to sell. As senior partner, however, he was able to insist on John publishing what James would, with restraint, later call 'injudicious speculations', such as an unreadable edition of the plays of Beaumont and Fletcher (rejected by Constable) and the posthumous *Collected Works* of Anna Seward, which even Lockhart described as 'a formidable monument to mediocrity'. The last straw was the *Edinburgh Annual Register*, begun in imitation of the *London Annual Register* and intended as another counterblast to the Whiggish *Edinburgh Review*. An unwieldy two-volume publication promising, in a vastly over-optimistic prospectus, to provide in-depth articles on history, literature, fine arts, science and something called 'Useful Arts', along with commercial, financial and statistical tables, the *Register* was a disaster from the start.

Even if all the contributors lined up by Scott had delivered, the journal would have been a nightmare to edit. As it was, deadlines were ignored and Scott had too many irons in the fire; he was involved in setting up a new Edinburgh theatre, and had recently taken on a new parliamentary appointment as Secretary of a Commission on the Administration of Scottish Justice, requiring lengthy visits to London. The Ballantynes on their own could not handle erudite material. As a result many of the articles were hastily cobbled together by Scott to fill space and, absurdly for an annual publication, the *Register* was usually about two years late. Nor did its extreme Tory bias go down well with readers, especially in London where John Murray acted as its distributor.

In 1812, when Murray washed his hands of it and withdrew his one-twelfth stake, the *Edinburgh Annual Register* was losing £1000 a year. It was a time when the prolonged War against the French was badly affecting the economic climate in Britain and the book trade was not immune. When Scott was belatedly forced to examine John Ballantyne's books, he was shocked to see how his partner's 'creative accounting' had hidden the mess the firm was in. The Scotts were far from the breadline; *The Lady of the Lake* had brought Scott around £10,000, he had the residue of his uncle's estate, £300 annually from his post as Sheriff and, on his appointment as Secretary to the Parliamentary Commission, his Clerkship salary had been increased to £1300. There were also the fees he earned from reviews and articles, and Charlotte's allowance of £600 a year from her brother in India. Scott should have been substantially better off than the 'whelp of a Lord Byron', who was deep in debt and desperately trying to sell his stately home. It is an indication of what it had cost Scott in handouts and 'loans' to keep John Ballantyne & Co. afloat that when he paid £4200 for Cartley Hole Farm between Melrose and Galashiels, he had to borrow half the sum from his brother, Major John Scott, and raise the rest on the security of *Rokeby*, a yet-to-be-published poem on which John Ballantyne & Co.'s future depended. It is no wonder that he remembered the years as Ashiestiel as the happiest of his life.

\* \* \*

Scott had invested much time and labour on the estate of Ashiestiel; in a few years he had built up the sheep farm, writing to George Ellis that 'long and short sheep, and tups, and gimmers, and hogs, and dinmonts make a perfect sheepfold of my understanding'. He planted trees and Charlotte kept chickens, with unfortunate consequences since there were

**1.** College Wynd, Edinburgh. Sir Walter Scott was born here, but was sent to Sandyknowe Farm near Kelso in the Scottish Borders when he was an infant because of his poor health.

(CASSELL'S *OLD AND NEW EDINBURGH*)

**2.** Smailholm Tower.

(BOB COWAN)

**3.** Engraving of Sandyknowe and Smailholm Tower by J. M. W. Turner, showing Scott as a young child with Aunt Jenny. This is the only known representation of her.

**4.** The Bath miniature. This is the only image of Sir Walter Scott as a child. John Gibson Lockhart said that it resembled Scott throughout his life, and the photogravure by Chantrey (fig. 24) suggests this is true.

(THE ABBOTSFORD TRUST)

**5.** George Square, Edinburgh, showing the house (second on the left) of Sir Walter Scott's father.

(CASSELL'S *OLD AND NEW EDINBURGH*)

**6.** The High School of Edinburgh. This building housed the school from 1778 to 1829, when it moved to Calton Hill.

(CASSELL'S *OLD AND NEW EDINBURGH*)

**7.** *Walter Scott, Esq. (1728–99), Father of Sir Walter Scott, 1st Bt.*, Scottish School.

**8.** *Mrs Scott of Raeburn* by John Watson Gordon. Sir Walter Scott's mother in old age.

**9.** The commemorative bust of Sir Walter Scott on a gable end of Waverley House (formerly The Garden) in Kelso.

**10.** Old College Quadrangle, south side 1789–1822.

**11.** *The Meeting of Robert Burns and Sir Walter Scott at Sciennes Hill House.* Besides Burns and Scott, we can see Dr Adam Ferguson (stoking the fire), philosophers Adam Smith and Dugald Stewart, physician Joseph Black, geologist James Hutton and dramatist John Home

**12.** Williamina Belsches (Lady Forbes) by Richard Cosway. Despite seeming to accept Sir Walter Scott's proposal of marriage in 1795, Williamina eventually married William Forbes in 1797.

**13.** *Lady Scott, née Charlotte Margaret Charpentier (1770–1828)* by James Saxon.

**14.** 39 North Castle Street. Sir Walter Scott and his wife Charlotte moved here in 1801 and remained until 1826.

(CASSELL'S *OLD AND NEW EDINBURGH*)

**15.** Sir Walter Scott's cottage at Lasswade by unknown artist. The cottage allowed Scott to engage in the country pursuits that he had enjoyed at his uncle's estate.

(SCOTTISH NATIONAL GALLERY)

**16.** Archibald Constable, Sir Walter Scott's publisher. Constable was also the commercial manager of the quarterly magazine *The Edinburgh Review*.

(CASSELL'S *OLD AND NEW EDINBURGH*)

**18.** George Gordon, Lord Byron. Byron was initially a rival of Sir Walter Scott but they later became friends.

**17.** William Erskine, Lord Kinneder, 1769–1822, a judge and Scott's friend, by William Nicholson.

(SCOTTISH NATIONAL PORTRAIT GALLERY)

**19.** John Gibson Lockhart, 1794–1854, son-in-law and biographer of Scott and Charlotte Sophia Scott, Mrs Lockhart, 1799 –1837. Painted by Robert Scott Lauder.

(SCOTTISH NATIONAL PORTRAIT GALLERY)

**20.** Cartley Hole Farm, known locally as 'Clarty Hole'. Sir Walter Scott changed the name to Abbotsford.

**21.** An incident during the visit of George IV to Edinburgh in 1822. A group of six unidentified figures, including two in Highland dress and one in the uniform of the Royal Company of Archers, by Sir David Wilkie.

**22.** Tartan suit in Ross tartan, made and worn for King George IV's visit.

**23.** Sir Walter Scott, by James Saxon. His favourite dog, a bull terrier called Camp rests on Scott's knee. The portrait was painted for his wife, Charlotte.

(SCOTTISH NATIONAL PORTRAIT GALLERY)

**24.** Sir Walter Scott, photogravure of the 1829 drawing by Sir Francis Leggat Chantry.

(THE SCOTT GALLERY: A SERIES OF ONE HUNDRED AND FORTY-SIX PHOTOGRAVURES TOGETHER WITH DESCRIPTIVE LETTERPRESS)

**25.** The Abbotsford family depicted in peasant dress, by Sir David Wilkie who visited Sir Walter Scott and his family at Abbotsford in 1817. Included in the group are Tom Purdie and Adam Ferguson, who commissioned the picture.

(SCOTTISH NATIONAL PORTRAIT GALLERY)

**26.** The Scott Monument in East Princes Street Gardens, Edinburgh, opened in 1844 and is the largest monument to a writer in the world. It has a series of viewing platforms reached by a series of narrow spiral staircases.

(BOB COWAN)

**27.** Sir Walter Scott's tomb at Dryburgh Abbey. When he died in 1832, he was buried next to his wife Charlotte who died in 1826.

(BOB COWAN)

hungry wildcats lurking close by. Despite this, she and the children loved the place, and Scott might have remained there, had it not been that oaks and sycamores grow slowly and that the land he was planting was not his. The seven-year lease on Ashiestiel was due to run out in the spring of 1811, and although an annual renewal was an option, Scott was by now hankering for a place of his own. He wanted to put down roots, both literally and metaphorically, for the benefit of his own descendants, not for those of someone else.

On 1 July Scott broke the news to John Morritt, an antiquarian landowner whom he had met on a visit to London in 1809, that he had 'bought a small farm value of about £150 yearly with the intention of "bigging [building] myself a bower" after my own fashion'. This was Cartley Hole, consisting of a rundown farmhouse with an incongruous classically styled portico, 110 acres of marshy haugh and a ragged fir plantation, on the bank of the Tweed between Melrose and Galashiels. The farm was known locally as 'Clarty Hole', meaning 'Dirty Puddle', though not for long. Scott, who soon began to refer to himself, half jokingly, as 'The Laird', changed the name to the grander Abbotsford, on the grounds that there was a ford on the Tweed below the house, and the land had once been owned by Melrose Abbey. Scott loved this kind of association; he also noted that at the nearby confluence of Tweed and Gala was the site of the last clan battle fought in the Borders, between the Scotts and the Kerrs in 1526. More delightful still was that the Huntly Burn, on whose bank Thomas the Rhymer had met the Queen of Elfland, ran nearby. Charlotte and the children, indifferent to such matters, wept bitterly on leaving Ashiestiel. The flitting, which took place in mid-May 1812, was hilariously described in a letter to another of Scott's titled friends, Lady Alvanley:

> *The neighbours have been much delighted with the procession of my furniture, in which old swords, bows, targets, and lances made a very conspicuous show. A family of turkeys was accommodated within the helmet of some preux* [gallant] *chevalier of ancient Border fame; and the very cows, for aught I know, were bearing banners and muskets. I assure your Ladyship that this caravan, attended by a dozen of ragged, rosy peasant children, carrying fishing-rods and spears, and leading poneys* [sic]*, greyhounds, and spaniels would, as it crossed the Tweed, have furnished no bad subject for the pencil, and really reminded me of one of the gypsey groups of Callot upon their march.*

To Daniel Terry, the theatrical actor-manager whose taste would strongly influence the later furnishing and decoration of Abbotsford, he wrote of 'twenty-four cart-loads of the veriest trash in nature, besides dogs, pigs, poneys, poultry, cows, calves, bare-headed wenches and bare-breeched boys'.

The first days at Abbotsford were, inevitably, chaotic. The house, into which Scott optimistically reckoned that 'by compression I think I can cram my family', was neglected and shabby, and the problems of accommodating and feeding husband, wife, four children and servants, while tripping over old helmets, muskets, banners and spears, were too much for highly-strung Charlotte. The children were fractious and she regularly lost her temper. The situation was made worse by Scott's immediately starting on improvements to the land, laying out gardens and planting trees as a prelude to building work on the house; within a year the noise of hammering and chiselling and the hazards of builders' rubble would be added to Charlotte's woes. She did not know it then, but as Scott's building fervour increased she was doomed to spend more than half of every year, for the rest of her life, in an architectural 'work in progress'.

Until the Court of Session rose in mid-July 1812 Scott had to be thirty miles away in Edinburgh during the week, but every Saturday evening he arrived back at Abbotsford, eager to see what progress had been made in his absence. At this stage his intention seems to have been relatively modest; he meant to improve the farmhouse without greatly enlarging it and, as he assured Joanna Baillie, 'keep the leeside of prudence in my proceedings'. To which Miss Baillie replied sceptically:

> ... that she doubted 'the Laird of Abbotsford has not told me honestly all the rooms that are to be in his new house, and that the museum-room has been omitted. Rob Roy's armour (for I suppose you have got it; pray let me know if you have), this purse, with its old coins, and many other things gathered and to be gathered, must require a place to be kept in ... .

In fact, Scott's remark about 'the leeside of prudence' was not to be taken at face value. He had in his own words been 'ruining himself' by buying yet more weapons and curios – including Rob Roy's purse and, he wrote to his daughter Sophia, 'some of the hair of Charles I cut from the head when his coffin was opened at Windsor'. He had also agreed to a hugely pricey plan for his 'cottage' proposed by William Stark, a young Glasgow architect, and compounded his own financial stress by buying, for a colossal £4000, the neighbouring property of Abbotslee.

Meanwhile, there was only one 'living-room' in the house, which had to serve as dining room, sitting room, schoolroom and study. In the long vacation, when Scott was not out digging in the garden and planting acorns and seeds sent to him by his aristocratic friends, he worked at a desk in the window, with a curtain pinned up behind his chair to give a semblance of privacy. His need was pressing; his edition of Swift for Constable was still unfinished, and John Ballantyne's increasingly shaky enterprise depended almost entirely on his input. Much depended on the success of *Rokeby*, a long poem inspired by visits to John Morritt's estate of that name in County Durham. In tandem with this work, he was writing a lighter romantic piece titled *The Bridal of Triermain*.

According to Lockhart, *Rokeby* was intended as 'a tale of the civil war, but with no reference to history or politics'. A tribute, no doubt, to Scott's large English readership, it was set just after the Parliamentarian victory over the Royalists at Marston Moor in 1644, and contains Scott's characteristic features of beautiful scenic description and dramatic action incorporating murder, vengeance, child abduction, a castle on fire and a young heroine torn between saving her father's life and entering a loveless marriage. What is missing is the intimate and loving sense of location that Scott had brought to his Scottish poems; although he knew the Rokeby estate, he was much dependent on Morritt, who was the dedicatee, to supply him with local and historical information.

For five years Scott had been the most fashionable poet in Britain, lionised in London and enormously popular in his native land. But public taste is fickle; perhaps some readers were tiring of Scott's convoluted plot lines and perceived provincialism, but there was also a new star in the sky. Fulfilling the promise of *English Bards and Scotch Reviewers* and with an image more romantic, sexy and scandalous than Scott's could ever be, Lord Byron had in 1812 published the first part of *Childe Harold's Pilgrimage*. Byron's poem was youthful, world-weary, melancholy, morally dubious and achingly modern, and the contrast with the dusty antiquarianism of *Rokeby* could scarcely have been more marked. Byron became the latest craze and, despite generally favourable reviews, the sales figures of *Rokeby* fell far short of what Scott was counting on to cover his expenses and shore up the fortunes of John Ballantyne & Co. His career as a poet was not yet over. *The Lord of the Isles* and *Harold the Dauntless* were still to come. But their tepid reception confirmed what Scott already knew, that in the world of poetry he was yesterday's man.

How Scott felt about his own verse is hard to know. Outward modesty had always been one of the devices he used to safeguard his privacy, and his most endearing characteristic was a healthy lack of 'literary' pretentiousness, probably born of his lifelong belief that soldiering was a higher calling. Although he worked hard at it, perhaps poetry was just something for which he found he had a lucrative talent. Indeed, the most amusing story told of this time says more about his attitude to child-rearing than about his private view of his achievement. James Ballantyne told Lockhart that he had once asked Sophia Scott what she thought of *The Lady of the Lake*. Her reply was, 'Oh, I have not read it. Papa says there is nothing so bad for young people as reading bad poetry.' Scott was a wise father; the young Scotts were never treated as 'celebrity' children. Indeed, in their earliest years, they seem scarcely to have known that their father was a writer at all. Scott reared them as outdoor children, teaching them to ride and – in the case of the boys – to hunt and shoot game. They were healthy and ordinary, and none of them ever showed a vestige of the literary precocity that had marked their father's childhood.

\* \* \*

*Rokeby*'s comparative failure was the final nail in the coffin of John Ballantyne & Co. In early 1813, as the long and expensive war against Napoleon dragged on, the national economy remained in the doldrums, the banking system in crisis and credit almost impossible to obtain. John Ballantyne without consultation sold some of Scott's precious copyrights to raise cash, putting Scott to the extra expense of buying them back. Although Scott's loyalty to the brothers was never in question, his letters to them at this time became ever more testy and by the summer he had had enough. On 25 July, having despaired of John, he wrote to James:

> *I have not proposed stopping a business which was,* ex facie [on the face of it] *profitable to others as well as to me until I made a very great struggle to keep it on. But I cannot support it any longer & any inconvenience directly affecting me would of course ruin the printing office also – to prevent which the stock of J.B. & Co. must be sold for its marketable value & all loss submitted to in silence.*

The upshot was that in August the Ballantynes (for of course Scott could not be seen to act in the matter) approached Archibald Constable to help them out of the hole the three partners had dug for themselves. Constable behaved with a blend of self-interest and magnanimity, offering £1300 for the more saleable items in Ballantyne's vast unsold stock. His conditions were that John Ballantyne & Co. stop trading at once, and that he should be allowed to buy a quarter share in the copyright of *Rokeby* for an additional £700. Constable also took it upon himself to prepare a report on the finances of the Ballantynes' publishing and printing operations, and reached the bleak conclusion that they must urgently raise £4000 to avoid bankruptcy. The consequences for Scott would have been nightmarish; his secret activities as a tradesman exposed, he would have felt obliged to resign from the Clerkship he had worked so hard to get, losing the precious income it brought him. He was given a short-term loan by his friend John Morritt and other well-wishers chipped in, but in the end Scott was forced to go cap in hand to the Duke of Buccleuch, who guaranteed a bank loan for £4000.

James Ballantyne lost money but saved the printing house. John, who had nothing to lose, closed one shop and opened another, where for the next seven years, he operated quite successfully as an auctioneer. Scott was the greatest loser financially, as he really deserved to be; he had employed the feckless John for his own ends and failed to supervise him. Few would disagree either with David Daiches' judgement that he had borrowed money from his friends under false pretences, for 'neither Morritt, nor Buccleuch, nor anyone except the Ballantynes had the remotest idea that Scott's troubles were largely the result of his financial involvement with a publishing and a printing firm'. It should have been, as Daiches concludes, 'a lesson and an awful warning to Scott', but it was not. The 'leeside of prudence' was forgotten, and by the year's end Abbotsford's first makeover was complete, with a new kitchen, laundry, stables and guest accommodation provided in an adjacent building, known as 'The Chapel' from a cross from an old church at Galashiels embedded in its wall.

\* \* \*

While the drama of John Ballantyne & Co.'s demise was being acted out in Edinburgh, and huge sums of money changing hands, Scott received a letter from the Marquess of Hertford. It contained an offer, on behalf of the Prince Regent, of the post of Poet Laureate, recently vacated by the literary nonentity Henry Pye. Such evidence of royal approval was flattering, but Scott heeded the advice of Duke of Buccleuch that 'the Poet Laureate would stick to you and your productions like a piece of court plaister [black sticking plaster]', and turned the honour down. In his reply to the Marquess, he suggested delicately that as he had paid legal positions, it should instead be offered to one of those who lives have been 'dedicated exclusively to literature, and who too often derive from their labours more credit than emolument'. The post went on his recommendation to the 'Lake' poet Robert Southey, who was ineffably delighted, even though the 'emolument' amounted to a mere £27 a year.

# CHAPTER 19

# The Great Unknown

*In truth, I am not sure it would be considered quite decorous of me, as a Clerk of Session, to write novels. Judges being monks, Clerks are a sort of lay brethren, from whom some solemnity of walk and conduct may be expected.*

~ Letter to J. B. Morritt, July 1815 ~

ALTHOUGH BY THE late eighteenth century the advent of circulating libraries had made novel reading as popular in middle-class Scotland as anywhere else, fiction had a slower start in Scotland than in England. For two hundred years after the Reformation in the 1540s, the teaching of the Presbyterian Church of Scotland was that only the Bible, the 'Word of God', contained the truth. The implication that all other story-telling was 'lies', and so the work of the Devil, cast a baneful shadow over imaginative writers and readers alike. Only the Puritan John Bunyan's *The Pilgrim's Progress* escaped censure, becoming a companion volume to the Bible in many a pious household. It was the mid-eighteenth century before Enlightenment ideas challenged this unpleasant doctrine, and among the strictest Presbyterians it took even longer to lose its power. Art in all its forms suffered to some degree, but the greatest obloquy was reserved for novels which patently were, in a literal sense, untrue – and in the Calvinist mind frivolous and a sinful waste of time.

By contrast, the Anglican Church in England had never after the Puritan period adopted such a hard stance, allowing both fiction writers and readers to flourish without a stifling sense of sin. The modern, non-didactic novel appeared first in the picaresque, or episodic contemporary tales of Samuel Richardson, Henry Fielding and Tobias Smollett (the last a Scot by birth but long resident in London), read by the adoles-

cent Scott during his convalescences in Kelso. As their influence diminished, however, novels set in past times became popular, many merging
with the 'Gothic horror' genre made popular by Mary Shelley, Horace
Walpole, Anne Radcliffe and Matthew 'Monk' Lewis. An example of this
kind of 'crossover' is the once-popular *The Recess; or A Tale of Other
Times* by the English Sophia Lee (1750–1824), set in the reign of Queen
Elizabeth I. Although the story features actual historical events, such as
the rebellion of the Earl of Essex in 1601, it transcends silliness in being
narrated by twin daughters of Mary, Queen of Scots by a secret marriage,
who have been brought up in the subterranean recess of a deserted
monastery.

This is far from the substance of Walter Scott, who admitted only the
influence of the Irish writer Maria Edgeworth (1768–1849) whose
*Castle Rackrent* (1800) has some claim to be the first regional and
seriously historical novel published in Great Britain. Scott's praise of
Edgeworth, who was not remotely a writer of his calibre, was excessive,
but genial Scott habitually overstated the merits of his contemporaries.
He thought Joanna Baillie was the greatest dramatist since Shakespeare.

In 1805, the year when *The Lay of the Last Minstrel* was published,
Scott was already at work on a prose romance, set in the Highlands
during the 1745 Jacobite Rising and tentatively titled *Waverley: 'Tis Fifty
Years Since*. Disappointingly, when he showed the first seven chapters to
Will Erskine, whose literary judgement he trusted, Erskine pronounced
them dull, an opinion backed up by James Ballantyne. Mildly discouraged, Scott turned his mind to other work. His poetry was flourishing
and Swift still unfinished, its completion delayed even further when
Henry Weber, whom Scott had adopted as his live-in secretary, had a
breakdown, produced a pair of pistols and challenged his benefactor to a
duel. Scott managed to disarm him, but Weber never recovered his sanity;
for the remaining five years of his life Scott generously paid his hospital
expenses, but was left to finish Swift on his own. The long task was
finally accomplished in 1814. During this period the only fiction he
worked on was *Queenhoo-Hall*, an unfinished novel by the antiquarian
Joseph Strutt (1749–1802) which John Murray had asked him to edit
and complete.

Intended by Strutt as a romance that would illustrate the manners
and customs of English people in the fifteenth century, the completed
*Queenhoo-Hall* was published in 1808 and flopped badly. Scott,
however, had learned from it. In the 'General Preface to the Waverley

Novels' (1829), he remarks of Strutt that 'by rendering his language too ancient and displaying his antiquarian knowledge too liberally, the ingenious author had raised up an obstacle to his own success. Every work designed for mere amusement,' he adds, 'must be expressed in language easily comprehended.' He further decided that 'the manners of the middle ages did not possess the interest which I had conceived, and was led to form the opinion that a romance founded on a Highland story, and dealing with more modern events, would have a better chance of popularity than a tale of chivalry. My thoughts, therefore, returned more than once to the tale which I had actually commenced ...'.

Although they were civil to each other, Scott had never really warmed to Constable, a self-made man indifferent to class distinction. But however little Scott relished the reconciliation, the fall of John Ballantyne & Co. forced him to return to Constable as his Edinburgh publisher. Constable, who regarded Scott with more detachment as a valuable contributor to his prosperity, wisely let past grievances rest, although he did not accede immediately to Scott's unabashed demands for a huge advance on a poem he had not even begun. Probably Constable had now to take into account the views of his new partner (and son-in-law) Robert Cadell, who regarded Scott's defection to John Ballantyne and Co. as a hostile act. When, in 1814, Scott anonymously published his first novel, there was no huge advance, only an agreement that the author would receive half of the profits.

\* \* \*

It should be noted, in reading Scott's – and by extension Lockhart's – version of the events leading up to *Waverley*'s publication, that in recent years eminent critics have questioned its veracity, citing discrepancies in dates, letters and paper watermarks as evidence of tale-spinning and the creation of myth. If so, the myth is a powerful one, and further evidence of Scott's imaginative capacity to turn his own life into a remarkably coherent story. According to his own account in the 'General Preface', after the adverse criticism of Erskine and Ballantyne in 1805, he had put the manuscript containing the first seven chapters in the drawer of an old writing desk which, on arrival at Abbotsford, was consigned to an attic to make room for new furniture. Not until the autumn of 1813 did Scott, searching for some fishing tackle to lend to a guest, pull out a drawer of the desk and find the long-forgotten manuscript. 'I immediately set to work,' he writes, 'to complete it according to my original intention.' This scene, like the one of Scott's meeting with Robert Burns in Professor

Ferguson's drawing room, was imprinted on the imagination of later readers by a famous painting by C. M. Hardie RSA which shows Scott, looking slightly furtive and as ever accompanied by dogs, bending over the desk with the manuscript pages in his hand.

Whatever the truth of the novel's gestation – which was certainly more complex than Scott's account admits – *Waverley* was different in both breadth and depth from anything that preceded it. Its subtitle altered to *'Tis Sixty Years Since* to take account of the ten-year gap between first idea and completion, it tells the story of Edward Waverley, a moony, quixotic young army officer on leave from his regiment, as he journeys from his ancestral home, Waverley-Honour in the south of England, through the Scottish Lowlands to the castle of Tully-Veolan in Perthshire. There he is entertained by the pedantic, staunchly Jacobite Baron Bradwardine, imagines himself in love with his daughter Rose, and meets the first of Scott's tragi-comic peasant eccentrics, the lyrical retainer Davie Gellatley. The scene darkens as Waverley is drawn into the more dangerous Highlands, where he falls under the spell of a cattle-rustling Chieftain, Fergus MacIvor of Glennaquoich, and falls in love with his beautiful, fanatically Jacobite sister Flora.

Of few fixed opinions and easily influenced, Waverley defects from the Hanoverian army in which he holds his commission to the Jacobite cause. He treasonably takes part in the Rising of 1745 led by 'Bonnie Prince' Charlie, along with Baron Bradwardine whose castle is destroyed in his absence by Hanoverian soldiers advancing towards Culloden. Saved from the worst consequences of his folly by the activity of Rose Bradwardine on his behalf, and the mitigating circumstance of his having saved the life of one Colonel Talbot at the Battle of Prestonpans, Waverley muddles through while, in the most harrowing yet noble scenes in the book, Fergus MacIvor and his henchman Evan Maccombich are savagely executed in the post-Rising reprisals at Carlisle. Rejected by Flora, Waverley transfers his affections to the less alarming Rose and the book ends on a note of harmony, with the castle rebuilt, the Baron pardoned and the houses of English Waverley-Honour and Scottish Tully-Veolan united.

No summary can convey the elements of comic chaos which leaven the serious theme, or the richness of historical ambivalence, exploration of motive and evocation of time and place developed by Scott in this remarkable book. *Waverley* may not be Scott's greatest novel, but in its warts-and-all portrayal of a 'hero' whom Scott himself called 'a sneaking piece of imbecility', it broke new ground in character realisation. It also sets out the preoccupations which had exercised Scott's mind almost since childhood and would be the substance of later novels: the marginalisation of the remoter parts of Scotland from the Lowland seats of power and prosperity, and the tension between the sweeping but violent romance of history in its periods of political and religious conflict and the safer but less stirring world of the post-1707 Union. Scott was drawn to both. On one hand he was a Scottish lawyer with Unionist loyalties, Tory sympathies and a deep fear of civil disorder. He had many English friends, and was not averse to cosying up to the descendants of George II and his brother, the 'Butcher' Duke of Cumberland. On the other hand, he could not dismiss the conviction that had he been alive in 1745, passion would have overcome caution, and he would have fought and died for the Stuart cause.

\* \* \*

*Waverley* was published anonymously on 7 June 1814. This was not unusual at the time; for reasons of modesty, diffidence or a desire to test the water a number of now well-known authors published anonymously or under pseudonyms, but few went so far as Scott in disclaiming his own work. Over the years he gave various reasons, besides the impropriety of a Clerk of the Court of Session's associating himself with the frivolity of fiction, for his reluctance to put his name to the book. He cited a fear of being discomfited should it fail to gratify public taste, and claimed that by 1814 he had fame enough, so that 'no degree of literary success could have greatly altered or improved my personal condition'. He might have added that he preferred not to have his work the main topic of conversation at every dinner he attended, and feel obliged to answer politely the questions every author dreads: 'Tell me, Mr Scott, where do you get your ideas?'; and worse, 'Mr Scott, I've written a book. Will you read it and advise me about finding a publisher?'

Scott went to great lengths to protect his anonymity. Lest his handwriting be recognised, his books were transcribed under James Ballantyne's supervision by 'confidential persons', proof corrections were copied by James onto a second set for the printers and, apart from his publishers and a few chosen confidantes, among them Will Erskine, J. B. Morritt and Lady Louisa Stuart, for the next 13 years no one knew officially the identity of the writer called 'The Great Unknown'. In fact, Scott's cover was quickly blown. No one who had read *The Lady of the Lake* was in much doubt as to the authorship of *Waverley*. Scott's fingerprints were all over it. Everybody who knows an author can hear a familiar voice in their work, and many people knew Scott. His friend Mrs Anne Grant of Laggan (1755–1838) immediately claimed to be 'satisfied from internal evidence that it is Walter Scott, and none other', while within weeks of publication the reviewer in *The Scots Magazine* was hinting heavily: 'Report assigns it to the most admired poet of the age and we see no reason that even such a writer could have to disown a perform-ance like the present.'

Even those further off were undeceived. Only three months after the book appeared, Jane Austen was writing indignantly in far-off Hampshire to her niece: 'Walter Scott has no business to write novels, especially good ones. It is not fair. He has Fame and Profit enough as a Poet ....' The Prince Regent guessed, and the adulation Scott enjoyed among the London literati would not have been offered to a poet already deemed to be *passé*. So why did Scott persist in deception for so long? Perhaps because he was afraid of criticism and certainly because he was amused by mystification and the stir it caused. And as he said, 'It was my humour'.

* * *

On July 29th 1814, Scott went on holiday. Leaving Charlotte and the children at Abbotsford, and the buzz of Edinburgh speculation behind him, he boarded the Lighthouse Yacht *Pharos* at Leith. Among his fellow passengers, all male and guests of the Commission of Northern Lights, was his friend Will Erskine, the Sheriff of Orkney; and in charge of the expedition was Robert Stevenson, engineer to the Commissioners, builder of lighthouses and the grandfather of Robert Louis Stevenson. During the next six weeks, while the Commissioners on board inspected lighthouses and the safety of shipping lanes, the *Pharos* carried Scott and his companions up the east coast to Shetland and back through Orkney and the Pentland Firth into the Minch. Visits were paid to lighthouses on Harris, Skye, Mull and Iona, Eigg and Northern Ireland, before the ship finally docked at Greenock on the Clyde. Scott compiled a detailed account of the voyage in the form of a diary, which he light-heartedly titled *Vacation 1814: Voyage in the Lighthouse Yacht to Nova Zembla, and the Lord knows Where*.

A curious observer of social customs, livestock and agriculture as well as landscape, Scott had a wonderful time. Unlike most of the passen-gers, he was only sick on the first night, and hugely enjoyed the company and the strange world of lighthouses, whaling ships, distant islands and the sea. He visited the Bell Rock and Skerryvore, explored the terrifying Smoo Cave at Durness, saw the Fairy Flag at Dunvegan, and at Sumburgh took childlike pleasure in sliding 'a few hundred feet' down a steep green slope on his bottom. He enjoyed breakfasts of 'excellent new-taken herring, equal to those of Lochfine [*sic*], fresh haddocks, fresh eggs and fresh butter, not forgetting the bottle of whisky, and bannocks of barley, and oat cakes, with the Lowland luxuries of tea and coffee'. The voyage was not without a spice of danger; although the war against Napoleon was temporarily halted, Britain was at war with the United States, and the *Pharos*, which carried guns for its protection, had two close encounters with America privateers in the Irish sea.

Most importantly for his writing, the voyage gave intensity to Scott's description of landscape in his new poem *The Lord of the Isles,* and provided a wealth of Shetland and Orkney folklore, scenery, antiquities, sports and customs. At Stromness he met Bessie Millie, an old witch who sold favourable winds to sailors for sixpence, and heard the tale of the buccaneer John Gow which seven years later would surface in *The Pirate*. The pleasure of Scott's holiday was marred by only one event, the unexpected news at Port Rush in Northern Ireland of the death of Harriet, Duchess of Buccleuch, at the age of forty. The wife of his old friend of Edinburgh Light Dragoons days, Scott had felt deep affection for this cultured, humorous and unstuffy young woman, who loved books and had done much quiet good in her short life. Pity for her husband and seven young children clouded the few remaining days of Scott's voyage.

Having completed the journey from Greenock to Glasgow on one of the new cutting-edge steamboats 'at a rate of about seven miles an hour, and with a smoothness of motion which probably resembles flying', Scott returned to Edinburgh where he found that the first edition of *Waverley* had sold out in five weeks. By November, three further editions had been called for. This success put Constable in a mellow mood, and he was now prepared to pay handsomely in advance for the poem Scott had been planning on the *Pharos*. He also agreed to take another tranche of John Ballantyne & Co.'s unsold stock, though well aware that he could not sell it either.

*The Lord of the Isles* is a verse tale based on the return to Scotland in 1307 of Robert the Bruce from exile in Ireland and his subsequent heroic struggle against the English. Woven clumsily into this historical narrative is the complicated romance of Edith of Lorn and Ronald, Lord of the

Isles. It has been suggested that Scott suffered some degree of 'writer's block' while composing the poem, and Scott himself said that the verses were 'ground out' with an effort akin to physical pain. The work proves the falling off of his poetic ingenuity; its couplets are leaden and syntax often horribly strained by the need to get rhyming words at the end of the line. *The Lord of the Isles* was not a huge success, and Scott seems to have accepted that as a poet he had written himself out. The conclusion is valedictory, and used by Scott to pay a final tribute to his friend and inspiration Harriet, Duchess of Buccleuch:

> *All angel now – yet litle less than all,*
> *   While still a pilgrim in our world below!*
> *What 'vails it us that patience to recall,*
> *   Which hid its own to soothe all other woe;*
> *What 'vails to tell, how Virtue's purest glow*
> *   Shone yet more lovely in a form so fair:*
> *And, least of all, what 'vails the world should know,*
> *   That one poor garland, twined to deck thy hair,*
> *Is hung upon thy hearse, to droop and wither there!*

CHAPTER 20

# Books, Byron
# and a Football Match

*I want to shake myself free of* Waverley *and accordingly have made a considerable exertion to finish an odd little tale within such time as will mistify [sic] the public I trust ....*

~ Letter to J. B. Morritt, 19 January 1815 ~

SCOTT WAS NOT long back from his trip on the *Pharos* when a new crisis in the printing business threatened to engulf him. In October 1814 James Ballantyne was served a distraint for debt which threatened the seizure of his property, and Scott again faced the horrible possibility of having his secret partnership exposed. After bailing out John only a year earlier, his own financial position was still dicey, yet he had no option but to come to the rescue again. It is small wonder that during the autumn he spent every available moment at his desk, or that *The Lord of the Isles* was so painfully 'ground out' of him.

Christmas that year brought a fright of another kind. Just as the Scott family were about to leave North Castle Street to spend the holidays at Abbotsford, 13-year-old Walter became ill with headache, fever and an ominous rash. A doctor diagnosed smallpox, then one of the most dangerous viral diseases on the planet. The boy would probably have died or been badly disfigured had not his parents had him inoculated in infancy, proving themselves both brave and enlightened. The great breakthrough in prevention by the English physician Edward Jenner (1749–1823) had been made only twenty years earlier and was not without its own complications. Walter recovered without infecting anyone else, but the number of references to his son's illness in letters of early 1815 show how rattled Scott had been. Years later he would tell Lockhart that he had written his second novel 'in six weeks over Christmas'. This would have been miraculous, at a time when he had so many distractions.

Scott was wise to 'shake himself free' of *Waverley*. When a first novel
has been very successful, there is often a temptation to repeat the winning
formula. Refreshingly, Scott resisted this – indeed, over a long career, he
only wrote one sequel. Leaving the complex national history of Scotland
aside for a while, his new book was, as he said, 'a tale of private life', set
in the 'recent past' of the 1760s and 70s. *Guy Mannering or, The
Astrologer*, unlike some of Scott's novels, grabs the reader's attention on
the first page.

The tale opens with a solitary young Englishman lost in a dark,
threatening landscape, from which he finds refuge at the New Place of
Ellangowan, a modern house close to the ancient castle of the Bertrams.
Here he is kindly received by the garrulous Laird, Godfrey Bertram, who
is anxiously waiting for his wife to give birth upstairs. Mannering is
introduced to the gawky, inarticulate 'Dominie' Abel Sampson and,
when the boy who will become the heir of Ellangowan and the lynchpin
of the story is born, to the fey gypsy Meg Merrilees, one of the most
haunting characters Scott ever created. When Bertram learns that
Mannering has studied astrology, he persuades him to cast the boy's
horoscope, which reveals that two catastrophes will threaten the heir:
one in his fifth and the other in his 21st year. The scene is set for a tale
richly complex yet built on the simple elements of fairy tale: a lost child,
a benign witch, false identity, friendship and love thwarted but undis-
mayed, the defeat of terrible villains and the final recognition and
restoration of the lost heir.

*Guy Mannering* teems with memorable figures: the grotesque but
faithful Dominie; the delightfully playful but deeply serious and humane
lawyer Paulus Pleydell; the irrepressible Liddesdale farmer Dandie
Dinmont with his brood of children and tribe of dogs; the wicked
smuggler Dirk Hatteraick, corrupt lawyer Gilbert Glossin and, towering over all, the gypsy matriarch Meg Merrilees – dispossessed, abused
yet faithful to death to the heir of the man who had evicted her and her
tribe from his land. Compared with these, the characters of Colonel
Mannering and the hero Henry Bertram, alias Vanbeest Brown, are
somewhat colourless, but Mannering's feisty, impudent daughter Julia is
one of Scott's more successful upper-class women. The harsh landscape
and wild sea coast of Galloway, where Scott had travelled when preparing his fateful defence of the Rev. Mr McNaught before the General
Assembly of the Church of Scotland, provide a chilly background to a
warmly human tale which culminates in what J. R. R. Tolkien in *Tree*

*and Leaf* describes as a 'eucatastrophe', the unexpected reconciliation which underlines the goodness at the heart of life.

*Guy Mannering* also illustrates one of Scott's greatest strengths, his use of the Scots language in what Henry Cockburn called 'the last purely Scotch age', before it was diminished and adulterated in the nineteenth century by the pernicious notion that English was the tongue of the educated. The vocabulary and biblical rhythms of the speech of Meg Merrilees, in particular, enhance her dignity and add a rich texture to Scott's prose, as in the famous denunciation of the Laird of Ellangowan as the gypsies leave his land:

> *'Ride your ways,' said the gypsy, 'ride your ways, Laird of Ellangowan – ride your ways, Godfrey Bertram! – This day have ye quenched seven smoking hearths – see if the fire in your ain parlour burn the blyther for that. – Ye have riven the thack off five cottar houses – look that your ain roof-tree stand the faster. – Ye may stable your stirks in the sheal-ings at Derncleugh – see that the hare does not couch on the hearth-stane at Ellangowan. – Ride your ways, Godfrey Bertram – what do ye glowr after our folk for? – There's thirty hearts there that wad hae wanted bread ere ye had wanted sunkets, and spent their life's blood ere ye had scratched your finger … . And now, ride e'en your ways, for these are the last words ye'll ever here Meg Merrilees speak, and this is the last reise that I'll ever cut in the bonny woods of Ellangowan.'*

The story that Scott wrote *Guy Mannering* in six weeks over Christmas 1814 is no doubt exaggerated. It is more likely, as Herbert Grierson suggested in the 1930s, that in the holidays Scott was 'giving form to a story over which he had been brooding for several months and probably composing in the intervals while he waited for the successive proofs of *The Lord of the Isles*'. Scott's account of the book's genesis, set out in the preface to the 1829 'Magnum Opus' edition that 'The tale [of the astrologer] was originally told to me by an old servant of my father's, an excellent old Highlander', is also questioned by modern critics, who point to a correspondence Scott was conducting in late 1814 with Joseph Train, a Supervisor of Excise in Galloway, an amateur anti-quarian and ardent admirer of Scott's poetry. It seems too much of a coincidence that a package from Train dated November 1814, con-taining accounts of Galloway gypsies, should include the local story of the astrologer, as Lockhart admits, 'almost in the words placed in the mouth of John MacKinlay in the introduction to *Guy Mannering*'. The mid-twentieth century critic W. M. Parker drew attention to the Annesley case, a court action of 1743 with striking similarities to the story of the lost heir in Scott's narrative, and more recently the scholar Professor Peter Garside has argued that Train's account arrived too late to be the basis of Scott's novel. In his view, it is most likely that Scott obtained the story from Tom Scott's wife, Elizabeth McCulloch, whose family had harboured the 'gypsy king' Billy Marshall on their land at Ardwall. If so, Scott's tale of the otherwise unmentioned 'excellent old Highlander' must be another instance, like the tale of the lost fishing tackle, of his inventing detail to give an extra spice of interest to his own story.

*The Lord of the Isles* was published on 8 January 1815, followed on 24 February by *Guy Mannering*, 'by the author of *Waverley*,' as Scott added to 'mistify' [*sic*] the public. The tepid reception of the poem and the electrifying success of the novel, which sold out its first edition of 2000 copies on publication day, reinforced Scott's belief that his future lay in prose. He would continue to weave beautiful lyrics into his novels and attempt an occasional longer poem, but his reputation – and his bank balance – could no longer depend on verse.

Despite Constable's successful marketing of *Waverley*, Scott had decided to take his second novel elsewhere. At this point John Ballantyne popped up again as literary agent, and successfully negotiated the sale of *Guy Mannering* to the London publisher Longman. Scott was paid £1500 for the rights to the first edition, and James Ballantyne of course was contracted as printer. Longman was forced to take £500-worth of John Ballantynes's unsaleable stock, and Constable was awarded the consolation prize of the Scottish marketing share. Although Scott informed the Edinburgh publisher that this arrangement need not be permanent, it was not the first or last time Constable had reason to feel aggrieved.

In early 1815, Scott's letters were full of plans for a long visit to London with Charlotte and 15-year-old Sophia. After some swithering over dates, the trio set off in April, Scott having persuaded Charlotte to travel by sea with the bribe that 'she shall have the difference of expence [*sic*] to save her from the horror of hackney coaches in London'. Charlotte may have rued her bargain, since the passage from Leith was, Scott wrote laughingly to Lady Abercorn:

*pleasant, bating three circumstances – 1st. That the wind was in constant and methodical opposition. 2nd. That a collier brig ran foul of us in the dark and nearly consigned us all to the bottom of the sea. 3rd. and last we struck on a rock and lay hammering for two hours until we floated with the rising tide.*

It was a heavy price to pay to avoid a few taxi rides. Scott and Charlotte stayed in Piccadilly with the Dumergues, friends of Charlotte's before her marriage, while Sophia was parked at Hampstead with Joanna Baillie and her sister Agnes.

Scott had business to attend to in London, but there was plenty of time for socialising, perhaps most notably with his former adversary Lord Byron. Happily, their mutual rancour had not endured. In 1812 John Murray, who published both poets and was keen to heal the rift between them, passed on to Scott some appreciative remarks made to Byron by the Prince Regent (later King George IV) about *The Lady of the Lake*. Scott's anger at being portrayed as 'Apollo's venal son' by the teenaged Byron had cooled over time, and he wrote on 16 July 1812 to thank him and invite him to visit Abbotsford. Byron replied, expressing regret for 'the evil works of my nonage' and an occasional correspondence ensued, although Byron never came to Abbotsford and it was not until 7 April 1815 that the two poets first came face to face. The encounter, which took place in the drawing room of 50 Albemarle Street, where John Murray was accustomed to keep 'open house' for his authors in the late afternoon, was a great success. Murray's young son, also John, later recalled the occasion in terms touchingly reminiscent of Scott's own youthful awe when he found himself in the same room as Robert Burns.

*I can recollect seeing Lord Byron in Albemarle Street. So far as I can remember, he appeared to me rather a short man, with a handsome countenance, remarkable for the fine blue veins which ran over his pale marble temples .... Lord Byron's deformity in his foot was very evident, especially as he walked downstairs. He carried a stick. After Scott and he had ended their conversation in the drawing-room, it was a curious sight to see the two greatest poets of the age – both lame, stumping downstairs side by side. They continued to meet in Albemarle Street nearly every day, and remained together for two or three hours at a time.*

They agreed, Scott said, about everything except religion and politics. He might have added morality, since by 1815 Byron's scandalous love life was the talk of the town, and Scott could scarcely have approved. As a sincere admirer of Byron's work, however, he was gratified by the friendship, which was sealed with an exchange of gifts. Scott gave Byron a Turkish dagger 'mounted with gold, which had been the property of the redoubted Elfi Bey', and Byron reciprocated with an enormous silver urn excavated from the long walls of Athens and containing human bones. This monstrous object, as casually removed from Greece as the Elgin Marbles, delighted Scott. He had a table specially made for it, and it is still on display at Abbotsford today. Some years later, Byron gave Scott a gift of another kind, the dedication of his verse drama *Cain*.

Byron was not the only celebrity Scott met in that summer. He called on Wordsworth and the then fashionable novelist Amelia Opie, but these meetings were eclipsed by an invitation to have supper at Carlton House, the residence of the Prince Regent. Scott, who had practice in flattering his social superiors without licking their boots, exerted his charm to entertain the monarch-in-waiting, and had a gratifyingly cosy evening – although his recollection that the Prince sang songs and called him 'Walter' was thrown into doubt when none of the other guests later contacted by Lockhart could remember anything of the sort. But the occasion had been successful, and on 23 May Scott wrote to acknowledge receipt of 'an elegant & valuable box with which it has pleased His Royal Highness the Prince Regent to honour me'. Thus was the connection between the dissolute Hanoverian prince and the Jacobite-sympathising though loyal subject of the Crown established, to mutual satisfaction.

The Scotts returned to Edinburgh on 11 June, a week before the Battle of Waterloo. On 27 July Scott was off again, this time accompanied by three younger men, his kinsman John Scott of Gala, Alexander Pringle of Whytbank and an advocate, Robert Bruce. They visited Cambridge on the way to Harwich, crossing to Hellevoetsluis in the Netherlands in a privately chartered cutter, then travelled via Antwerp to Brussels. Before leaving home, again using John Ballantyne as his agent, Scott had hurriedly arranged to subsidise his tour by writing an account of it, which he would disguise as a series of letters from 'Paul', a 'cross old bachelor' travelling abroad, to his rusticated family in Britain. In *Paul's Letters to his Kinsfolk*, Scott used his alter ego to voice his own reaction to the places he visited, notably the field of Waterloo and Paris in its aftermath. Despite his talking up the courageous exploits of the British and disparaging of the French, his treatment of the Emperor Napoleon was remarkably even-handed, and his most critical remarks were reserved for the brutal behaviour of the conquering Prussians. Yet with typical fairness, he felt obliged to concede that the French had treated them very badly.

\*　\*　\*

The year 1815 had been a vigorous, exciting year for Scott and it closed on a note of good cheer, with the Laird at Abbotsford invited to organise a football match. The suggestion came from the Duke of Buccleuch, who proposed that his brother-in-law, the Earl of Home, would captain a team of farmers and shepherds from among their own tenants against a team from Hawick, Selkirk and Gala. The Duke's part was to provide a refreshment tent and throw up the ball to start the match, which was to be played on a wide field at Carterhaugh, near the junction of the Ettrick and Yarrow. Scott was in his element, advising the Ettrick team and making sure that all the players had sprigs in their bonnets, heather for Ettrick, pine for their opponents. Many sprigs were required, since the 'Carterhaugh Ba'' game played on 4 December between the 'Men of Ettrick' and the 'Men of Yarrow' was less a football match as now understood than a game of mega-rugby with few rules and hundreds of participants on each side. It lasted for five hours and was watched by 2000 spectators, among whom were the entire Buccleuch family and almost every other titled person in the Borders. Naturally Scott could not conceive even a football match without giving it a twist of historical pageantry; pipes skirled, the players marched and the ancient war banner of the Buccleuch family was paraded on the pitch. As he proudly told J. B. Morritt:

> *My boy Walter carried the Duke's standard and as he was dressed in forest green and buff with a green bonnet and an eagle's feather in it, a large gold chain with a medal, and otherwise gallantly armed and mounted he really made a very handsome figure. He is you know a good horseman and really became the old banner well, looking more like an Esquire of old than a high school boy.*

Scott wrote a terrible poem, 'Song, on the lifting of the banner of the House of Buccleuch, at a great Foot-ball Match at Carterhaugh', which was printed and distributed among the spectators:

*... Then strip, lads, and to it, though sharp be the weather,*
  *And if by mischance you should happen to fall,*
*There are worse things in life than a tumble on heather*
  *And life is itself but a game at foot-ball.*

*Then up with the banner, as forest winds fan her,*
  *She has blazed over Ettrick eight ages and more;*
*In sport we'll attend her, in battle defend her,*
  *With heart and with hand like our fathers before.*

As far as anyone knew or cared, the score was a draw.

# CHAPTER 21

# Changing Horses

*The last of my chargers was a high-spirited and very handsome one, by name Daisy. He had, among other good qualities, one always particularly valuable in my case, that of standing like a rock to be mounted. When he was brought to the door, after I came home from the Continent, instead of signifying, by the usual tokens, that he was pleased to see his master, he looked askant at me like a devil; and when I put my foot in the stirrup, he reared upright, and I fell to the ground rather awkwardly. The experience was repeated twice or thrice, always with the same result.*

~ John Gibson Lockhart,
*Memoirs of the Life of Sir Walter Scott, Bart., 1837–38* ~

LONG AFTER THE Edinburgh Light Dragoons had ceased to be an important part of his life, Scott had kept a warhorse, a tall, strong and courageous animal bred for the cavalry charges which were a vital component of historic battle plans. There was an element of swank in this; the charger was a status symbol dear to Scott the keen-as-mustard part-time officer. The rejection by his warhorse immediately after his reality-check at Waterloo seemed strangely significant, especially when the animal allowed Tom Purdie to mount him without protest. But after trying again a week later with the same result, Scott realised sadly that he must part with Daisy. 'Wars and rumours of war being over,' he added ruefully, 'I resolved to have done with such dainty blood. I now stick to a good sober cob.'

Since his sickly childhood and adolescence, Scott had enjoyed robust health, walking, climbing and riding in all weathers, getting soaked to the skin and never allowing his lame leg to curtail any activity. Recently in London, however, he had excused himself from an appointment with John Murray on the grounds of 'the day being execrable and my rheumatics troublesome'. At 44, he realised, he was no longer young. The swapping of his battle charger for a short-legged horse presaged a new phase of life, and the dominant character in his next book was a man in middle age.

At the close of 1815, Scott began a letter to James Ballantyne:

*Dear James – I'm done, thank God, with the long yarns*
*Of the most prosy of Apostles – Paul,*
*And now advance, sweet heathen of Monkbarns!*
*Step out, old quizz, as fast as I can scrawl!*

Even if *Paul's Letters to his Kinsfolk* had been a chore rather than a pleasure, the book sold reasonably well. Its completion freed him to get on with a more congenial task, writing his third (and personal favourite) novel, *The Antiquary*. Scott had already written in *Waverley* a tale harking back to the time of his grandparents, and in *Guy Mannering* one within his parents' recollection. The action of *The Antiquary* takes place in what to Scott was 'the present', the years leading up to the threatened French invasion of Britain in the 1800s. Set on the east coast of Scotland in the environs of Arbroath (Fairport) and the red cliffs nearby, it features some of Scott's most brightly evocative incidents: a fraught stagecoach ride from Edinburgh's High Street to Queensferry; a thrilling rescue from a tidal surge on the sands at Halket Head; a nightmare in a haunted room; the richly funny scene in the mail office at Fairport where nosy gossips gather to tamper with incoming letters, avid to learn their neighbours' private business.

*The Antiquary* has been criticised for having in the young man known as 'Lovel' a colourless romantic hero, for tending to melodrama and lacking a coherent plot line. But it has the quality that the novelist and critic E. M. Forster (1879–1970), who belonged to the generation that undervalued Scott, reluctantly identified as his great strength: 'He could tell a story. He had the primitive power of keeping the reader in suspense and playing on his curiosity.' He makes us, adds Forster, ask constantly: 'What next? ... And then?' This is certainly true of *The Antiquary*, but its chief joy is not its tangled plot but its protagonist, Jonathan Oldbuck, the 'sweet heathen' and 'old quizz' of Monkbarns. It has been claimed that he was 'based' on George Constable, he who had been in love with Aunt Jenny at Prestonpans long ago, and some of

Constable's eccentricities may have found their way into the story. But what makes Oldbuck so entertaining is the sense that Scott was guying himself. The Antiquary is middle-aged, finicky, an avid collector of dusty antiquities and full of abstruse and sometimes dubious historical lore. An early disappointment in love is offered as reason for his outrageous but amusing misogyny, his only characteristic which Scott clearly did not share; the Antiquary is what his creator might have become had he not moved on after his love affair with Williamina Belsches.

The tale has other memorable characters; the aged 'Blue Gown' or licensed beggar Edie Ochiltree with his courage, fearless impudence and expressive Scots speech; the Antiquary's tetchy spinster sister Miss Grizelda Oldbuck; the hairdresser Caxon left, after a change in fashion, with only three wigs in the parish to tend, and the demented old fisher-wife Elspeth Mucklebackit, whose history is at the hub of the book's melodramatic closing chapters. There are moments of absurdity featuring Edie Ochiltree and a ludicrous trickster named Dousterswivel; and of tragedy – the drowning and funeral of the fisherman's son, Steenie Muckle-backit, and the wild grief of his mother are poignantly described. More painful still is the bitter response of the bereaved father to Oldbuck's word of encouragement on finding him soon back on the shore mending the 'auld black bitch of a boat' in which his son perished:

> And what wad ye have me do, unless I wanted to see four children starve, because ane is drowned? It's weel for you gentles, that can sit in the house with handkerchers at your een when ye lose a friend, but the like o' us must to our work again, if our hearts were beating as hard as my hammer.

In the end, as in *Guy Mannering*, all works out well. Lovel becomes an Earl and gets married, the old age of Edie Ochiltree is provided for and, in a scene of delightful farce involving a bonfire, a false alarm and Lovel revealed as a dashing army officer. The French do not land at Fairport and everyone goes home to breakfast.

\* \* \*

The years 1815 and 1816 were a time of astonishing creativity for Scott. They saw the publication of *Guy Mannering*, *Paul's Letters to his Kinsfolk* and *The Antiquary*, along with a vast amount of journalism, including articles for the *Encyclopaedia Britannica* which was now owned by Constable, the whole of the 'History' section of the *Edinburgh*

*Annual Register* and a typically generous review in the *Quarterly* of Jane Austen's *Emma*. Scott always admired in Austen a quality he knew that he lacked. Lamenting her early death, he wrote in his *Journal* in 1826: 'The Big Bow-wow strain I can do myself like any now going; but the exquisite touch, which renders ordinary commonplace things and characters interesting ... is denied to me.' At this time he was also writing his last long poem *Harold the Dauntless*, and embarking on a new fiction project which saw 'The Author of *Waverley*' reinventing himself with a new publisher.

Gratified as he was by the sales figures of his first three novels, Scott was still beset by financial anxiety. James Ballantyne's marriage in 1815 was made conditional by the bride's brother on his being clear of financial liabilities. This resulted in Scott's assuming James's share of their joint debts and becoming sole partner in the printing firm, while retaining James as an employee at a salary of £400 a year. People who had made loans when John Ballantyne & Co. collapsed in 1813 were beginning to press for the return of their money. He needed cash, not only to keep creditors at bay, maintain 39 North Castle Street and educate his sons, but also to finance his grandiose plans for Abbotsford.

Constable had done well both for the author and himself with the first 'Waverleys', and Scott had no intention of breaking with him at this point. But neither did he want to put all his eggs in one basket, and felt free to negotiate with other publishers, provided that the books were not advertised as 'by the Author of *Waverley*'. James Ballantyne was chosen to open negotiations with William Blackwood (1776–1834), Constable's only serious competitor in Edinburgh, who was also Scottish agent for John Murray in London. (Apparently John Ballantyne was not chosen because both Blackwood and Murray disliked him.) Scott's name was not mentioned, but when Blackwood heard that part of the deal was to be his acceptance of £600-worth of John Ballantyne's unsold 'trash' he guessed who the prospective author must be. Unimpressed by the promise of 'something totally different in style and structure' and keen to cash in on a winning formula, Blackwood offered a four-book deal, each volume to contain a tale set in a different area of Scotland. Scott's precious anonymity was to be protected by the introduction of a pedantic fictional schoolmaster whom Scott (as brilliant as Dickens in the invention of outlandish names) called Jedediah Cleishbottom – translatable as Whackbehind. The four stories 'edited' by Cleishbottom, were supposedly written by his deceased colleague Peter Pattieson, who in turn had heard them from the landlord of the village inn – hence the title *Tales of my Landlord*. It is not surprising that many modern readers become bored by this prosy 'apparatus' which merely delays the opening of the story proper; now that we know the books were all Scott's, his mystifications and disguises seem tedious. The best advice probably remains that given to children in the days when Scott was still read in schools. Skip the introductions, and go in at the third chapter.

As things turned out, *Tales of my Landlord* did not conform to plan. Of the four intended stories, only two materialised; *The Black Dwarf*, which occupied the first volume, and *Old Mortality*, which extended to fill the other three. In 1797, on an outing with Adam Ferguson, Scott had visited a real-life dwarf named David Ritchie who was then living in a moorland cottage near Manor in Peeblesshire. The young men had been quite alarmed by their taciturn and reluctant host, and Scott had never forgotten him.

*The Black Dwarf* is not Scott at his best, although the character of the misanthropic but secretly romantic Elshender the Recluse, later revealed as Sir Edward Mauley, is sensitively drawn. The scenes describing his existence at Mucklestane Moor in Liddesdale, where he has withdrawn to escaped the taunts of his neighbours and live among less cruel creatures, are also affecting. Many of the ballads included in the Border *Minstrelsy* echo through *The Black Dwarf*, but Scott found it difficult to compress his convoluted plot into one volume and towards the end seems to have run out of steam. The tangled conclusion, in which wrongs are righted and lovers united by the noble intervention of the dwarf, who then mysteriously disappears, lacks dramatic credibility. When he read the manuscript, Blackwood was appalled. Finding that John Murray agreed with him, he not only had the temerity to request that it might be rewritten, but also to make suggestions as to how it might be done.

This was a new experience for the gentlemanly Scott, and when he got wind of the tradesman's 'impudent proposal' he was outraged. 'Tell him,' he fumed to James Ballantyne, 'that I belong to the Black Hussars of literature, who neither give nor receive criticism.' Blackwood was not normally a timid man, but on this occasion he was so unnerved by his author's vehemence that he apologised profusely and published *The Black Dwarf* as it stood. Perversely Scott, writing anonymously in the *Quarterly*, gave it a bad review.

*   *   *

In the autumn of 1816, in his other world of the law, Scott began to hanker after a new job. His post as Clerk of the Court of Session was not onerous but often tedious, and he had in his sights a promotion to the Bench as a Baron of the Scottish Court of the Exchequer. This would make him a judge and importantly, for an ambitious Border laird, give him the title of Lord Scott. In December he petitioned the Duke of Buccleuch for his support, writing honestly if cynically that 'there is a difference in the rank, and also in the leisure of a Baron's situation; and a man may, without condemnation, endeavour at any period of life to obtain as much honour and ease as he may comfortably come by'. On this occasion, however, the Duke declined to help him and Scott was passed over. During the next few years he would see a number of his contemporaries promoted, but his own career in Law never progressed beyond his Clerkship.

\* \* \*

With one ambition denied him, Scott threw his energy into another. Buoyed up by a legacy in 1816 of £3000 from his brother Major John Scott, and by the optimistic belief that the huge advances and royalties his novels commanded would settle his debts, as well as allow him to realise his plans for Abbotsford, Scott engaged in another round of land acquisition and home improvements. Abbotsford, once intended as a modest country cottage, was about to have its first makeover as 'a small Scottish manor'. Thirty labourers were employed to carry out a major refurbishment influenced by the ideas of the English architect Edward Blore (1787–1879), and a new range of buildings rose up alongside the original farmhouse. Blore's antiquarian interests were in tune with Scott's, and the exterior of this transitional Abbotsford was replete with towers and turrets and Gothic arches. Inside were a new dining room, a conservatory, much-needed guest bedrooms, basement kitchens and, as Joanna Baillie had predicted, an armoury. The work took two years to complete, and again one feels sorry for Charlotte. She had been in indifferent health since the birth of Charles in 1805 and now suffered from chronic asthma. It could not have done her any good to spend half the year inhaling builders' dust and the other half among the windblown reek of Edinburgh.

As he built his dream house, Scott's lust for land remained unaffected by his precarious bank balance. He had bought adjoining Abbotslea the year he moved from Ashiestiel, and in 1817 added Kaeside and Toftfield, of which he wrote: 'I have bought a good farm adjacent to Abbotsford and beautifully situated so I am now a considerable Laird and Walter may be a rich one.' In fact, Kaeside and Toftfield were considerably more than farms. They were small estates with fishing and shooting rights, houses and cottages and tenants who now became Scott's. Toftfield, which Scott renamed Huntly Burn, had a house large enough to accommodate his old friend Adam Ferguson and his sisters; and Chiefswood, where Sophia Scott would live in the early years of her marriage, was another substantial dwelling. Scott was trying to make concrete a romantic place of his own imagination, where the march of time had been suspended and he would rule like a clan chief of old, no longer warlike but insistent on deference and loyalty in exchange for kindness and generosity. It was a doomed riposte to modernity, but in its limited, *Brigadoon*-like way, it seems to have worked. Few of Scott's contemporaries of any social class had a bad word to say about him, and his patriarchal notions were tolerated at Abbotsford in exchange for benevolence and security of tenure. But there was a price to pay. Sustaining his elaborate fantasy depended on Scott's ability to write and keep writing, on retaining public favour and holding his creditors at bay.

# CHAPTER 22

# Old Mortality

*As to Covenanters and Malignants, they were both a set of cruel and bloody bigots and had notwithstanding those virtues with which bigotry is sometimes allied. Their characters were of a kind much more picturesque than beautiful. Neither had the least idea either of toleration or humanity, so that it happens that as far as they can be distinguished from one another, one is tempted to hate most the party which chances to be uppermost at the time.*

~ Letter to John Richardson, 6 December 1828 ~

THE UNSUCCESSFUL *BLACK Dwarf* was published alongside a novel which has a strong claim to be considered Scott's best, *Old Mortality*. In his first three books, Scott had concentrated on the eighty years between the Jacobite Rising of 1745 and his own life time. In *The Tale of Old Mortality* (its original title) he moved further back in history to the Scotland of the late seventeenth century, a dismal period shattered by civil war, religious intolerance and fanaticism. For *Waverley* he had had the advantage of meeting very old people who remembered the events of 1745 and hearing their conversation, which in turn coloured his narrative. *The Antiquary* was, at the time, a modern novel. For *Old Mortality* Scott was dependent on written accounts, family legends, the attitudes which had filtered down to him through his father's stern observance, and the Church of Scotland services he had been forced to attend in his youth.

As a man, Scott had none of his father's strictness. He disliked the austerity of Presbyterian worship, with its psalm singing and lengthy, judgemental sermons. His mother had been brought up Episcopalian and, after his marriage to Charlotte and his father's death, Scott quietly joined the small Episcopalian congregation of St George's in York Place, Edinburgh. He loved the rich texture of the liturgy, and at Abbotsford read prayers to his family and guests from the Episcopalian prayer book. But although his belief in God was unwavering, he did not attend church regularly and was never a narrow sectarian. He managed to retain an appreciation of the good points of Presbyterianism, its high principles and willingness to suffer for them and – once he had left it – a nostalgic affection for its eccentricities. Scott found extreme religious posturing absurd as well as distasteful, yet given his opinion of extremists as spelt out in his letter to John Richardson, the great strengths of *Old Mortality* are its even-handedness and the dignity he allowed even to his most ridiculous characters.

After the Restoration of King Charles II to the throne of Great Britain in 1660, the Covenanters, representative of extreme Presbyterianism and for 13 years the ruling power in Scotland, had been much reduced in numbers and strength by factional fighting. In 1650 their supremacy ended in a terrible defeat at Dunbar by an English army commanded by republican supremo Oliver Cromwell. Yet as late as 1679, the year in which the action of *Old Mortality* occurs, this diminished 'remnant' remained obdurate and valiant for their version of truth, up in arms against the Episcopacy forced upon them by Charles's preference for liturgy and bishops. The Covenanters' nemesis now was John Graham of Claverhouse, Viscount Dundee (1648–89), who had taken command of the 'Malignant' Royalist forces operating against them in the south west of Scotland. This dark, subtle and ruthless soldier was admired by Scott, who had a portrait of him on his study wall and wrote the poem which gave him the nickname, 'Bonnie Dundee'.

The idea for the story seems to have originated with Joseph Train, who had provided Scott with information for *Guy Mannering*. His suggestion was that Scott should write the story of Claverhouse's anti-Covenanting campaign as told by 'Old Mortality', in real life one Robert Paterson, an itinerant stonemason who had devoted his life to restoring the weathered epitaphs on the memorials of the Covenanters. Train later told Lockhart that Scott knew nothing of Paterson previously, which is at odds with Scott's own claim that he had encountered the old man in Dunottar kirkyard in 1797. Whatever the facts, Train's suggestion of 'Old Mortality' as narrator was not accepted, and the old mason appears only in the 'Jedediah Cleishbottom' apparatus which precedes the narrative.

Although it opens with a disarming scene of farce, the most striking aspect of *The Tale of Old Mortality* is its sombre realism. So soon after his visit to the field of Waterloo, Scott was in no mood to give a gloss of glamour to the atrocity of war. The hero, Henry Morton, begins as a moderate Presbyterian. Only in protest against his arrest and treatment by Claverhouse's soldiers does he join the Covenanters. His sin had been to shelter a murdering fanatic, John Balfour of Burley, because his father had been Burley's comrade-in-arms. For this act of conscience Morton is condemned to death, escaping only through the intervention of the Royalist Lord Evandale, his friend and rival in love.

The object of the young men's affection is one Edith Bellenden, granddaughter of ultra-Royalist Lady Margaret of Tillietudlem. But this strand of interest pales in a narrative of cruelty and slaughter, torture and execution, in which neither side emerges as morally superior to the other. Scott tempers his enthusiasm for Claverhouse as a soldier with ambivalence about his methods, while in the terrifying figures of brutal John Burley and the mad Covenanter preacher Ephrahim Macbriar he exposes the suffering and persecution which had led to the religious extremism of the period. *Old Mortality* resonates powerfully in today's intolerant and war-torn world.

Fortunately such almost unbearable truth to life is leavened by Scott's irresistible comic impulse; he understood as well as Shakespeare the need for emotional release. The characters of imperious Lady Margaret Bellenden, forever reliving the fleeting visit of King Charles II when 'his Most Sacred Majesty partook of his disjune [breakfast] at Tillietudlem', and her ploughman Cuddie Headrigg, tasked with toning down the dangerously outspoken evangelical ranting of his mother Mause, are hugely entertaining, while the cockiness of the manipulative maidservant Jenny Dennison is a pleasing contrast to the insipidity of her aristocratic mistress Edith. As always Scott's handling of the flexible, expressive Scots language is trenchant, although for a modern reader of *Old Mortality* it is perhaps too obviously a device used to differentiate the speech of the Covenanters (uneducated, lower-class) from the English of the Royalists (formal, educated and born to rule). In fact, in the seventeenth century Scots was spoken at every level of society.

With all its incidental richness, however, Scott's subject, as much as Wilfred Owen's a century later, was 'The pity of War'. Played out against the bleak moorland of Lanarkshire, the tragedy of the Covenanters' hopeless stand against the ruthless professional armies of Claverhouse at Drumclog and the Duke of Monmouth at Bothwell Brig is unsparingly unfolded, while the torturing of Ephrahim Macbriar haunts the memory as disturbingly as the execution of Fergus MacIvor at Carlisle. In such a tale, the romantic interest is rendered almost incidental by horror. Henry Morton and Edith Bellenden are the weakest characters in the book; Scott informs the reader that Henry Morton has changed his allegiance twice, but fails adequately to explore his reasons, while Edith emerges as one of Scott's famous 'walking gowns', a well-dressed, painfully virtuous cold fish. Like Flora McIvor's, her speech, as John Buchan remarked of *The Black Dwarf's*, is 'a language which was never yet on sea or land', and the only mystery is why two men were crazy about her.

Many theories have been advanced to explain Scott's inability to portray romantic love convincingly, ranging from Edwin Muir's suggestion that his imagination was frozen by Williamina Belsches's rejection to the slightly bizarre conviction of modern historian Richard Michaelis that Scott 'deliberately under-characterised his heroes and heroines', making them 'representatives of the societies, classes and cultures that produced them rather than fully-fledged characters'. Perhaps the delightful conclusion of the American critic Agnes Repplier (1855– 1950), who loved Scott, is closer to the truth:

> *Sir Walter Scott always shook hands with his young couples on their wedding-day and left them to pull through as best they could. Their courtships and their marriages interested him less than the other things he wanted to write about – sieges and tournaments, criminal trials, and sour Scottish saints.*

Always a man of action and with a phenomenal capacity for hard work, between 1814 and 1817 Scott had been pushing himself to the limits of endurance. He was making a vast amount of money from his writing, but financial anxiety was never far away and his lifestyle was not healthy. He had a hearty appetite and enjoyed colossal breakfasts of cold meat, eggs, fish, rolls, butter and cream. Although he ate less if at home with his family in the evenings, he gave and attended dinner parties regularly, drinking whisky and wine in quantities then considered moderate but now known to be dangerous. Nor did he have a regular pattern of exercise; for six months of the year in Edinburgh he led a sedentary life at the Clerks' table in court and at his desk at home, while in the country he pushed his heavy, broad-chested body to extremes, planting and felling trees, riding and tramping across the Border hills, getting chilled and soaked to the skin. Even at Abbotsford he spent long hours at his desk, and nowhere did he ever get sufficient sleep. It was no wonder he had rheumatism, or that there was worse to come.

On 1 March 1817, Scott wrote to Joanna Baillie, asking her to forward a letter to her brother, Dr Matthew Baillie, a distinguished London doctor who was Physician in Ordinary to King George III. In explanation, he revealed that recently he had been having terrible bouts of stomach cramp. He (and Charlotte) were sleepless. 'Last night in particular,' he wrote, 'the agony was so great that I fainted, and truly I thought the grim skeleton was about to take my harp out of the Minstrel's hand. I have no desire,' he added ruefully, 'to quit this wicked world either upon short warning or so early in life.' Scott had tried to combat his alarming symptoms by drinking hot water, but on 5 March, long before Dr Baillie received his letter, he suffered a spectacular collapse at a dinner party in his own house. The attack of pain was so violent that it forced from him 'a scream of agony which electrified his guests', and sent him to bed 'roaring like a bull-calf'.

Doctors were summoned and Scott subjected to the same nightmarish and futile treatments he had endured in his youth. Heated salt was poured over his body 'so hot that it burned my shirt to rags', he told Morritt later. In the absence of any specific diagnosis, he was blistered and bled and treated with opiates which dulled the pain but left him giddy, suffering from tinnitus and without sense of taste. As during his adolescent illness, he was prescribed a starvation diet which weakened him further, and it is unsurprising that Scott, who was described three months later as 'worn almost to a skeleton ... his countenance, instead of its usual healthy colour, of an olive brown', brooded about his own mortality. He gave morbid thought to his obituary, and consoled himself with the Latin saying *sat est vixisse* – 'It is enough to have lived.'

It is difficult to be conclusive about the causes of illness in the premodern period, but Scott's description of his symptoms suggests that he had gallstones, which would plague him at intervals for the next three years. But his determination to work was unquenchable, and before he even had time to convalesce he was back at the Clerks' table. In July, the month when he was described as a green-faced skeleton, he travelled to Loch Lomond to visit Rob Roy's Cave and the scenes of the folk hero's exploits around Glenfalloch and Aberfoyle – the territory already made famous by *The Lady of the Lake*. His new project was another 'Waverley' novel for Constable, who haggled mightily over Scott's terms but was really pleased to have him back. Remarkably, in the circumstances, *Rob Roy* is one of Scott's sprightliest and consistently entertaining works.

To a reader expecting to be plunged immediately into the colourful adventures of Rob Roy MacGregor (1671–1734), the half-mythical Highland cattle thief, the title is misleading. Set at the time of the first Jacobite Rising in 1715, the action takes place in the North of England as well as in the Trossachs and Glasgow – *Rob Roy* is the only one of Scott's novels to centre on Scotland's great commercial metropolis. For the first time, Scott uses a first-person narrator, a young Englishman named Frank Osbaldistone. Frank has quarrelled with his father due to his preference for poetry over the drudgery of making money in the family business – a familiar theme of Scott's – and is sent off to cool his heels at Osbaldistone Hall in Northumbria. In his uncle Sir Hildebrand's slovenly, hunting-mad household, he meets six cousins (five witless oafs and a scheming, dastardly villain named Rashleigh). Also living in the house is Sir Hildeband's niece, Diana Vernon, whose name Scott unusually abbreviates as 'Die', darkly beautiful, opinionated, Roman Catholic and fervently Jacobitical. Die's speech is as highfalutin as Isabella Wardour's, but her style and feistiness captivate the impressionable Frank from the moment he meets her, fetchingly dressed and mounted for the hunting field.

Osbaldistone Hall with its echoing chambers and mysterious priest-hole is creepily Gothic, but more prosaic Glasgow, where Frank is drawn when his father's business gets into trouble and Rashleigh flees to Scotland with some vital papers, provides the best scenes in the book. From this point, Frank has constantly at his elbow a crafty and unlovable servant, Andrew Fairservice, whose self-serving impudence is only partially mitigated by his loyalty. Although the Gothic atmosphere persists in the town jail and the shadowy Cathedral crypt, it fades against the ordinariness of the household and personality of Frank's new acquaintance Bailie Nicol Jarvie, one of the most entertaining characters Scott ever invented. Presbyterian, Whig, passionate only in his belief in the peace and prosperity offered by the Union of 1707, Bailie Nicol Jarvie's business is the trade with the West Indies and America which had made Glasgow suddenly prosperous.

Much of the book's comedy lies in the Bailie's ambivalence. He fears above all the restless Jacobitical clansmen lurking beyond the Highland line, excluded from Lowland prosperity and personified in the Bailie's kinsman, the notorious Rob Roy – the 'Them' and 'Us' perception that has lasted well into modern times. Yet Bailie Nicol is not immune to the romance of the glens; he is, like Scott himself, an establishment figure with a sneaking admiration for the 'daft reiks' of Highlanders like Rob. As he admits wistfully:

> *It is a queer thing, but I think the highland blood o' me warms at thae daft tales and whiles I like better tae hear them than a word o' profit, Gude forgie me! But they are vanities, sinfu' vanities and, moreover again the statute law – again the statute law and the gospel law.*

For all the intricate weaving of plot and subplot, the staid Glasgow burgher's inner struggle between caution and romance and his nervous relationship with the flamboyant, lawless cattle thief from Balquhidder are the heart of the book. Yet it is decency and loyalty, rather than any conscious heroism, that finally compel the Bailie to leave his home comforts and accompany Frank beyond the Highland line. At the clachan of Aberfoyle and in the wild mountains beyond, his pithy commentary on his adventures, both funny and touchingly brave, is one of the book's chief joys.

As usual in a Scott novel, in the end everything works out in true love's best interest. The Jacobites rise up and are put down with Hanoverian efficiency. Rob Roy kills the villainous Rashleigh, order is restored, and Frank – the book's least colourful character – goes meekly back to his father's counting house. Subsequently, since all of Sir Hildebrand's other sons have died in the Rising, he also inherits Osbaldistone Hall. In a last Gothic flourish, Frank rescues Die Vernon from a French convent and, in an exit even more abrupt than usual, they shake hands with Scott on their wedding day.

# CHAPTER 23

# The Honours of Scotland

*The extreme solemnity of opening sealed doors of oak and iron, and finally breaking open a chest which had been shut since 7th March 1707, about a hundred and eleven years, gave a sort of interest to our researches, which I can hardly express to you, and it would be very difficult to describe the intense eagerness with which we watched the rising of the lid of the chest, and the progress of the workmen in breaking it open, which was neither an easy nor a speedy task.*

~ Letter to John Wilson Croker, 7 February 1818 ~

ROB ROY, WITH its catchy title suggested by Constable, was published in January 1818. It was an immediate success, its original print run of 10,000 copies selling out in a fortnight. The critics were kind, praising in particular Scott's characterisation of Bailie Nicol Jarvie and Andrew Fairservice. As usual, it was left to Francis Jeffrey to carp in the *Edinburgh Review* that Diana Vernon was improbably opinionated and witty for her age, in the male-dominated society where she had grown up. Yet it was her excitingly unladylike liveliness that delighted readers, making her the ancestor of many sparky, unconforming Victorian heroines to come. The book's income enabled Scott to pay off some debts including his rather large one to the Duke of Buccleuch, but with his children growing up and Abbotsford eating money as fast as he earned it, the need to write was as imperative as ever.

Even when sick and overburdened with work, Scott's passionate embellishment of his 'small manor house' went on unchecked. With architect William Atkinson (1774/5–1839) now in charge and egged on by his theatrical friend Daniel Terry, Scott was gradually filling up the new rooms and courtyard with the antiquities he adored – stained glass portraits copied from a ceiling in Stirling Castle, plaster copies of gargoyles at Melrose Abbey, the old fountain from the Cross at Edinburgh which, he exulted to Terry, 'flowed with wine at the coronation of our kings and on other occasions of public rejoicing'. There were the mementos he had brought from Waterloo to be accommodated; three regimental banners were found in a cupboard at Abbotsford during the recent refurbishment of the house. He acquired more weapons, armour, pictures, skulls, snuff boxes, stuffed animals and a blotter book containing a thin strand of Napoleon's hair. And although he would never have spare money to emulate his friend Richard Heber's library, he bought valuable old books for the new shelves in his 'sanctum'.

Why did the possession of these objects, some of dubious provenance and many downright gruesome, matter so much to Scott? It is not uncommon for historical novelists to feel a spiritual connection between common objects and their former owners, or to sense that handling them gives an insight into the mind of their makers. Yet in such obsessive and indiscriminate hoarding Scott took this inspiration to extremes, and one can only suppose that what John Buchan called his 'burning reverence for the past' made his response unusually intense.

Yet for all his love of magic and Gothic horror and his use of them in poetry and fiction, Scott had a mind informed by the Enlightenment and his real-life experience of the supernatural seems to have been slight. Once in 1793, he wrote in a late work titled *Letters on Demonology and Witchcraft*, he had been spooked at Glamis Castle by the eerie feeling that his bedroom was 'too far from the living and too close to the dead', and in April 1818, in the middle of Abbotsford's refurbishment, an incident occurred that he accepted as paranormal. A London cabinet-maker named George Bullock had been enlisted by Terry to make some fine furnishings for Abbotsford, but died suddenly at home before his work was complete. On two successive nights, Scott and his wife were awakened by loud noises which, he said, 'resembled half-a-dozen men hard at work putting up boards and furniture'. But when, armed with a sword, he went searching for an intruder, 'nothing could be more certain than that there was nobody on the premises'. Only when he heard the date and time of Bullock's death did he make a connection, and marked what he called 'the coincidence'. Scott did not see ghosts round every corner, and seems to have felt more imaginative curiosity than fear of them.

Meanwhile, undeterred by the chaos of building work, the visitors, invited and uninvited, who would always be a feature of Abbotsford life, poured in, among them the American writer Washington Irving, the artist David Wilkie, even Lord Byron's deserted wife. Abbotsford being 'partly uninhabited,' Scott informed Terry, 'I intend to fit up my neighbouring farmhouse (that sounds grand) at Kaeside to accommodate a part of my family & therefore can promise you & Mrs Terry a sort of accommodation'. Scott's hospitality became legendary and, when inclined to feel sorry for Charlotte, it must be remembered that she did not actually have to wash the sheets and do the cooking.

By 1818, Scott was also having to give serious thought to the future of his 17-year-old son Walter, the heir of Abbotsford and future keeper of his father's legacy. An idea of sending him to boarding school in England had come to nothing, and Scott must have realised over the years that his son, a vain lad known within his family as 'The Laird of Gilknockie', had inherited his love of sport and horses but neither his intellect nor his capacity for hard work. Scott may have felt some regret over Walter's disinclination for the 'family business' of Scottish law, yet he must have known since the great football match at Carterhaugh that the boy's preference was for prancing about on horseback, dressed up in fancy clothes and carrying a banner. Scott, whose own love of similar pastimes has been noted, and who had no doubt fed Walter with chivalric tales, agonised briefly over his moral welfare in the lax ambience of an officers' mess, but then gave way gracefully. On 19 July 1819, the by then 18 year-old was commissioned as Cornet, or colour-bearer, in the 15th (The King's) Hussars, at an initial cost to his father of £1300. (The practice of buying commissions in the British Army, largely to preserve the exclusivity of the officer class, was abolished in 1871.) Walter's upkeep in a fashionable and notoriously expensive regiment was another burden which Scott would now be obliged to bear, but he was proud to have a soldier son, and keen to assist the young officer's army career. It was left to the Laird of Gilknockie's sisters to giggle at him posing in his fancy uniform – a response easily understood by viewing the hilarious portrait of 'Walter Scott the Younger' 'in full Hussar puff' painted by Sir William Allan (1821).

* * *

Scott had been so pleased with Constable's promotion of *Rob Roy* that he decided to trust him with the next series of *Tales of My Landlord*. This decision was particularly pleasing to Constable, who was peeved by Blackwood's incursions into territory he considered his; the publication of *Blackwood's Magazine* as a Whig counterblast to the *Edinburgh*

*Review* also offended him, especially since he had been lampooned as 'The Crafty' in its pages. Scott was paid an initial £4000 for four volumes, his original idea being to devote three to *The Heart of Midlothian* and one to a story centred on the Honours of Scotland, also known as the Scottish Regalia and the Scottish Crown Jewels. This tale was not in the end included, but Scott did not abandon the subject.

In the years since 1815, Scott had visited London on a number of occasions, on business both literary and legal. Taking the royal gift of a jewelled snuff box as encouragement, he had been careful to cultivate his acquaintance with the Prince Regent through presentation copies of his novels and occasional flattering correspondence. There had been more intimate dinners at Carlton House, during which Scott had talked up the German Prince's descent from the dashing Scottish Stuarts, and politely pressed his case for a project dear to his heart.

After the Union of Parliaments in 1707, the Honours of Scotland had disappeared from public view, but not from public consciousness. Consisting of Crown, Sceptre and Sword of State, these powerful symbols of nationhood dated from the end of the fifteenth century, and had last been used for their proper purpose at the Coronation of Charles II at Scone in 1651. Subsequently, the Honours had become part of the panoply of the old Scottish Parliament, and their cursory banishment to a strongroom in Edinburgh Castle had represented a severance from old custom and dignity which many Scots still resented. There was a persistent rumour that the Honours had been secretly removed to London – a move, as Scott knew, certain to stoke anti-English sentiment further. It was as a means of ending such divisive speculation that Scott suggested to the Prince Regent a search of the Castle and the uncovering of the Honours. The Prince obligingly agreed to set up a commission of inquiry, and at the close of 1817 regally granted permission.

On 4 February 1818, before invited guests including Scott and his daughter Sophia, an old oak chest in the Crown Room was opened and the quietly beautiful Honours of Scotland revealed for the first time in more than a century. For most it was a moment of deep emotion, but famously one of the commissioners present thought flippantly to put the Crown on the head of a young lady present. This impious gesture was stopped only by Scott's cry of 'By God, No!' John Buchan speaks of Scott's belief that the unveiling of the Honours was 'a ceremony of sacramental gravity', and once again his 'burning reverence for the past' was revealed.

\* \* \*

*The Heart of Midlothian* was published seven months after *Rob Roy*, with Scott so absorbed in the story that, despite his ill health, he adopted the habit of writing after dinner as well as in the early morning. In a way, the book was an act of expiation. Scott had taken to heart a scathing series of articles in the widely read *Edinburgh Christian Instructor*, in which Dr Thomas M'Crie, a formidable Church historian, had attacked as 'false and distorted' Scott's depiction of the Covenanters in *Old Mortality* as murderous yet laughable fanatics. Scott countered with a self-defensive article in the *Quarterly*, but seems to have been troubled by the anguish of M'Crie's criticism. Sensitive to having caused gratuitous pain, in his new book he set out to show more dignified qualities in the Covenanters fifty years on from the hideous events of 1679.

The inspiration of the *The Heart of Midlothian* (the reference is to the grim Tolbooth prison adjacent to St Giles' church in Edinburgh's High Street) had come to Scott in a letter of early 1817 from a Mrs Thomas Goldie of Craigmuie, the wife of a Government official. She told him the true story of Helen Walker, a farm labourer's daughter who in 1738 had journeyed on foot from Dalquhairn in Dumfriesshire to London on behalf of her younger sister Isobel, who was sentenced to death for the murder of her newborn child. In Scottish law at that time, such a sentence might have been commuted, had the accused revealed her pregnancy before the birth, but Helen Walker had refused to perjure herself by pretending that Isobel had done so. Presenting herself at the London house of the Duke of Argyll, she persuaded him to petition the King, who granted the prisoner the only thing that could save her – a royal pardon.

This story gave Scott the core narrative of *The Heart of Midlothian*. He renamed the sisters Jeanie and Effie Deans and moved the scene to Edinburgh, where their father appears as David 'Douce Davie' Deans, an upright and pious veteran of Bothwell Brig, now settled as a poor cattle-grazer in a cottage at the foot of Edinburgh's St Leonard's Crags. But although his fighting days are long gone, the Covenanting zeal for absolute truth is still strong in Davie, as in his plain and hard-working elder daughter Jeanie. Called as a witness in her sister's trial for the murder of her illegitimate child, Jeanie refuses to lie under oath to save beautiful Effie, who is imprisoned in the Tolbooth to await execution. Jeanie sets out barefoot and wrapped in a tartan plaid to walk to London intent, in the absence of King George II in Hanover, on pleading with

Queen Caroline for her sister's life. In Scott's story the Duke of Argyll appears merely as an intermediary, and the great scene where Jeanie meets the Queen face to face, impressing her deeply with her simple Scots eloquence, is the emotional highlight of the book.

The tale begins with Scott at his best in a stunningly vivid account of the riots of 1736, when an Edinburgh mob responded to the reprieve of Captain John Porteous – found guilty of ordering the Town Guard to fire on bystanders at a public execution – by storming the Tolbooth, dragging Porteous from hiding and hanging him in the street. As often in a Scott novel, the more wicked characters are most memorable; the baby-selling Meg Murdockson and her insane daughter Madge Wildfire, the evil George Staunton who marries Effie and the savage son who improbably survives to kill his father, are all more lively than Douce Davie, his heroic but humourless elder daughter and her earnest divinity student admirer. Although Jeanie's tramp to London is enlivened by kind acts and dangerous encounters, and Scott is skilful in contrasting Scots and English traits of speech and character, *The Heart of Midlothian*'s subplots are complicated and the book overly long. The final volume, in which Jeanie, now a minister's wife, and her aged father are resettled in a pastoral paradise as tenants of the Duke of Argyll, is an anticlimax, though revealing as the working-through of a Scott ideal; the reconciliation of past and present through the benevolence of the aristocracy and the grateful acknowledgement by the people of the benefits of the Union. Less charitably, the reviewers of *Blackwood's Magazine* and *The British Review* remarked that the book was spun out to its detriment because Scott had been paid for four volumes in advance.

* * *

In 1818 Scott's friend the Prince Regent, who been his mentally ill father's stand-in for eight years, was among the most unpopular men in England. In Scotland, which he had yet to visit, he barely registered in the public consciousness. A vain, hugely overweight figure in fashionable clothes, 'Prinny' was notorious in London for his extravagance, vanity and scandalous sexual behaviour. At a time of widespread economic depression and poverty, contempt for his excesses had naturally hardened into public hostility. Only Scott's veneration of Royalty and mission to preserve Scottish identity while promoting the Union would have induced him to cultivate such a grossly unattractive man. Yet without approving of the Prince's lifestyle, and capable of private disloyalty (in a letter to John Morritt he repeated the jibe of London fashion idol 'Beau'

Brummell by referring to the Prince as 'our fat friend'), Scott knew that he was also a cultured man who took an interest in the arts. The Regent was well-read; he knew Scott's work and was doubtless gratified by the complimentary portrait in *The Heart of Midlothian* of his grandmother Queen Caroline (who actually disliked the Scots and advocated hard punishment for the lynching of Captain Porteous). The unusually good publicity he had earned through the restoration of the Honours had further put him in Scott's debt. Something more than a snuffbox was required, and in December Scott received news of an honour which the Prince was 'minded' to bestow on him. He confided in the Duke of Buccleuch:

> *I have received an official intimation that the Prince Regt. is desirous*
> *of conferring a high mark of his favour upon Mr W. Scott and proposes*
> *to confer on him the rank of a Baronet of Great Britain. I feel the*
> *honour very gratifying, and although the rank itself can be of little*
> *consequence to me individually, yet it may be very different with*
> *respect to my family, especially as Walter has declared for the army a*
> *line in which* le petit titre vaut toujours quelque chose. *It may also help*
> *my own views towards the court of Exchequer should a favourable*
> *opening occur.*

It is quite usual for people to express their own unworthiness of a title which privately delights them. But Scott rather gives the game away when he says that the prospect of being 'Sir Walter Scott' is of little consequence, only to admit a couple of lines later that if he decides to renew his application to be a judge, it will be a useful addition to his curriculum vitae. As to his family, he must have known that Charlotte would love to be Lady Scott, and his view that the 'small' hereditary title of Baronet might be useful to Walter in his posh regiment shows merely that he knew the way of the world. The poignancy is in knowing with hindsight that young Walter's army career never hit the heights that he and his father had imagined, and that rather than handing the title down to a line of descendants, he would be its only inheritor.

# CHAPTER 24

# Breaking the Circle

*When the last Laird of Ravenswood to Ravenswood shall ride*
*And woo a dead maiden to be his bride,*
*He shall stable his horse in the Kelpie's flow*
*And his name shall be lost for evermoe!*

~ Prophecy from *The Bride of Lammermoor*, 1819 ~

IN THE LAST month of 1818, when Scott received word of his pending title, a death occurred in India which distressed Charlotte, particularly because it left her without a single blood relation. Scott sympathised, but was too honest to pretend about his own feelings. He had never met his brother-in-law, who was already settled in the service of the East India Company when the Scotts married in 1797, and was really only interested in the terms of Charles Carpenter's will. Mr Carpenter, he noted with pleasure, had 'with great propriety' settled the life interest on his estate to his own childless wife, and the capital, estimated by Scott to be approximately £40,000, to be divided on her death among Charlotte's four children. Scott was particularly pleased with the provision for Sophia and Anne: '£10,000,' he confided to Morritt, 'will secure my daughters the choice of marrying suitably or of an honourable independence as single women.' Unfortunately, Scott's castle-building in the air remained just that. As it turned out, he had been vastly over-optimistic about the amount of the inheritance – not that it mattered since, to his annoyance, Charles Carpenter's widow remained stubbornly alive. She outlived not only the elder Scotts but all their children, dying at a great age in 1862.

The year that had brought good fortune at its end gave way to a much more difficult period. Scott had never been entirely free from stomach cramps since his spectacular collapse in North Castle Street, and by March 1819 the pain had again become so disabling that he was unable to travel to London to receive his baronetcy. He suffered acute pain, jaundice and 'tension of the nerves all over the body'; the dreary, useless treatments, violent laxatives, scalding baths and huge doses of laudanum left him weak and depressed. John Gibson Lockhart, who had first met him a year previously, remarked on his physical deterioration during that time; by Easter,

> *he had lost a great deal of flesh – his clothes hung loose about him – his countenance was meagre, haggard, and of the deadliest yellow of the jaundice – and his hair, which a few weeks before had been but slightly sprinkled with grey, was now almost literally snow white.*

Astonishingly, this wreck of a human being managed to go on working; the third series of *Tales of My Landlord*, consisting of *The Legend of Montrose* and the much more accomplished *Bride of Lammermoor* were published by Archibald Constable and his London partners in late June 1819.

Lockhart gave a dramatic account of Scott's dictating the whole of *The Bride of Lammermoor* to William Laidlaw and John Ballantyne, when in such agony that he could not afterwards remember having written it. This story is now regarded by many scholars as Romantic myth-creation. It dates from a time when the opium-induced writings of Coleridge and Thomas de Quincey were trendy, and study of the original manuscript has proved that only the final chapters were in fact dictated. Yet the depression and hopelessness that flood the narrative are so foreign to Scott's usual style that it is hard not to suppose that overdoses of laudanum temporarily affected his normally robust imagination. This was noted by the English critic Alethea Hayter, who wrote in *Opium and the Romantic Imagination* (1968) that 'the difference between the strong-hearted, unglamorous Jeanie Deans, the heroine of Scott's previous novel, and the lovely but feeble Lucy Ashton, heroine of *The Bride of Lammermoor* ... is almost an allegory of the difference between Scott's imagination in its natural and in its opium-influenced condition'.

*The Bride of Lammermoor*, like *The Heart of Midlothian*, derives from a true story. This one Scott had heard as a child from his great-aunt and his mother. It concerned the family of the jurist Viscount Stair (1619–95), a supporter of the Covenant whose daughter Janet Dalrymple had fallen in love with Royalist Archibald, Lord Rutherfurd.

Her angry parents, objecting to Rutherfurd's principles but more to his poverty, forced the unhappy young woman into an arranged marriage with David Dunbar of Baldoon in Wigtownshire; the wedding took place in the Church of Old Luce in 1669. There is some confusion about what happened that night, whether the bride stabbed the groom or vice versa, but Dunbar was seriously wounded and his wife of a few hours, discovered bloodstained and raving, died shortly later without recovering her reason.

No novel demonstrates more clearly than *The Bride of Lammermoor* the power of a great writer to transform the bare bones of a story into art. In his version, Scott fast-forwards the action, building his narrative on the clash between a long-established social order, now in retreat, and the rise of the triumphant *nouveaux riches* in the period between 1688 and the Union of 1707. He relocates the scene from west to east and recasts the doomed lovers as Edgar Ravenswood, last of an aristocratic family fallen on hard times since the end of the Stuart dynasty, and Lucy Ashton, daughter of Sir William and Lady Ashton, an upwardly mobile couple who have appropriated the Ravenswood estate. Archibald, 'The Master of Ravenswood', now lives in a half-ruined tower at nearby Wolf's Crag with one servant, Caleb Balderstone, the only convincingly comic character in a tale with darker preoccupations.

Although in its main aspect Gothic, *The Bride of Lammermoor* is enriched by folk elements which suggest the dark working of primitive powers. An interweaving of distinctively Scottish supernatural motifs unsettles the narrative, lifting it high above a cheaply sensational Gothic tale. The deathly old hags in the graveyard, whom Ravenswood overhears spelling out his doom, are the witches of Calvinist nightmare, and the blood-soaked raven falling dead at the lovers' feet is an omen of death to come. There is no escaping predestination, and the lowering atmosphere of bleak sea coast and murky wood is a fearful metaphor for nature's indifference to human struggle. The principal characters evoke pity, but all are flawed; Ravenswood's wounded pride, his rival Bucklaw's blundering insensitivity, Sir William's moral cowardice and Lucy's terrible passivity in the face of her mother's devilish plotting all lead remorselessly to the fulfilment of prophecy: the death of Edgar Ravenswood in the quicksands of the Kelpie's Flow. In an unforgettable image, all that remains of his life and the vanished past it represents is one sable feather floating on the rising tide.

\* \* \*

On 11 May, Scott had been well enough to attend the opening of the court for the start of its summer session. Shortly afterwards, he was confined to bed by an attack of pain so severe that he believed he was about to die, and actually gathered his family to say goodbye before resigning himself to his fate. Once rumour hit the streets, it was widely supposed that *The Bride of Lammermoor* would be Scott's swan song, and in a scene of macabre farce the self-important Earl of Buchan, now owner of the burial rights at Dryburgh, visited North Castle Street intent on assuring the dying man that he would personally superintend his funeral. Mercifully Scott survived such humiliation and over the next few months made a gradual recovery; he attributed this to the ministrations of a new physician Dr Dick, who – wrongly – diagnosed kidney disease and treated Scott with calomel. This mercurous drug, widely used in nineteenth-century medicine, is so dangerous that it causes symptoms ranging from loosening of teeth and bloody diarrhoea to brain damage and renal failure. The quantities prescribed for Scott were 'small', which was just as well, since the lethal dose is one gram. Scott was of course unaware of this; even when his mouth 'began to fester' he blamed the weather and continued to take calomel at intervals for the rest of his life.

By September, Scott's normal health was apparently restored, although the severity of his suffering was written on his diminished physique; at 48 he looked like an old man. Despite some disappointment at the initially slow sales of *The Bride of Lammermoor*, which had been reviewed in *Blackwood*'s as a 'pure and magnificent tragic romance' but by others less effusively, Scott decided that he should commission William Atkinson to design a further enlargement of Abbotsford and buy for £30,000 the estate of Faldonside. To raise extra money, he sold his copyrights, 16 in number, to Constable for £12,000. This may have seemed an easy way to raise cash, but it was ill-advised, since Constable was now free to publish new editions of the 'Waverley' novels without paying a penny of profit to the author. Scott's chronic desperation for money would force him to write 14 books in the next six years, disparagingly dubbed 'impromptu novels to buy farms' by Carlyle in 1838.

And not only to buy farms. Scott's insatiable lust for antiquities was unabated and money was spent not only on more weapons, including the sword of Montrose and a set of Indian clubs, but also on keys from Loch Leven Castle, a wallet embroidered by Flora Macdonald, and even a fragment of oatcake salvaged from the site of the Battle of Culloden. Scott had recently risen from what he thought was his deathbed. Did he not worry that if he had died, his unfinished house would have presented night-marish problems, and the end of his earning capacity would have left his family in sadly reduced circumstances, especially if even his copyrights belonged to someone else? If so, he repressed his fears. Despite the reflection he saw in the mirror, with improved well-being his optimism bounced back; his confidence about his own constitution and ability to go on earning the enormous sums which publishers were paying him was unquenchable. For a few years yet, it would seem that he was right.

\* \* \*

As if to counterbalance his own returning vitality, 1819 was a year of loss for Scott. In April the Duke of Buccleuch died of tuberculosis in Portugal, where he had gone in the hope that a milder climate might arrest his disease, at the age of 47. He had survived his Duchess by only four years, leaving young daughters and his heir, a boy of 13. Scott, with his highly coloured view of feudal loyalty and pride in his distant kinship with his 'Chief', was genuinely distressed. His letters to the Duke, of which there were many, may nowadays seem sycophantic, but he owed the friend of his youth many kindnesses, and when he told the Duke's brother that 'the world seems a sort of waste without him' they were not idle words.

Then around Christmas, within a few days of each other, a Rutherford uncle died, snatched out of life in the act of stroking his cat, followed by his sister, Scott's favourite aunt. Finally Scott's mother died suddenly at the age of 87. Outlived by only two of her many children, Anne Scott had remained alert and lively until the day before she died of a stroke, and had been busy preparing presents to give to her family and friends at New Year. Scott wrote to Lady Louisa Stewart:

> If I have been able to do anything in the way of painting the past times, it is very much from the studies with which she presented me. She connected a long period of time with the present generation, for she remembered, and had often spoken with, a person who perfectly recollected the Battle of Dunbar and Oliver Cromwell's subsequent entry into Edinburgh [events which had taken place in 1650].

It has been suggested that the death of his mother in some way liberated Scott's imagination from its exclusively Scottish focus, but this is questionable since he had written the book on which the suggestion is based before old Mrs Scott died. Perhaps he had tired of the complications of a small nation's history. Perhaps his long visits to London in the years since Waterloo and his widening circle of English friends gave him a perception of a shared, British past. The travel restrictions of the long war with France had prevented him from being European in culture, but its need for whole-island solidarity had made him British. He saw nothing amiss when young Walter joined a predominantly English regiment, and his friendship with the Prince Regent (who, after the death of the Duke of Buccleuch, he began to address as his 'Chief') was evidence of his practical loyalty to the British Crown. Whatever the reason, 1819 did prove a turning point in Scott's career. Although he would still return occasionally to Scottish locations and events, he embarked on a series of novels featuring periods of English history. These are now little read outside universities and, despite the best of them, *Kenilworth*, *Woodstock* and *Peveril of the Peak* remaining richly readable, are unlikely to return to popularity any time soon. The best, and until the end of the twentieth century best-known, though perhaps more through films, television series and boys' comics than the printed version, is the one published by Constable in 1820, *Ivanhoe*.

* * *

*Ivanhoe* presented new challenges for Scott. Set in the reign of King Richard I 'The Lionheart' (1157–99), the action centres on 1194, the year when the King returned to England after a long absence in Palestine as a leader of the Third Crusade. In his absence, his power had been usurped by his brother Prince John, who a few years later would succeed him as King. The book deals with tensions between the native Anglo-Saxons and the conquering Normans who had swept the country after the Battle of Hastings in 1066, the two groups separated by language and culture as well as nationality. The hero, Wilfred of Ivanhoe, is the son of Cedric, an Anglo-Saxon nobleman who dreams of restoring the Saxon royal house by marrying his ward Rowena to Athelstane of Coningsburgh, a descendant of King Edward the Confessor. Inconveniently for this plan, Ivanhoe and Rowena are in love with each other, and Ivanhoe, having quarrelled with his father, has become a Crusader knight whose valour wins the approval of King Richard.

One thing *Ivanhoe* has in common with Scott's earlier novels is that the less elevated the characters' rank, the more entertaining they are. While insipid, blue-eyed Rowena is another of Scott's 'walking gowns' and Ivanhoe a pillar of chivalric virtue, Gurth the swineherd and Wamba the Jester are literary cousins of Cuddie Headrigg and Davie Gellatley. All that is missing is the magic of the Scots tongue. It had been easy enough for Scott to indicate class distinctions in his previous novels by contrasting the Scots speech of one group with the high-flown English of another. In *Ivanhoe* and its successors this was not possible. Scott tried to differentiate by using on the one hand words derived from Anglo-Saxon and on the other words of French and, aware of the chief defect of Strutt's *Queenhoo-hall*, aimed for a less affected style. The fact remains that the dialogue of *Ivanhoe*, with its peppering of phrases such as 'Gramercy for thy courtesy' and 'By my halidom!' – what a character in a Josephine Tey novel called 'talking forsoothly' – makes modern readers groan. It is too obvious that Scott's literary-historical language was invented; it is without the warmth and intimacy of living speech.

It is easy, however, to see why *Ivanhoe* was a film-makers' dream. The pageantry of a great tournament, in which Prince John's supporters get their comeuppance at the hands of Ivanhoe and King Richard, the magnificent wickedness of the chief villains, Sir Brian de Bois-Guilbert and Baron Front-de Boeuf, the machinations of Templar knights and even the appearance of Robin of Locksley, alias Hood, were the very stuff of boyish adventure.

More depth is given to this tale by the introduction of Jewish characters, Isaac of York and his daughter Rebecca, whom Ivanhoe rescues from a planned ambush while on a secret visit to the house of his estranged father Cedric. Scott had leant heavily on William Shakespeare's *The Merchant of Venice* in drawing these people, and while it is true that he makes a noble figure of the daughter, he unfortunately resorts to Shakespearean stereotype in his depiction of the father. Isaac is a usurer (not unusual, since all other professions in England were closed to Jews) and, more damagingly, a profiteer who had amassed a vast fortune by charging extortionate interest on loans to Crusader Christians. His daughter, a devout Jewish healer, secretly falls in love with Ivanhoe, who finds himself in a love triangle with Rebecca and Rowena.

Scott's partisans point to his powerful portrait of Rebecca as a healing and conciliatory force as evidence that he was not anti-semitic. Yet it is worth remembering that Scott was a man of his time; there were no Jews in his social circle, and his references to individual Jews in his personal writings quite often betray the casual anti-semitism endemic in British society before it was pulled up short by the Holocaust. In a *Journal* entry of 1826 he refers to an Edinburgh drawing-master of his youth as 'a little Jew animalcule', and his railing against the London gold merchants William Abud & Son, who in 1825 made difficulties over money Scott owed, conflates their unsporting persistence in pursuit of the debt with their Jewishness. He affects not to be able to spell 'Abud', using 'Ahab' and 'Abut' at random, and is not above remarking offensively, 'they are Jews, I suppose; the devil baste them for fools with a pork griskin'. Scott was sorely tried, but this is not tolerant language. In Isaac of York, with his long grey beard, wrinkled skin and 'mean and unamiable' demeanour, he perpetuates the negative characteristics depressingly present in English literature since Geoffrey Chaucer wrote 'The Prioresses Tale', Shakespeare imagined Shylock, and Christopher Marlowe invented the psychopathic Barabas in *The Jew of Malta*.

Of course Scott's presentation of Rebecca, the beautiful, courageous daughter of the venal Jew, is entirely sympathetic, yet it too stresses Jewish 'otherness'. Rebecca's dark good looks, her dress – yellow turban with ostrich feather, dress of flowered silk and flamboyant jewellery – are all in vivid contrast to the blue-eyed Saxon fairness and simple attire of Rowena. Rebecca behaves with courage and dignity through unspeakable ordeals, including abduction and a trial for witchcraft, and her nobility is beyond question. We do not know how Scott conceived the character when he began *Ivanhoe* (here there was no real-life prototype), but sometimes, as they write, authors fall in love with their own creations. One senses that Scott fell in love with Rebecca. He also respected her integrity; there was no forced conversion for the sake of a 'happy ending'. What Scott conveys best, and what also separates his Jews from the Jews of Shakespeare and Marlowe, is his awareness that historic persecution had made both Isaac and Rebecca what they are. There is a parallel here with the persecution of the Covenanters, which had led to extremes of one sort or another in the Scottish character, and 'Rebecca's Hymn' with its allusions to burning faith and contrite hearts would have struck a familiar chord in any Presbyterian soul.

At the end of *Ivanhoe*, the Saxon hero chooses to marry Saxon Rowena. Isaac and his daughter, who has decided to give her life to good works, resume their wandering course by leaving abusive England in the hope of greater safety in the tolerant Islamic Caliphate of Cordova in southern Spain. The marriage of Ivanhoe was historically inevitable – a Christian Crusader knight would not marry a Jew, nor would Isaac have permitted such a marriage for his daughter. This did not prevent indignant readers from writing to Scott to claim that he had got the ending wrong and that Ivanhoe should have married Rebecca.

# CHAPTER 25

# The Third Son

*He reached Edinburgh late in April, and on the 29th of that month he
gave me the hand of his daughter Sophia.*

~ John Gibson Lockhart,
*Memoirs of the Life of Sir Walter Scott, Bart.*, 1837–38 ~

THE SUCCESS OF *Ivanhoe* was phenomenal. Within two weeks of its
publication in December 1819 it had sold 10,000 copies, making huge
profits for the author and the publishers, Constable & Co. in Edinburgh
and Hurst, Robinson & Co. in London. Reviewers were as enthusiastic
as readers, with even the caustic Francis Jeffrey purring that the book
showed 'at least as much genius as any of those with which it must now
be numbered'. For Scott, emerging from a year of grinding illness, the
New Year must have seemed like a new lease of life.

In April 1820, after long delay, he was at last able to travel to
London to receive his Baronetcy from King George IV, as 'Prinny' had
become on his father's death in January. Gratifyingly, when Scott kissed
his hand, the King remarked, 'I shall always reflect with pleasure on Sir
Walter Scott's being the first creation of my reign'. During this visit,
Scott received further honours which cemented his status as a figure of
the British Establishment. At the King's request, he sat to Sir Thomas
Lawrence (1769–1830) for a portrait destined for the Great Gallery at
Windsor Castle, and to Sir Francis Leggatt Chantrey (1781–1841) for
the marble bust said above all others to 'preserve for posterity the cast of
expression most fondly remembered by all who ever mingled in his
domestic circle'. He was back in Edinburgh in time to host 'a jolly party'
to celebrate the marriage of his twenty-year-old daughter Sophia.

Two years earlier, in the summer of 1818, Scott had met at an
Edinburgh dinner party a dark, saturnine young man with whom he

discussed the German poet Goethe. This was John Gibson Lockhart, the son of a Church of Scotland minister who had won a Greek medal at the University of Glasgow before being awarded, at the age of 13, an Exhibition to Balliol College, Oxford. There he took a first-class degree in Classics, but was prevented from applying for a Fellowship because he was not an Anglican. In 1815 he had arrived in Edinburgh to study Scots Law, and by the time he met Scott was an unemployed Advocate eking out his meagre fees by journalism, chiefly for *Blackwood's Edinburgh Magazine*.

The high Tory politics and satirical tone of *Blackwood's* 'Maga' suited Lockhart's talent for invective, and he quickly formed an alliance with another irreverent young man, John Wilson (1785–1854) who wrote under the pseudonym 'Christopher North'. In the very first edition, with the co-operation of the 'Ettrick Shepherd' James Hogg, the young men had produced in mock-biblical prose a sensationally tasteless satire on public figures in Edinburgh, entitled 'The Chaldee Manuscript'. As Lockhart later wrote smugly, 'It fell on Edinburgh like a thunderbolt', simultaneously offending the Whigs and scandalising the then large membership of the Church of Scotland. Although Scott was uneasy about this kind of journalism, his first impression of Lockhart was favourable and, probably remembering his own failure at the Bar and in hope of diverting the young man's talents into safer channels, he arranged for him to do some work on *The Edinburgh Annual Register*. Lockhart continued to please; within three months he was invited to stay at Abbotsford, where he met Lord Melville, as well as his host's daughter Sophia.

Although posthumously he has had a few apologists, it cannot be denied that throughout his life Lockhart was disliked by almost everybody who knew him. Even his kindly biographer Marion Lochhead failed to dispel the 'floating dislike' identified by Professor George Saintsbury in 1916. This was sixty years after his obituarist Harriet Martineau (1802–71) had gone for the jugular. 'It was Lockhart's own callousness which made the sensitiveness of others so amusing to him,' she remarked, adding that 'the well-connected and vigorous and successful had nothing to apprehend from the *Quarterly*, but as sure as people were in any way broken or feeble, as sure as they were old, or blind, or deaf, or absent on their travels, or superannuated, or bankrupt, or dead, the *Quarterly* was upon them'. Yet the amiable Scott found things to like about the handsome if sneery Lockhart, writing to Mrs

Clephane that 'he is a very clever fellow, well informed in ancient and modern lore, has very good manners and is I think, likely to make a very distinguished figure in society'. This last of course mattered to Scott, particularly if Lockhart aspired to marry his daughter.

It is not hard to see what attracted Lockhart to Sophia. He was dazzled by the friendship of her father and was keen to take advantage, personally and professionally, of a marriage alliance with the Abbotsford family. Sophia was neither particularly beautiful nor well-educated; Scott had admitted frankly of his daughters, 'I was so terrified for their becoming young lionesses at second-hand that I left them in a good measure to their natural gifts'. Sophia was a home-loving girl who played the harp and sang Scottish airs to please her father, and she was certainly guided by him in her marriage choice. Despite the conventionally flowery tone of their prenuptial correspondence, there seems to have been no overwhelming ardour between Lockhart and Sophia. On the day of her engagement, Sophia wrote briskly to her former governess: 'I have at last made up my mind to marry Mr Lockhart. That I might have made a much higher marriage in point of rank and wealth I have little doubt but I am not one who can be persuaded that happiness can depend on these two alone.' Most importantly, 'Papa has a high opinion of him, and his opinion is all the world to me'. Perhaps the most striking thing about the Lockharts' relationship is its uncanny resemblance to that of Scott and Charlotte – unequal in intellect and short on passion, but affectionate and companionable in its way. Sophia moved into Lockhart's house in Great King Street, and not long afterwards Scott gave them the tenancy of Chiefswood, a substantial country house on the Abbotsford estate. Their closeness suggests that Scott saw Lockhart as an adopted son, one who shared his literary interests in a way that neither unintellectual young Walter, nor clever but indolent Charles, ever could.

It was not long, however, before 'the Scorpion', as Lockhart was named in the infamous 'Chaldee Manuscript', got himself – despite warnings from his father-in-law to tone down his scurrilous journalism – into serious trouble. In November one John Scott, the (unrelated) editor of *The London Magazine*, who had a history of trading insults with Lockhart in print, went too far, insinuating that the recently ennobled Sir Walter was the driving force in *Blackwood's* 'hoaxing and masquerade'. Further abuse was hurled on both sides until, in January 1821, Lockhart went thundering off to London to demand that John Scott either apologise or fight a duel. John Scott declined to apologise, but while arrangements were made for the (technically illegal) encounter, Lockhart returned to Edinburgh – probably summoned by Sir Walter to comfort Sophia, who was in the last stages of a difficult pregnancy. Shortly afterwards, when John Scott finally agreed to a duel, Lockhart declined to leave his wife. Tragically, the convention of duelling insisted that the meeting went ahead, in Lockhart's absence, between John Scott and Lockhart's unfortunate 'second', his old college friend Jonathan Christie. Scott was shot in the stomach and died in agony ten days later. Christie fled abroad, but soon returned, gave himself up to the police, stood trial and was acquitted. Lockhart's reputation as an honourable man was, however, in tatters, while Sir Walter, who had psyched his son-in-law up instead of calming him down, and who insisted coldly that the dying John Scott was a 'poltroon' who had deserved all he got, has not entirely escaped the opprobrium of his biographers.

On 14 February 1821, Sophia gave birth to Scott's first grandchild, John Hugh Lockhart, an apparently healthy child on whom his grandfather doted. Through the *Sturm und Drang* of the last few months he had continued to write as usual; 1820 had seen *The Monastery* and its sequel *The Abbot* in print. The novels of 1821 would be *Kenilworth*, a magnificent evocation of tragic events during the reign of Queen Elizabeth I of England, and the delightful though now little-read *The Pirate*.

\* \* \*

Seven years had passed since Scott's holiday on board the *Pharos*, and the detailed journal he had kept then suggests that he intended it as notes for a future novel. In Orkney he had heard the story of the eighteenth-century pirate John Gow who, after a bloody career on the high seas had returned to Orkney on his ship the *Revenge*, renamed it the *George* and restocked it at Stromness while masquerading as 'Mr Smith', a respectable trader. In this role he courted and exchanged vows with a Miss Helen Gordon. Only fate intervened; Gow was recognised by a visiting sea captain and one of his own crew fled to Kirkwall, where he denounced his captain to the authorities.

At once Gow reverted to his pirate trade, attacked the mansion house of Clestrain, plundered it and abducted two women. Next he sailed to the Isle of Eday intent on attacking Carrick House, but here his luck ran out. The *George* grounded on the shore opposite the house, and after a long stand off Gow was forced to surrender. He was taken to London, imprisoned in the Marshalsea and hanged at Execution Dock on 11 June 1725. Many elements of this story were used by Scott in *The*

*Pirate*, although the novel is much more than the sum of these parts.

Unusually for Scott, the book took some months to write. He had to make two trips to London, one on legal business and the other to attend the Coronation of George IV, and was preoccupied by the building at Abbotsford, now entering its final phase. He also had other literary commitments; he spent time on a collection of seventeenth-century letters, edited the *Northern Memoirs* of Richard Franck (*c*.1624–1708) and wrote about the life and works of Tobias Smollett for Ballantyne's Novelists' Library. This series of cheap reprints of popular works had been the brainchild of John Ballantyne for whom, in spite of all the grief he had caused him, Scott had always had a soft spot. Flamboyant, irresponsible John died of tuberculosis, cheerful to the last, in June 1821. After his funeral in Canongate kirkyard, Lockhart quotes Scott as saying, 'I feel as if there would be less sunshine for me from this day forth'.

Scott's biggest problem with *The Pirate* was that he found the information in his 1814 journal inadequate and had to summon Will Erskine, Sheriff of Orkney and Shetland, to fill him in on old Norse lore and superstition with which to flesh out the tale of the pirate Gow. The result was a story, set at the end of the seventeenth century, rich in the atmosphere of an isolated, sea-girt society that had failed to keep pace with the changes in modern life. Scott's 'Zetland' is a place where improved methods of agriculture and even the abandonment of paganism in favour of Christianity are slow to take hold in a resistant and superstitious society. The mysterious and unsociable incomer, Basil Mertoun, evokes resentment among his neighbours, while the tension between the Udaller Magnus Troill, who holds his land by right of ancient Norwegian law, and the 'enlightened' agriculturalist Triptolemus Yellowley, who is in the pay of an absentee Scottish landlord, underlines mutual suspicion and incomprehension between the self-contained Northern Isles and mainland Scotland less than 200 miles away.

The chief theme of *The Pirate*, however, is a romantic one, concerning the love of the Shetland Udaller's daughters, Minna and Brenda, first for the same man, the handsome Mordaunt Mertoun, then Minna's for the eponymous pirate Clement Cleveland. Towering over all, with her spells and curses and prophecies, is one of Scott's daftest creations, the witch-like Norna of the Fitful Head. Scott denied indignantly suggestions that he had tried to recreate Meg Merrilees; if he did, he certainly came a cropper. Meg is never less than magnificent, Norna quite preposterous. The book rumbles with dark island superstition. The power to change the wind has been transferred from the old woman Scott had seen in 1814 to Norna, while much is made of the belief that it was dangerous to save a man from drowning because he would live to do his rescuer harm. Merton and Cleveland save each other from drowning, and do each other harm.

On its publication in 1822 and since, *The Pirate* has never been short of critics. The plot has been dismissed as implausible and the interpolation of indifferent verse, put into the mouth of the ineffably tedious 'bard' Claud Halcro, seen more as an impediment than an enrichment. More seriously, Scott's intention of dramatising, in the person of the pirate, a clash between exotic and insular cultures has rightly been judged a failure. Cleveland's nobility has been questioned in the brutal context of real-life piracy, and the ethereal high-mindedness of his lover Minna Troill dismissed as anaemic and dim. Robert Louis Stevenson, ever grumpily ungenerous to his great predecessor, called *The Pirate* 'a ragged, ill-written book', while the American writer James Fenimore Cooper (1789–1851), usually Scott's ardent admirer, was so disgusted by Scott's wonky grasp of seamanship that in protest he wrote *The Pilot* (1823), the first great sea-story of the modern age. And whatever his views, it is hard to believe that Stevenson's *Treasure Island* (1883) owed nothing to Scott's book.

What is it, then, that makes *The Pirate* such an entertaining read? Partly it is the reappearance after *Ivanhoe* and *Kenilworth* of pithy Scots speech, particularly in the mouths of Mrs Baby Yellowley, the comically parsimonious sister of farmer Triptolemus, and the hypocritical pedlar Bryce Snailsfoot. Partly it is Scott's evocation of a stripped landscape, shadowy sky and growling, untameable sea. Most of all it is the sense that, for all his desire to stamp authenticity on the islands (which led one critic to complain that the book worked better as an essay on Shetlandic customs than as a novel), the historical setting matters less than Scott's success in conveying the self-containedness of an imagined world. As much as J. R. R. Tolkien's Middle-earth and Terry Pratchett's Discworld, the islands of *The Pirate* exist within a magical circle, where the distinction between legend and reality dissolves and disbelief is willingly suspended for a while.

\* \* \*

In 1821, Scott's sons were on the receiving end of much paternal advice, which no doubt bored them as much as the hectoring of Walter Scott WS had bored their father thirty years before. Young Walter had been posted to Dublin, charged with countering the unruliness of starving Irish insurgents; Scott, with his terror of civil disobedience, was as fretful as if Walter was about to go into battle against a dastardly and well-armed foe. He had heard rumours about officers of the 18th Hussars drinking excessively, and that twenty-year-old Walter was 'paying attention to one young lady in particular. I beg you will do nothing that can justify such a rumour as it would excite my highest displeasure should you entangle yourself or any other person,' he thundered. But his chief gripe was expense; young Walter's lifestyle was costing his father dearly, and he was constantly reminded that he was not a rich young officer with money to burn. The best he could expect was 'to draw on me for £20 or so'.

Charles, still being tutored at Lampeter in Wales and enjoying sport more than construing Latin, was reminded to consider study 'the principal object – many men have read and written their way to independence and fame, but no man ever gained it by exclusive attention to exercises or to pleasure of any sort'. Another letter warned the 16 year-old that 'labour is the condition which God has imposed on us in every station in life – there is nothing in life that can be had without it ... as for knowledge, it can no more be planted in the human mind without labour than a field of wheat can be produced without the previous use of the plough'. It is not hard to guess why Charles did not write home as often as Papa thought he should.

Privately, of course, Scott boasted about his boys. 'Walter is really what you call un beau cavalier,' he told Lady Abercorn, 'with the advantages of a good figure in all the exercises he has steady good sense & temper.' It was perhaps stretching the truth slightly to add that 'having spent three years with a rollicking Irish regiment of cavalry he has never given me a moment's uneasiness either by over expence [sic] or otherwise'. When Charles, aged 19, went up to Oxford – a place far, far removed from the rowdy, egalitarian University of Edinburgh which his eleven-year-old father had entered forty years before – Scott bragged to all his posh friends.

The adopted son was not spared his share of advice. In response to his father-in-law's concern, Lockhart had reduced his contributions to *Blackwood*'s, but had declined to sever completely his connection. Meanwhile Scott, along with a number of other right-leaning officers of the law, had got into a scrape of his own. Ill-advisedly he had become a secret financial backer of a new weekly Tory publication, the *Beacon*, compared with which *Blackwood*'s was positively tasteful. First published in January 1821, the *Beacon* immediately established a reputation for often libellous vilification of leading Whigs, one of whom, James Stuart of Dunearn (1775–1849), was so incensed by the spleen directed against him that, according to Henry Cockburn, 'he caned the [paper's] printer in the street'. The feud between Stuart and the *Beacon* continued in print, and when it was discovered that Scott had backed the publication another aggrieved Whig, James Gibson, challenged him to a duel. This probably fatal encounter was averted only when the *Beacon*'s other backers disassociated themselves from the enterprise. The matter did not end there, however, and subsequently a duel was fought between fiery James Stuart and Alexander Boswell of Auchinleck (1775–1822), who had been unmasked as his chief tormentor. Boswell was the son of Dr Johnson's biographer and a close friend of Scott, who was badly shaken by his death and angry at being tainted by association in the affair. Scott congratulated himself on having kept Lockhart out of the matter, but used the occasion to emphasise to his son-in-law the perils of needlessly provocative journalism. 'I hope,' he wrote, 'that this catastrophe will end the species of personal satire and abuse which has crept into our political discussions. The lives of brave and good citizens were given to them for other purposes than to mingle with such unworthy affrays.' Remembering Scott's own harum-scarum youth in Edinburgh in the 1780s, it is hard to resist the thought that he had turned into his father.

Even with Scott's tireless efforts to promote his career and bring him to the attention of London Tories with the power of patronage, Lockhart never achieved the distinction for which his natural ability might have fitted him. He attempted fiction without having a great novelist's gifts and, although he was a perceptive critic, his reviews were often marred by sarcasm and mockery. His essay on Burns has been recently condemned as mendacious and unjust, while his implication in the trashing of Keats and a venomous review of Tennyson's 1833 *Poems* are discreditable. Even his second-best book, *Peter's Letters to his Kinsfolk* (1819), a fascinating survey of Edinburgh society in the early 1800s, contains passages of breathtaking impertinence. Had Lockhart not married Sophia Scott and lived to write his father-in-law's biography, today he would scarcely be remembered at all.

CHAPTER 26

# The Chevalier's Heir

*Sir Walter, practical, and with a strong grasp of real life in his poetry,
was always endeavouring to live in a world of fiction. His Abbotsford
... and the reception of the king in Edinburgh were continuous efforts
to transplant himself into another age.*

~ James Hogg, *Domestic Manners and Private Life
of Sir Walter Scott*, 1834 ~

IN 1822 NO reigning sovereign had set foot in Scotland since Charles II
in 1651. The Jacobite Risings had passed, with fleeting visits by the Stuart
'Old Pretender' in 1715–16 and his son 'Bonnie Prince Charlie' in 1745–
46. By the end of the eighteenth century Scots had, with varying degrees
of enthusiasm, settled for the rule of the Stuarts' German cousins, the
Protestant descendants of King James I and VI in the female line.

Scotland nonetheless remained a country divided. North of the
Highland line, running north-east from Balmaha on Loch Lomond to
southern Aberdeenshire, lived a sparse Gaelic-speaking society that
had been cruelly used and culturally suppressed by the London
Establishment after the defeat at Culloden. Wearing tartan and carrying
weapons by civilians had been banned. The 'heritable jurisdictions'
which had allowed clan chiefs to be sole legislators and judges of their
own adherents were abolished, along with the custom whereby a
tenant's allegiance to his chief included a duty of military service. With
feudal ties loosened, a number of chiefs, some of whom who had impoverished themselves to help the Jacobite cause, evicted their tenants and
sold their land to sheep farmers from the south. The effect of these
'Clearances', which saw mass emigration and almost forced recruitment
of dispossessed tenants to the Highland regiments of the British army,
are remembered and bitterly resented by many Highlanders to this day.

On the south side of the Highland Line, in the country of Bailie Nicol Jarvie rather than that of Rob Roy, the English and Scots-speaking Lowlands might have been a thousand miles away. The fertile Borders and the east coast farmlands of Angus and south Aberdeenshire were rich with sheep, cattle and crops, and as the Industrial Revolution of the late eighteenth century took hold, Glasgow and the whole area between the rivers Forth and Clyde became a powerhouse of coal mining, iron smelting and maritime trade. Dundee's jute mills thrived on trade with India, and small towns like Alloa and Paisley became prosperous centres of woollen and silk manufacture. The universities flourished, and Edinburgh, long merely a titular capital, developed as the hub of the Enlightenment. This society had its downsides; workers were exploited and the unrest provoked by French revolutionary ideas erupted sporadically into violence. But in the main, this southern Scotland was a douce and law-abiding place.

No one was more aware of the starkness of division and mutual distrust between Highlands and Lowlands than Scott, who had reaped many benefits from the Union, and deliberately used its mechanisms to promote both his own and his son's interest. His friendship with the King and association with prominent London Tories had hooked him into court and political circles, and his 'English' novels were calculated to appeal to a southern readership. Yet imaginatively he had lived so intensely in the romantic worlds of feudalism and Jacobite sentiment that his Scottishness remained the most important part of his sensibility. When he was called on to orchestrate an event where he saw the possibility not only of celebrating the Union, but also effecting a symbolic reconciliation between Gaels and Lowlanders, Jacobites and Hanoverians, and indeed his own conflicting personae, he had no hesitation about which way to go.

The unpopularity in London of dissolute, extravagant and overfed George IV peaked in the year of his Coronation, 1821. The enormous cost of the ceremony to the public purse would have caused even more controversy, had it not been eclipsed by an unseemly incident during which the King's estranged wife, Caroline of Brunswick, was turned away as she tried to force her way into Westminster Abbey. It was widely known that George had a succession of mistresses, and that in 1795 he had even gone through a secret ceremony of marriage with one of them, Maria Fitzherbert. But his arranged marriage to Caroline, despite mutual hatred, was legal and her public humiliation won him few friends.

In the wake of this fiasco and in an atmosphere of Radical unrest, the Government, in an attempt to get the King away from London and restore some dignity to his office, arranged a number of provincial tours. These included an 18-day visit to Ireland which – despite beginning only a few days after the death of Queen Caroline on 7 August 1821 amid whispers that she had been poisoned – was a great success. A visit to Scotland, of which Scott and Lord Montagu were chief promoters, was pencilled in for 1822, but the King, who was suffering from gout, dithered over whether he should go north or south to attend a Congress of Nations in Vienna. Scott became so convinced that no visit was in the offing that he arranged his summer holiday as usual. When it was suddenly announced on 22 July that the King would be arriving in Edinburgh in the middle of August, panic seized the Town Council and sent the Lord Provost scuttling to North Castle Street to ask for help.

It was in many ways a good move. No one was better qualified than Sir Walter Scott, recently steeped in the pageantry of a royal visit in *Kenilworth* and full of knowledge of heraldry, ceremony and theatrical effects to change grey, sober-suited Edinburgh into a scene of colour, music, excitement and romance. Rising to the challenge, Scott chose as his chief assistants William Murray, the actor-manager of the Theatre Royal, and Colonel David Stewart of Garth, a veteran of the Napoleonic war and an expert on the Highland regiments. The theme was to present George IV, the great-nephew of Culloden's 'Butcher' Duke of Cumberland, as a Stuart prince and, even more contentiously, a Highlander.

Initially, enthusiasm for the 'Celtification' (Lockhart's word) of the city was muted. Even as the kilted and Gaelic-speaking Highlanders summoned by Scott began to appear on the streets, most of the middle classes were either hostile or indifferent. Rumours of the King's far from private life did not prejudice Presbyterian Edinburgh in his favour, nor did the scandal of the Highland Clearances endear the swaggering chiefs to the largely Whiggish urban intelligentsia. Yet faced with the extravaganza of bright tartans, skirling bagpipes and parade of 'traditions' (such as the Company of Archers) invented on the hoof by Scott, and not least with the delight of poorer citizens unused to such entertainment, bourgeois disapproval melted into amusement.

Seizing the moment, Scott wrote, printed and circulated *Hints Addressed to the Inhabitants of Edinburgh, and others, in Prospect of His Majesty's Visit. By an Old Citizen*. After unblushingly assuring his fellow Scots that 'King George IV comes hither as the descendant of a long line of Scottish kings' and 'with the blood of the heroic Robert Bruce -- the blood of the noble, the enlightened, the generous James I in his veins', Scott proceeds not to hint, but to lay down the law about dress codes, procedure and behaviour at the levee and drawing room planned for the Palace of Holyroodhouse, balls, military reviews and 'Gathering of the Clans' with which he proposed to exhaust the unhealthy, overweight King. Ladies are told how many feathers to wear in their headdresses, and not to overdo the tartan, while those northern gentlemen privileged to appear in their ancient costume 'must be careful to be armed in the proper Highland fashion – steel wrought pistols, broadsword and dirk'. Civilians are instructed to wear 'Blue Coat, White Waistcoat and White or Nankeen Pantaloons, and in their hats a St Andrew's cross 'by way of cockade'. Pressing orderly behaviour on 'the populace', Scott reminds them that 'our gracious King throws himself, as it were, into the arms of his people. He has no guard but their love, no security but their sound sense and manly respect.' The *Hints* deserve to be read less for their entertainment value, which is considerable, than for their insight into the fantasy world of Walter Scott.

The visit was, in the event, a triumph. From the moment that the King's yacht, HMY *Royal George,* anchored at Leith in an August downpour, a population swollen by countless visitors flocked to see him, and gratification at his unaccustomed popularity made him gracious. Tartan mania infected even the most cynical and the King, enchanted by his new role as a Jacobite monarch, appeared in the costume which provides the abiding image of him in Scotland – a vast kilt and coat in a gaudy new 'Royal Stewart' tartan created for him, an enormous furry sporran and, most memorably, flesh-coloured tights; the full fig, including weapons and jewellery, cost £1355. He was painted in heroic pose by David Wilkie, who tactfully slimmed him down and omitted the tights, and by J. M. W. Turner, who followed him around with a sketch-book. The London caricaturists had a field day.

It was not only the King who was exhausted by a seemingly endless round of levees, processions, banquets and balls. The organisation of such a colossal enterprise was not without cost to Scott, who had to sort out complaints and huffs over precedence, supervise costume, oversee catering and do a lot of entertaining on his own behalf. (The Suffolk poet George Crabbe (1754–1832), whom Scott admired and had invited to visit Abbotsford, turned up unexpectedly at North Castle Street on the day of the King's arrival. Never having seen a Highlander he was, to put it mildly, baffled.) Poor Charlotte was suffering from breathlessness and swollen ankles and, just before the King's arrival, Scott developed an irritating rash which covered his body but mercifully not his face. It put paid to his hopes of wearing a kilt, however, and he had to settle for trews in Campbell tartan, to which he claimed a right through his great-grandmother, Mary Campbell of Silvercraigs.

Scott's pleasure in the King's arrival was also marred by the death on the same day of his old and much-loved friend Will Erskine, who had recently been elevated to the Bench as Lord Kinneder. The circumstances were tragic; grieving after the death of his wife, Erskine had become the victim of an untrue and slanderous rumour that he was the secret lover of an apothecary's wife. The effect of this calumny on a shy and nervous sensibility was dire; Erskine developed what Scott called a 'fever of his spirits' which quickly reduced him to a shadow of his former self. The usual treatments of cupping and blistering made things worse, and 'on the morning of the King's arrival,' Scott told Joanna Baillie, 'he waked from sleep and took a kind leave of his servants (his family were not allowed to see him) ordered the window to be opened that he might see the sun once more, and was a dead man soon after'. Whether Will Erskine died naturally or committed suicide is not known.

At the time, Scott had no space to grieve. The King's yacht was in the Leith roads and private feelings must be suppressed. As things turned out, the day of rain-soaked pageantry ended in a moment of farce. Invited, on board HMY *Royal George*, to exchange healths with the King in cherry brandy, Scott afterwards dared to ask if he might have the royal glass as a memento. This was permitted, and Scott put the glass into the tail-pocket of his coat. Arriving home late at night and completely exhausted, he threw himself into a chair and emitted a loud howl. Charlotte thought he had sat on a pair of scissors, but the only casualty was the glass, which was smashed to smithereens.

Since there had been no time to renovate the royal sleeping apartments at the Palace of Holyroodhouse, the King was quartered at Dalkeith Palace, where he gave private audiences, held intimate dinners with Scottish music and dancing, and annoyed the teenaged Duke of Buccleuch by using him as a message boy. He went to church at St Giles', where he was obliged to listen to the Moderator of the Church of Scotland, Dr David Lamont, preach a sermon on the sins of fornication, wrath and mendacity, and of the duty of husbands to love their wives. His last public appearance was at a venue more to his taste, the Theatre Royal, where he had a jolly and relaxed evening watching an adaptation of Scott's *Rob Roy*.

On 29th August, again in lashing rain, His Majesty paid a brief visit to Hopetoun House, the seat of the Earl of Hopetoun, where he and his entourage dined, although the outdoor entertainments arranged for him had to be abandoned because of the downpour. He played with the Earl's ten children and, in a last ceremonial act, knighted Adam Ferguson and Scotland's greatest painter Henry Raeburn. At six o'clock he boarded HMY *Royal George* at South Queensferry and vanished into an east coast haar.

No doubt George IV carried back to London happy memories of his fortnight as a Jacobite King. He must certainly have had the impression that Scotland was a Highland kingdom, dominated by tartan-clad chiefs and their loyal clansman, and been gratified by his reception as super-chief of a country of which he had seen nothing outside a twelve-mile radius of Edinburgh. He would never return, or know that when the illuminations were dismantled, the ashes of bonfires cleared and gaudy finery put away in wardrobes, Edinburgh would return to its sober-suited, mercantile ways. Yet as the visitors dispersed and the clansmen with their bagpipes faded back into the mountains, it seems clear that the romanticising of the Highlands started by *The Lady of the Lake*, *Waverley* and *Rob Roy* had, in two colourful weeks, become vital to the self-image of the nation.

Although Highlanders accounted for a very small percentage of Scots, and Scott had been scrupulous in not forcing the burghers of Edinburgh into tartan clothing, it was not the medieval-style garb of the Knight Marischal's attendants or the Royal Company of Archers that defined the pageantry of the King's visit, or any awareness of the diversity of contemporary life. It was the clothing, language and bearing of the men of the north. It did not matter that the dress code of the Edinburgh Celtic Society, of which Scott was a prominent member, was savaged as inauthentic by Alastair Macdonell of Glengarry, the most haughty and quarrelsome of the chiefs. 'Highland costume' as pre-scribed by the Society caught the imagination and is nowadays *de rigeur* at almost every Lowland wedding.

Sir Walter Scott was much blamed, during the long years of his unpopularity, for a 'Celtification' of Scotland which skewed reality and obscured the majority culture. No doubt the emphasis on Highlanders in

Scott's great pageant of 1822 led to false perceptions, not least among visitors from abroad, but it is unreasonable to link his management of the King's visit to the distasteful 'tartan tat' peddled in tourist outlets today. Yet is hard to look at contemporary Scotland without supposing that, for all its contradictions and reliance on myth, many Lowland Scots are comfortable enough with a 'Highland' identity which includes the playing of bagpipes on city streets, ubiquitous kilts and evening classes in Gaelic. Scott was anxious to consolidate a Union between Scotland and England under the descendants of George IV, while celebrating the cultural integrity of his countrymen. For almost two centuries, his vision went largely unquestioned, but perhaps the real division had always been within Scotland itself. If so, as the British ideal comes under pressure, Scott's great Celtic festival may best be seen as a gesture of Scottish reconciliation, an early manifestation of the romance of a shared identity which has recently gripped our nation.

\* \* \*

Fittingly, Scott's last word on the Jacobites can be found in his great novel of 1824, *Redgauntlet*. There had long been rumours, though no actual proof, that Prince Charles Edward Stuart had visited Britain in disguise in the early 1760s, and around this intriguing idea Scott built his story, imagining conspiratorial preparations for a third Jacobite Rising at that time. Central to this enterprise is the mysterious Herries of Birrenswork, alias the Lord of the Solway Lakes, alias the eponymous Redgauntlet, a fanatical Jacobite who has never accepted the failure of the Stuart cause.

It has been remarked as a weakness of *Redgauntlet* that although the action takes place in the mid-eighteenth century, the atmosphere Scott creates is that of his own youth in the 1790s. Scott's way of circumventing this anomaly was to be unspecific about dates, and to general readers it is scarcely a problem at all. They are immediately drawn into the world of the two young heroes, the Law student Alan Fairford and his friend Darsie Latimer, who lodges in the house of Alan's father, Writer to the Signet Saunders Fairford. It has been suggested that the younger Fairford represents Scott in his student days, when his father was constantly breathing down his neck, and the carefree Darsie his friend Will Clerk. Just as probably the two young men represent different persona of Scott himself, the serious Law student who got up at dawn to study for his Bar exams and the 'gangrel scrapegut' of whom his father despaired. In this, his most introspective book, Scott finally lays the ghost of his long-dead father, recalling a relationship at times comic and abrasive, yet loving even in the moments of deepest exasperation.

Two things, apart from the main plot which involves the kidnap of Darsie by his uncle, Alan's desperate attempts to rescue him and a mysterious triangular love affair, make *Redgauntlet* the most haunting of Scott's novels. One is the cavalcade of vividly realised characters: Poor Peter Peebles, the ragged plaintiff driven crazy by years of litigation; the outwardly placid Quaker Joshua Geddes, whose peaceful principles are sorely tried by his fiery nature; Redgauntlet's thuggish retainer Cristal Nixon; the educated sea captain Nanty Ewart; the moonlighting smugglers Thomas Trumbull and Father Crackenthorp; the old Jacobite Pate-in-Peril and the blind fiddler Wandering Willie, whose tale of his grandfather Steenie Steenson's visit to Sir Robert Redgauntlet in hell stands as the best Scottish ghost story ever written.

Then there is the spirit of place, Scott's evocation of the weird Solway coast with its shivering quicksands, the Quaker's garden where every creature is safe, the secluded Catholic house of Fairladies across the Border in Cumbria, the inn of Father Crackenthorpe, the moonlit Firth and above all Scott's 'own romantic town'.

*Redgauntlet* is a book about hopeful, vigorous youth, but it is also about the end of old men's dreams. The once bonnie Prince is faded, sick and stubborn, without power to inspire; the Jacobites who have mustered reluctantly at Redgauntlet's bidding think of their estates and one by one excuse themselves from reviving a spent and lacklustre Cause. Only the ageing Redgauntlet, fanatical but loyal, is willing to follow his master into exile in France. In a final irony, it is revealed by the arrival of Colonel Campbell, the officer sent to break up the conspirators' meeting and escort the Prince to the shore, that the Government of George III has all along known of the plot to launch a third Rising – and decided that it was too paltry to be worth taking action against.

# CHAPTER 27

# A House of Dreams

*It is a kind of Conundrum Castle, to be sure and I have great pleasure in it, for while it pleases a fantastic person in the stile* [sic] *and manner of its architecture and decoration it has all the comforts of a commodious habitation.*

~ *Journal*, 7 January 1825 ~

THE WRITING OF *Redgauntlet* had been preceded by a period of frenetic composition for Scott. Since 1821 he had had no thought of defection from Archibald Constable as his publisher; Constable was eager to pay him vast sums in advance for his work, money he badly needed as his schemes for Abbotsford became ever more grandiose. There was also young Walter's army career to be advanced, with his father paying for his promotions (Walter's captaincy alone cost him £5000), buying horses, financing his studies in Germany and at Sandhurst, while fretting simultaneously about his associating with unsuitable women and his failure, so far, to find a wealthy wife. Charles too was proving a drain on the parental purse; after some angst about whether he should join the Foreign Office or the Indian Civil Service, Charles was entered at Brasenose College, Oxford. Here he found a patron in Scott's old friend Richard Heber, now Member of Parliament for the city, although this relationship came badly unstuck when in 1826 Heber was exposed as homosexual and forced to flee abroad.

Toiling in the morning hours and sometimes late at night, Scott wrote and published *The Fortunes of Nigel* in 1822, *Peveril of the Peak* and *Quentin Durward* in 1823, and *St Ronan's Well* in 1824. The range of these novels is impressive, from London in the reign of James VI and I in *Nigel*, to Derbyshire at the time of the 1678 Popish Plot in *Peveril*, and from the France of Louis IX in *Quentin* to an early nineteenth-century Scottish spa town in *St Ronan's Well*. Scott was interrupted briefly during the writing of *Peveril* by the King's visit and, in the aftermath of Will Erskine's death, admitted that he laboured to finish it; *St Ronan's Well*, Scott's only attempt at a 'contemporary' novel, despite a famous depiction of the doughty old innkeeper Meg Dods and an ending as tragically intense as that of *The Bride of Lammermoor*, is an unusually depressing book. It was not well received, and Scott was wounded by its negative reviews. *Quentin Durward*, the story of a young Scottish archer at the court of one of the craftiest, most superstitious yet able monarchs in French history, is in the tradition of *Ivanhoe* but a more subtle and plausible book. The first of Scott's novels to have any real impact in France, it caused an outbreak of tartan fever in Paris and kick-started Scott's acceptance as an important European novelist.

John Sutherland, in *The Life of Walter Scott*, reckons that with *Redgauntlet* Scott had written himself out as a novelist and that from then on his best writing is to be found in the *Journal* which he began to keep in November 1825. This is perceptive, yet there were good works still to come, chief among them *The Chronicles of the Canongate*, where are found *The Fair Maid of Perth* and Scott's most accomplished shorter stories, 'The Highland Widow', 'The Two Drovers' and 'The Surgeon's Daughter'. Yet it is true that none of Scott's work after *Redgauntlet* ever achieved the melding of passion and objectivity which is the hallmark of great novels, among which is this magnificent book.

\* \* \*

As he reached his early fifties, Scott, generally upbeat about his own health, was becoming aware that he 'had reached the other side of the hill'. A candid and unflattering portrait study of 1823 by Andrew Geddes (1783–1844) suggests how much the stress of the previous year had affected him. His once clear eyes are reddened and strained, his cheeks puffy and his mouth downturned. After Will Erskine's death he had written to Daniel Terry complaining of 'a whoreson thickening of the blood and a depression of spirits', and the rash which plagued him during the King's visit took two months to fade. His lame leg was weakening and giving him pain; and though in the Borders he could still ride for miles on his mare Sibyl Grey and spend hours helping Tom Purdie to thin the woods he had planted, walking was not the pleasure it once was. He probably had high blood pressure and was putting on weight. Yet however ill and downhearted he felt, Scott would not, could not, rest from his labours. He had more tales of the Crusaders, *The Betrothed* and

*The Talisman* to write, and there seemed no limit to the advances Constable was prepared to offer.

As ever, Scott needed money. Abbotsford was entering its last phase of expansion, and in the building of this 'romance of a house' no expense could be spared. Scott insisted on supervising every detail. His correspondence with Terry in 1824 was all about acquisitions. For the drawing room, hung with hand-painted Chinese wallpaper, he was 'only ambitious to have one fine mirror over the chimney-piece; a smaller one will do for the other side of the room'. The curtains were to be made of crimson damask silk, and Lady Scott had 'seen some Bannockburn carpets, which will answer very well'. Scott fussed about fringes and curtain rings, loops and tassels; Terry's other commissions included a white marble table to support Chantrey's bust, cases of antlers and 'a parcel of caricatures which can be bought cheap', to paper the lavatories.

For the library, green curtains were considered, but red chosen. Intricate carvings copied from Rosslyn Chapel were made to decorate the ceiling, which was painted to match the Jamaican cedar of the bookcases. Scott, who referred to them as 'presses', was pleased with these, although they reminded him of 'the awful job of arranging my books'. There were now upwards of 7000 of these: chapbooks from his childhood, bound manuscripts of Border ballads from the *Minstrelsy* days, books of history, witchcraft, folklore and chivalry, antiquarian books which are now priceless, and manuals of tree planting and cultivation. In the study he placed his dictionaries and encyclopaedias, alongside the huge bespoke desk he had brought to Abbotsford from Ashiestiel. Elsewhere in the house, coats of arms of his ancestors and their related families were painted for the entrance hall, where they hung alongside 'lions rampant and griffins volant'. A chair made of wood from Robroyston, where the patriot William Wallace was captured in 1305, was presented by Joseph Train, and an Italian mosaic given by Archibald Constable.

Scott did not get quite everything he wanted. An attempt to acquire a fireplace from Stokesey Castle in Shropshire, through the agency of his friend Mrs Mary Ann Hughes, was rebuffed by its owner Lord Craven, leading Scott to defend himself. 'Though a professed pedlar in antiquarian matters I really feel none of the paltry spirit of appropriation which induces men of that class to disjoin curiosities from the place to which they are fitted by association for the poor gratification of calling them their own,' he wrote huffily. He had felt no such scruples when removing Roman bas-relief heads from the fort at Penrith, or accepting Byron's Greek funerary urn.

Outside, once the original cottage was gone, a walled garden was laid out, 'a sort of plaisance' with medieval-style gateways and colonades, their cornices carved with flowers. There was a wide gravel drive for carriages, shrubs and yet more trees. Abbotsford, Scott told Mrs Hughes proudly, 'thrust its lofty turrets into the skies'. Walls and towers were ornamented with stone thistles, crosses, monograms and heraldic shields. The quality of the workmanship was superb, but Scott's interferences took their toll on his architect. 'I believe Atkinson is in despair with my whims,' he told Lord Montagu, 'for he cries out Yes-yes-yes in a tone which exactly signifies No-no-no-by no manner of means.'

Fortunately Scott did not live so much in the past that he could not appreciate the comforts of modern living. Abbotsford had water closets, bells that worked by air pressure to summon servants and, most famously, a private gasworks which provided lighting indoors. Scott was clued up about this cutting-edge technology, since he was a director of the Edinburgh Oil Gas Company, but Lockhart, who hated it, wrote:

> *Dinner passed off and the sun went down, and suddenly, at the turn of a screw, the room was filled with a gush of splendour worthy of the palace of Aladdin; but, as in the case of Aladdin, the old lamp would have been better in the upshot. Jewelry [sic] sparkled, but lips and cheeks looked cold and wan in this fierce illumination; and the eye was wearied, and the brow ached, if the sitting was at all protracted. I confess, however, that my chief enmity to the whole affair arises from my conviction that Sir Walter's own health was damaged, in his latter years, in consequence of his habitually working at night under the intense and burning glare of a broad star of gas.*

Through the whole period of rebuilding and refurnishing, visitors had come, stayed for weeks and departed, just as usual. Lord and Lady Minto, Sir Humphry and Lady Davy, the Terrys, Ballantynes, Constables and the Scott-worshipping Mrs Hughes all had their turn. The 'Ettrick Shepherd' James Hogg came for a couple of nights, referred to unkindly by Scott as 'a pig on a string' and his table manners deplored by Lady Scott. An uninvited 'party of indescribable dandies' found no favour, but room was gladly made for 'Mr and Mrs Skene, two Miss

Swintons, one Miss Skene and one Miss Rae'. All seemed happy to share the inconvenience of noise and piles of rubble and the headache-inducing smell of paint and turpentine.

A visit which gave Scott enormous pleasure was from his fellow novelist and long-time correspondent Maria Edgeworth, who stayed in the summer of 1823 with her brother and two half-sisters. They had long admired each other's work, and now were happy in each other's company. Lockhart memorably described Miss Edgeworth as 'a little, dark, bearded, withered, active, laughing, talking, impudent, fearless, outspoken, honest, Whiggish, unchristian, kindly, ultra-Irish body', while she put Scott irresistibly in mind of Whuppety Stoorie, the Scottish Rumplestiltskin. The Irish writer was frank about the Scotts too; she thought Lady Scott overdressed and over-rouged, and she did not take to Anne. It seems not many people did; the dark, sharp-tongued young woman, alone among Scott's children, apparently suffered a delusion of vicarious celebrity. But Maria loved Sir Walter, 'one of the best-bred men I ever saw', although she was mystified as to when he ever found time to write.

* * *

At Christmas 1824, the Laird of Abbotsford held a gigantic house-warming party to celebrate the completion of his 'romance in stone'. There was feasting of medieval splendour, the 'twelve days' were spent in hunting and shooting, the evenings in music, games, ghost stories and recitations by Scott of ballads old and new. Presents of food and clothing were distributed to Scott's tenants and the poor, while pennies and treats were handed out by the Laird to the children at New Year. One of the guests, a naval officer named Basil Hall, wrote of this holiday that 'surely if Sir Walter Scott be not a happy man, which he truly seems to be, he deserves to be so'. Scott was indeed happy; in Abbotsford he had everything he had ever desired.

On 7 January 1825, what John Buchan called 'the first and last ball which Scott saw in Abbotsford', was held in the library to celebrate an event close to his heart, the engagement of young Walter. His fiancée was Miss Jane Jobson of Lochore, an heiress wealthy enough to please even her prospective father-in-law. As Andrew Lang observed cattily in 1906, 'The name of Jobson is neither suggestive of wealth nor of heraldic additions to the quarterings of the Scotts', and indeed the same thought seems to have occurred to haughty young Walter who, before committing himself, had wanted to know whether the Jobsons were 'in trade'.

For this he received a stiff talking-to from his father:

> *Upon* [Miss Jobson's] *connections I would just remark that we are but
> cadets of Raeburn who are the cadets of Harden and therefore, though
> gentlemen, are much like what the French call Gentillatres and the
> Highlanders Duniewassels. In the present day, there is no aristocracy
> so strong as that of wealth or talent, and no one thinks
> of making some sacrifices of the prejudices of birth to acquire the
> former.*

The chief attractions of Miss Jobson, to Scott at least, were that she
was the niece of Sir Adam Ferguson and had a 'fortune of £50,000 in
land'. Such a match for young Walter would relieve his father of at least
one of his financial burdens, and hopefully continue into a third generation the line of Sir Walter Scott. The only disadvantage was that the
young lady had an extremely disagreeable mother, who made difficulties
and was not nearly impressed enough by the prospect of an alliance with
the Scotts of Abbotsford. Sir Walter and Sir Adam nonetheless pressed
on and arranged the marriage, so forcefully that the young couple had
little option but to imagine that they were in love. In fact, Jane was as shy
and socially insecure as Walter was vain and arrogant, and there is not
much evidence of passionate attachment on either side.

The most ominous part of the marriage settlement was that, apparently at the insistence of the Jobsons' lawyers, Scott was forced to make
over Abbotsford to Walter and his heirs, reserving for himself only the
life-rents on the estate and the right to raise a mortgage on it no greater
than £10,000. That Scott failed to tell James Ballantyne, whose resources
were much depleted by his secret partner's need for cash, seems in retro-
spect reprehensible, but it appears that Scott, at the pinnacle of his
achievement, signed away his 'romance in stone' still without a thought
that his luck might one day run out.

# CHAPTER 28

# Dark Days

*As I walked by myself*
*I talked to myself*
*And thus my self said to me.*

~ Written on title page of Scott's *Journal*, 20 November 1825 ~

A YEAR PASSED, and, in the darkening autumn of 1825, Scott's mood changed from delight in dreams come true to loneliness, depression and anxiety about the future. After protracted negotiation about the terms of his employment and some unpleasantness with a London literary establishment that disliked his reputation, John Gibson Lockhart had finally been confirmed as editor of the *Quarterly Review*. This meant a move to London and Scott, who had never been far from Sophia even after her marriage, had to endure parting not only with her and Lockhart, but with his painfully delicate grandson Johnny. Sophia, who had lost a baby girl only two days old in 1824, was again pregnant and Scott's anxiety was acute. The Lockharts decided to leave North Castle Street early on a December morning before anyone else was up, sparing Scott 'the red eyes and blowing of noses' which he hated. But as they settled in to a new life in Pall Mall, Scott, who had lobbied ceaselessly for his son-in-law's appointment, was left feeling empty and sad.

At home, the main cause of anxiety was the deterioration in Charlotte's health. She had suffered from asthma for years, and more recently had been showing symptoms of pulmonary oedema, commonly called 'water on the lungs' and an indicator of heart failure. She too was being treated with the poisonous drug calomel and increasing doses of opiates to which she had probably, through no fault of her own, become addicted. The rouge on her cheeks, which drew unkind remarks, was a pathetic attempt to conceal the fading of her complexion. She bravely tried to keep up appearances, but in private she was not an easy patient. Her daughter Anne, fated to be the only child left at home with her parents, was worn out by the demands of looking after her.

It was against this dreary background that Scott decided in November 1825 to start keeping a journal. Perhaps the prospect of committing his thoughts to a 'handsome lockt [sic] volume' appealed because he was missing intimate conversation with the Lockharts. Or perhaps he was inspired by the recently published *Diary* of Samuel Pepys (1633–1703), which Lockhart had asked him to review for the *Quarterly*. The 'lockt volume' no doubt gave Scott a sense of privacy but, as he admitted in the first paragraph he wrote in it, he also knew that after he was dead it would sooner or later become public property. It would have been natural for Scott to view his *Journal* as an exercise in self-image management, an attempt to manipulate the perception of the future.

This makes it all the more remarkable that the diary Scott kept during the last six years of his life, although naturally it has self-defensive moments, is in the main a searingly honest account of horrifying events and his feelings of pain, humiliation and 'the cold sinkings of despair' as his carefully constructed life disintegrated and his health failed. Professor David Hewitt points out in his Introduction to *Scott on Himself* that the *Journal* has the coherence of a natural tragedy, moving from the height of prosperity through ruin to the heroic attempt to do what was right, leading in turn to physical and mental destruction. It is also full of the humour, acute observation and interest in humanity that made Scott so well loved in his own lifetime.

In the summer of 1825, Scott had gone with Anne and Lockhart to Ireland. The priority was to visit Walter, who was now installed with Jane in the grandest of garrison lodgings in St Stephen's Green, Dublin. A return visit to Maria Edgeworth at Edgeworthstown in Co. Longford was also planned. Scott, who had just finished the introductory chapters of his latest project *The Life of Napoleon Buonaparte*, was in holiday mood. Lockhart remarked that on the voyage from Glasgow to Belfast he 'was always as full of glee on any trip as a schoolboy', and his delight in reunions with his family and old friend, later described in the first pages of his *Journal*, was palpable. Scott had by now become used to the attentions of those whom Lockhart calls 'noblemen and gentlemen', and was unsurprised by the invitations he received to attend dinners and to visit great houses – although Anne, who had never been abroad before, was mightily impressed. What touched and amused Scott was the enthusiasm of ordinary Irish folk. According to Lockhart:

> *If his carriage was recognised at the door of any public establishment, the street was sure to be crowded before he came out again, so as to make his departure slow as a procession. When he entered a street, the watchword was passed down both sides like lightning, and the shopkeepers and their wives stood bowing and curtseying all the way down.*

Scott warmed to these generous, friendly people, but was appalled by the poverty he witnessed, describing it as 'on the extreme verge of human misery'. 'Their cottages,' he added, 'would scarce serve for pig-styes, even in Scotland.'

The Irish visit was followed by a leisurely journey home through North Wales and the Lake District, where they visited Wordsworth at Rydal Mount and Southey at Keswick, arriving back at Abbotsford on 26 August. Scott noted that the trip had cost him £500, because they had travelled 'in great style'. It would be the last time he could afford to throw money about, and the last time he would have a carefree holiday with members of his family.

\* \* \*

The closing months of 1825 were a time of national financial anxiety. The British economy had at last recovered from the depression that followed the end of the Napoleonic Wars, and a growth of confidence was encouraging investors to venture large sums on dodgy stock market shares. The mania for speculation had spread to the book trade, with publishers rumoured to be gambling huge sums in South American mining shares, railways and gas supply companies. This period ended with a stock market collapse; banks went out of business, deposits were lost and panic spread among investors great and small. The danger of all this hit home to Scott when he heard a rumour that Constable's London correspondents, and by association his own publishers, Hurst, Robinson & Co., had ventured a breathtaking £40,000 in the beer-making staple hops.

Scott's fears were compounded by his involvement over many years in a method of payment widely used in business in the early nineteenth century known as 'accommodation bills', which were an easy way of raising cash quickly. For example, Scott (using James Ballantyne & Co.

as a cover) would make out a credit note for money to be paid at a future date. The bill would be endorsed by Constable, who would make out a counter-bill to be endorsed by Ballantyne. One or both bills could be converted to cash at a bank at a discount. The assumption was that the money would be used to expand the businesses, but in fact Constable and Ballantyne, as well as Scott, had diverted cash to improve their private properties – Constable at Polton on the outskirts of Edinburgh and Ballantyne in Edinburgh's St John Street. Accommodation bills had two snags. They could be sold on to a third party unconnected to the original signatories (which is why Scott became the debtor of William Abud & Co.). There was also a rule that if either of the signatories failed to repay his debt, the other became responsible for both bill and counter-bill. Thus if Hurst, Robinson & Co., Archibald Constable & Co. and James Ballantyne & Co. collapsed with disastrous knock-on effect, Scott, as James Ballantyne's sole partner, might find himself responsible for vast debts that, having spent so lavishly, he could not possibly cover.

Too late Scott admitted to himself and his *Journal* on 22 November that 'I had a lesson in 1814 that should have done me good, but success and abundance erased it'. Still, he comforted himself with the thought that he was owed £10,000 in rents and publishers' payments before Midsummer 1826, and assured young Walter that he had no personal debts, so was 'not afraid of the slightest injury. If the money horizon does not clear up in a month or two,' he wrote, ' I will abridge my farming &c. I cannot find there is any real cause for this ... .' Even so, he took the precaution of raising the £10,000 allowed him by Walter's marriage contract, ostensibly to settle personal debts, but more probably to prop up James Ballantyne, who confided that he had only enough cash left to pay wages and bills for one more week. In his *Memoirs of the Life of Sir Walter Scott, Bart.*, Lockhart inserts at this point a story of Scott driving through the night to confront Constable at home in Polton, and returning at dawn in great relief to announce: '*All is right.* [Constable] is as sound as Ben Lomond.' This account is nowadays regarded as invention, the insinuation that Constable lied being a part of Lockhart's prolonged and shabby campaign to protect Scott's reputation by vilifying his publisher and printer, James Ballantyne.

Scott's optimism was short-lived. His *Journal* entry for 18 December states that 'Cadell has received letters from London which all but positively announce the failure of Hurst and Robinson so that Constable & Co. must follow and I must go with poor James Ballantyne for company. I suppose it will involve my all.' He now felt it necessary to warn Charlotte and Anne of trouble ahead. 'Anne,' he wrote bleakly, 'bears her misfortune gallantly and well, with a natural feeling, no doubt, of the rank and consideration she is about to lose.' Charlotte's initial incredulity was followed by hysterical reproach. '[Lady Scott] did not afford me all the sympathy I expected,' recorded Scott huffily.

Christmas 1825 passed in painful contrast to the conviviality and merry-making of the previous year; now Scott had only had his fractious wife and unhappy daughter Anne for company. He felt too unwell to meet the Scotts of Harden, and on Boxing Day he suffered an attack of pain so acute that he feared an inflammation of his kidneys. Dr Clarkson, however, diagnosed 'a gravellous tendency', probably small stones in the kidneys or gallbladder, and treated him with more calomel. After 24 hours the pain subsided, but anxiety about his health continued to oppress him. He stopped drinking wine and cut back on whisky and water 'for fear of a tendency to a diabetes' and instead smoked two cigars in the evening, believing that they acted as a sedative. No one round the dining table that Christmas felt inclined to eat.

The year 1826 opened stressfully. Not only was Scott ill, but Constable was confined to bed with gout, and James Ballantyne, cruelly disabused of his belief that Abbotsford stood between him and ruin, developed a stomach ulcer. On 5 January Scott had a frightening experience. 'To my horror and surprise I could neither write nor spell, but put down one word for another and wrote nonsense. I was much overpowered at the same time, and could not conceive the reason.' Once his head cleared, he reassured himself that the painkiller he had taken the previous night was to blame, but it is more likely that he had suffered a temporary blocking of the blood vessels in the brain. In medical parlance this is now called a transient ischaemic attack, but is still generally known as a minor stroke.

Eventually, badgered by everybody, Constable dragged himself out of bed and, in a last desperate throw of the dice, on 13 January travelled to London in the hope of raising loans against valuable copyrights he held. Such was the financial chaos in the capital, these attempts were unsuccessful. Five days later he came back to Edinburgh to discover that Hurst, Robinson & Co. had refused to accept one of his accommodation bills. This, Scott realised, 'infers the ruin of both houses. We will soon see.' By 17 January both Constable and Ballantyne had run out of money and stopped all payments. On the 22nd, Edinburgh awoke to the electrifying news that the great Sir Walter Scott had been a partner in the business of James Ballantyne & Co., and was now a ruined man.

\* \* \*

Public reaction was mixed. Scott was a vastly popular figure both in Edinburgh and the Borders, and personal sympathy was not in short supply. When the enormity of his personal debt – almost £170,000 – sank in, offers of donations and loans poured in to 39 North Castle Street. Young Walter, to whom his father's calamity came as a bolt from the blue, offered to raise a £50,000 mortgage on Abbotsford, while Jane offered to sell Lochore to help her father-in-law. John Morritt, the Duke of Buccleuch, the Duke of Somerset, and Scott's legal colleagues offered help. The butler William Dalgleish said he would work for nothing and Sophia and Anne's former music teacher, Mr Poole, offered the few hundred pounds which were his life savings. Affecting as these proofs of benevolence were, Scott found the idea of charity repellent. Whatever the future held, he would not stoop to that.

Magnanimity was not, of course, the only reaction to Scott's plight. Dorothy Wordsworth's shrill denunciation of Sir Walter's trade connection was far from unique, although Henry Cockburn, in *Memorials of his Time*, recorded the shock more elegantly:

> *The opening of the year 1826 will ever be sad to those who remember the thunderbolt which then fell on Edinburgh in the utterly unexpected bankruptcy of Scott, implying the ruin of Constable the bookseller, and of Ballantyne the printer. If an earthquake had swallowed half the town, it would not have produced greater astonishment, sorrow and dismay. Ballantyne and Constable were merchants, and their fall, had it reached no further, might have been lamented merely as the casualty of commerce. But Sir Walter! The idea that his practical common sense had so far left him as to have permitted him to dabble in trade had never crossed our imagination.*

It was against this background that Scott, on 24 January, steeled himself for a public appearance in the Court of Session. Cockburn, who was there, recalled 'no look of indifference or defiance; but the manly and modest air of a gentleman conscious of some folly, but of perfect rectitude, and of most heroic and honourable resolutions'. Some of his colleagues smiled and said good-day. Some looked as if they were attending a funeral. Some shook his hand, and again there were offers of help. Scott then made a remark which has become part of his legend: 'No! This right hand shall work it off.'

Which was all very noble and Scott's dignity and stoicism are rightly praised. Yet there are aspects of his behaviour more open to criticism. He was not above pressing Sandy Ballantyne of the *Kelso Mail* to hand over £500 which he had salvaged from the wreck of his brother's business, and he showed no concern for the smaller tradesmen to whom money was owed and who were seriously discommoded or put out of business by their loss. His major creditors behaved with great generosity, agreeing to set up a trust into which Scott would pay his earnings until his debts could be paid in full. His old friend and one-time rival Sir William Forbes, whose bank was Scott's largest creditor, was appointed chairman, and the administrator was Scott's solicitor John Gibson. Although Abbotsford was safe because it belonged to young Walter, Scott felt obliged to sell 39 Castle Street and technically his library, furniture and antiquities also belonged to the creditors' trust. Nonetheless he was able to go on living at Abbotsford rent-free, and to keep a proportion of his earnings – his legal salaries and income from essays and reviews – for personal use. James Ballantyne did not come off badly either. His business, which had a full order book, was also taken over by the creditors' trust, but he was paid a salary of £400 a year and allowed the occupancy of his house in St John Street.

The greatest loser was Archibald Constable, to whom Scott owed so much and to whom, egged on by Lockhart, he now showed an implacability at odds with his reputation. It was Constable whose vision made possible projects like the 'Magnum Opus' edition of the 'Waverley' novels and who commissioned *The Life of Napoleon*. This work, with novels from Scott's backlist, was originally intended for *Constable's Miscellany*, a groundbreaking series of affordable editions of classic works. It was Constable's partner and disloyal son-in-law, the wily and ambitious Robert Cadell, who reaped the benefit. Constable's last desperate bid to wrest from the trust the rights to *Woodstock* and *Napoleon*, which Scott had promised him, was defeated in a court ruling. Humiliated and excluded, deprived of his fine mansion at Polton and bereft of his life's work, the most innovative publisher of his age was dead within 18 months. Scott did not send condolences and refused to attend the funeral.

\* \* \*

After the sale of 39 North Castle Street and its contents in February 1826, Scott turned down offers of accommodation by James Skene and other friends, opting to move into Mrs Brown's lodging house at 6 St David's Street. His bed was crawling with bugs and dogs barking kept him and the faithful Dalgleish awake at night, but Scott was happy enough to have a place to write without the distraction of other people's domestic arrangements. He was probably secretly relieved too to be away from the harrowing sight of Charlotte's decline, which became more dramatic after she was rusticated at Abbotsford.

True to his determination to pay off his debts, Scott pushed on late into the night with *The Life of Napoleon*. He finished *Woodstock*, a spritely tale of Cavaliers and Puritans featuring poltergeists and King Charles II ludicrously disguised as a Scottish page named Louis Kerneguy, which shows no sign of the terrible strain he had been under. And he made time to write the *Letters of Malachi Malagrowther*, provoked by a British government decision, in the wake of the recent bank failures, to stop banks other than the Bank of England from issuing banknotes under £5. Scott was among those afraid that this prohibition would disadvantage Scotland, where gold was scarce and small bank-notes widely used. In three letters to the *Edinburgh Weekly Journal*, later issued in pamphlet form, he launched a vitriolic and not-very-anonymous attack on the proposal – much to the annoyance of his London Tory friends. The result was victory. 'The projected measure against the Scottish bank notes has been abandoned, the resistance being general,' he noted triumphantly in his *Journal* on 13 May.

The day after this entry was written, Charlotte died at Abbotsford, aged 56. Scott had known for some weeks that her death was imminent; on 17 April he warned his son Walter that 'I must in the course of no long period lose the companion of so many years of pain and pleasure'. In the last months of her life, Charlotte had been enduring fits of coughing lasting more than two hours, and was being treated for heart failure with digitalis, which made her sick, as well as calomel and laudanum. It is little wonder that she was confused and irritable, though it was left to Lockhart to remark that 'it seems but too evident that mental pain and mortification had a great share in hurrying her ailments to a fatal end'. Scott's behaviour at this time has been criticised as unsympathetic, and it is probable that Charlotte's reproaches got under his skin. It was also unfortunate that so late in life the sensitive matter of her parentage was again raised. In March, Scott had received a letter from Lord Downshire's London solicitor, Thomas Handley, informing him that there was a large sum held in Chancery for Lady Scott, dependent on proof of her paternity. At a time when Scott was staring ruin in the face, he may have distressed his dying wife with questions; Anne Scott testified that her mother's last words were 'Lord Downshire' and 'father'.

Scott returned to his bug-infested Edinburgh lodgings on 11 May for the opening of the Court of Session the following day. The Clerks were short-handed, since Sir Robert Dundas was absent with migraine and Robert Hamilton with gout. Scott might have sought leave of absence too, but he had left Charlotte deeply asleep and, as is common after a very protracted illness, he was probably unaware how near the end really was. He had no communication with home during the next three days, and it was only on the 15th that he wrote in his *Journal*: 'Received the melancholy intelligence that all is over at Abbotsford', and the 16th before he wrote one of its most affecting passages:

> *I have seen her. The figure I beheld is, and is not, my Charlotte – my thirty years' companion. There is the same symmetry of form, though those limbs are rigid which were once so gracefully elastic – but that yellow mask, with pinched features, which seems to mock life rather than to emulate it, can it be the face that was once so full of lively expression? I will not look on it again.*

The funeral took place at Dryburgh Abbey on 22 May, and a week later, accompanied by Charles and Anne, Scott returned to Edinburgh. Although twenty years ago he had admitted to Lady Abercorn the lack of passion in his relationship with Charlotte, he had been fond and protective of her and amused by her foibles, at least until the last bitter days of her life. Now he was profoundly affected by her loss.

> *I do not know what other folks feel, but with me the hysterical passion that impels tears is of terrible violence – a sort of throttling sensation – then succeeded by a state of dreaming stupidity, in which I ask myself if my poor Charlotte can actually be dead.*

Yet now the stoicism, the hiding of his feelings behind a carapace of self-restraint which he had learned as a child at the High School of Edinburgh, reasserted itself. On the eve of Charles's departure to Oxford, he took himself in hand: 'I have been wont to say "My Mind to me a Kingdom is". I am rightful monarch and God to aid, I will not be dethroned by any rebellious passion that may rear its standard against me.'

# CHAPTER 29

# Tales of a Grandfather

*Some great authors now will think it a degradation to write a child's book – I cannot say I feel it such. It is to be inscribed to my grandson and I will write it not only without a sense of its being infra dig, but with a grandfather's pleasure.*

*~ Journal, 8 May 1827 ~*

ONE OF SCOTT's favourite Latin quotations was *agere et pati fortia Romanum est* – 'To act and to suffer bravely is the Roman way', and in the months and years following Charlotte's death they came to define him. Even before the court rose for the summer of 1826, whenever he was not at the Clerks' table he was closeted in his room at Mrs Brown's, covering sheet after sheet of manuscript. In a fortnight he finished the third volume of *The Life of Napoleon* – about 250 printed pages – wrote a lengthy review of John Galt's *The Omen* for *Blackwood's Magazine*, and started to write the *Chronicles of the Canongate* for his new publisher, Cadell & Co. It had not taken Robert Cadell long to get back on his feet and acquire a new London correspondent, Simpkin & Marshall.

On 17 June, Scott paid a brief visit to Abbotsford, where he slept for the first time in the bed he had shared with Charlotte. 'This was a sore trial,' he confided to his *Journal*, 'but it was necessary not to blink such a resolution.' He was pleased to find Anne more composed than she had been in the aftermath of her mother's death; her cousin Anne, daughter of Scott's brother Thomas, had come to help out in the last days of Charlotte's life and had stayed on for a while to keep Anne company. Even during a five-day visit, however, Scott toiled through a heatwave to get forward with *Chronicles of the Canongate*. For this book he invented a new narrator, Chrystal Croftangry, and much of his own pain is evident in the development of a sad, middle-aged and disillusioned character who had wasted a fortune and, afraid of being imprisoned for debt, fled to lodgings in the debtors' sanctuary of Holyrood Abbey. To him are told, by his friends Mrs Bethune Baliol and Miss Kate Fairscribe, the tragic tales of 'The Highland Widow', 'The Two Drovers' and 'The Surgeon's Daughter', their common theme the diaspora of Scots, in the post-1745 period, to seek their fortunes elsewhere.

Six months after Charlotte's death, Scott decided that he needed a holiday, although a holiday for Scott was never much more than moving his work elsewhere. *Napoleon* kept growing; he had completed the four volumes originally agreed with Constable, but the work soon outgrew the format of the *Miscellany* and would eventually expand to nine volumes. He wanted to research further in the archives of the Foreign Office, which held important documents about Napoleon's imprisonment on St Helena, and then go on to Paris to quiz those who had known Napoleon. He would take with him Anne, who needed a holiday more than anyone. On the eve of his departure, Scott got a fright. He thought he saw the ghost of Charlotte and heard her voice crying 'Scott, do not go!' He ascribed this '*hysterico passio*' to disruption of his quiet routine, but it rattled him to the extent that he muddled up his papers and mislaid his money. The following day, 13 October, father and daughter left Abbotsford and, after a short visit to Rokeby, arrived in London on the 17th.

Apart from research, Scott had three main objectives on the visit. One was to solicit patronage for Charles, who was about to graduate and who – despite his expensive education – was still without any career prospects. Another was to see Lockhart and Sophia in their new house in Pall Mall and to meet his second grandson, Walter Scott Lockhart, born on 16 April. Most of all, he was anxious to spend time with six-year-old Johnnie, whose frail health had been causing anxiety for some time and for whom his grandfather, remembering his own sickly childhood, had a tender fellow-feeling. It was never precisely said what ailed Johnnie Lockhart, other than that he had a spinal complaint, but the recurrence of fever, increasing debility and the presence of an abscess on his neck suggest that the disease was osteomyelitis. In an age without antibiotics, this was an incurable infection of the bone leading to early death. Scott found Johnnie cheerful though recumbent; the child's condition was painful to see, as was the strain placed on his parents. Sophia was now plagued by rheumatic pain, and worried constantly about the health of her family, while Lockhart, whatever his failings in his professional life, was an anxious and devoted father.

Scott stayed in London for a week, did his research, sat for the second time to Sir Thomas Lawrence, met the Duke of Wellington, went to Daniel Terry's Adelphi theatre and met Owen Rees of Longman, Hurst, Rees & Orme. He had negotiated an advance of £11,000 with Longman for the rights to *Napoleon*, but that money belonged to the creditors' trust, so he was pleased to hear that Rees had found a French translator for the book who was willing to pay £100 for the privilege. Scott, who was for ever doing little sums in the margins of the *Journal*, reckoned that this money would enable him to break even on what was proving a rather expensive journey. On 20 October, he travelled to 'The King's Cottage', later known as Royal Lodge, at Windsor, where he had a private audience with his old, and now even fatter, friend. Mutual admiration was as strong as ever. 'He is,' wrote Scott, 'the model of a British monarch ... desires the good of his subjects, is kind toward the distressed and moves and speaks "every inch a king".' Scott stayed the night, walked next morning with the King's secretary, Sir William Knighton, and was gratified to hear that royal patronage would be available to get Charles a vacancy in the diplomatic service.

In the last days of October, Scott moved on to Paris where, as well as interviewing Napoleon's colleagues, he had an amicable meeting with Fenimore Cooper, the American who had been so rude about *The Pirate*. He went with Anne to see Rossini's 'Ivanhoé' at the Odéon and 'Rosamunde' at the Comédie Française, saw King Charles X on his way to chapel at the Tuileries, and received a deputation of actresses who came 'with a bouquet like a maypole and a speech full of honey and oil'. Scott was tiring of French compliments, but Anne was naturally thrilled – though not as thrilled as when, back in London, she was invited to dinner with the Duke of Wellington. 'Anne,' wrote her amused father, 'could not look enough at the *Vainqueur du Vainqueur du monde*.' The Conqueror of the Conqueror of the world had been immensely helpful to Scott, providing him with the details of Napoleon's Russian campaign.

On 15 November, Scott was present at a 'conclave of doctors' who had come to examine Johnnie Lockhart. 'They give good words,' he wrote, 'but I cannot help fearing the thing is precarious, and I feel a miserable anticipation of what the parents are to undergo. It is wrong, however, to despair. I was myself a very weak child, and certainly am one of the strongest men of my age in point of constitution.' This had always been Scott's boast, but already time and overwork were taking their toll on a body constantly pushed beyond its limitations. He was exhausted and hankering to get home. Late hours and heavy meals were disagreeing with him, and he wished 'for a sheep's head and a whisky toddy against all the French cookery and champagne in the world'.

Scott and Anne arrived at Abbotsford at three in the morning on 23 November, and two days later went on to Edinburgh. A furnished house in Walker Street had been rented for the winter, which Scott found comfortable and convenient compared with Mrs Brown's. Within a week he developed a bad cold, as often happened when he returned from the country to a sedentary life in stuffy rooms. He had not recovered from the fever and headache it brought when he was stricken by what he called 'cholera morbus', causing stomach pains, cramps and diarrhoea. He slept badly and could scarcely drag himself to court. To crown all on December 23rd, the day he left Edinburgh again for Christmas at Abbotsford, he awoke with agonising rheumatism in his good knee and on arrival had to be carried into the house. It was a wretched end to a year that had brought financial ruin and Charlotte's death. Even a long visit from Walter and Jane could not lift Scott's spirits.

Now the resolution 'to work and suffer' became a reality for Scott. So much illness made him aware of mortality. 'There is some new subject for complaint every moment; your sicknesses come thicker and thicker; your comforting or sympathising friends fewer and fewer … . The best is, the long halt will arrive at last, and cure all.' But before the long halt came, he had to pay off his debts. He doubled the number of pages he had originally vowed to write each day; as well as writing in the early morning, he was now writing in the afternoons after court and the evenings when he was at home. He wrote all day on Sunday and on the Wednesdays when he had no court duties, until writing became a compulsion which he could not have broken had he tried.

The astonishing thing is how much else he managed to pack into his work-dominated routine. He attended meetings of the Oil Gas Company and the Scottish Union Fire and Life Insurance Company, of which he was a governor. He took a hands-on interest in the Edinburgh Academy, founded by Henry Cockburn and Francis Horner to promote the teaching of Greek, and of which Scott became an enthusiastic director in 1825. He attended meetings of the Bannatyne Club, which he had initiated to publish editions of historic Scottish literature, and of the Celtic Society, founded to promote Highland culture by Colonel David Stewart of Garth. He was an enthusiastic member of the Royal Society of Edinburgh and of the New Club. And he dined out with friends – the

Skenes, the Dundases, the Clerks – stumbling over the uneven, ill-lit pavements of the New Town, sometimes muddling dates and arriving on the wrong day. It was at a benefit dinner on 23 February in aid of the Theatrical Fund that Scott finally and formally acknowledged his authorship of the 'Waverley' novels. Some fuss was made but, since he had already confessed all to his creditors the previous year, the revelation was not much of a surprise. Scott dismissed it wearily: 'The joke had lasted long enough and I was tired of it.'

*The Life of Napoleon Buonaparte*, the work of only one year, was published in nine volumes in 1827 by Longman in London and Cadell in Edinburgh, and printed, as ever, by James Ballantyne. Scott had long since abandoned his youthful fear and hatred of Napoleon, and his mature view of his subject was admirably measured. He praised Napoleon's military genius, and his commitment to improving French education and communications. To the profound annoyance of many of his fellow Tories, however, he refused to present 'the little Corsican' as a bloodthirsty monster, stressing instead his mild temperament and patriotism. Scott attributed Napoleon's downfall to his growing conviction that he was a man of destiny, whose arrogant ambition and self-obsession led to catastrophe in Russia's merciless winter snow. *The Life of Napoleon* was a universal commercial success, and while modern readers outside academia may baulk at its length, a recently published one-volume abridgement, skilfully edited by Richard Michaelis, gives access to this balanced and compassionate work.

\* \* \*

In the summer of 1827, Johnnie Lockhart's helpless doctors recommended sea bathing and fresh air. Sophia wanted to take the children to the south coast and suggested that Scott and Anne should join them there. Scott, who was overwhelmed with work, ruled out such a disruption in his routine, and the outcome was a sisterly spat between Sophia and Anne. Sophia came north with Johnnie, but refused to go to Abbotsford; instead they took lodgings at 8 Melville Street, Portobello. On 9 June, Scott went down to greet them with 'a bottle of wine and a flask of Maraschino', but he was not best pleased. He could not understand the point of Sophia's 'lying on a couch in a cage at Portobello', as he described her lodgings, when neither she nor the boys bathed in the sea. 'The place is a stew pan in hot weather, a watering pan in rainy weather and affords the accommodations of a piggery at all times,' he wrote sourly to Lady Louisa Stuart. For Scott the only pleasure of the visit was the time he spent with Johnnie, telling him the stories from Scottish history which he was already planning to turn into a book.

\* \* \*

Scott's idea for *Tales of a Grandfather* was to write a book primarily for children, which he did not feel 'a degradation', but at the same time to make it appeal to an adult audience. This is, as he found, the most difficult task known to a writer and initially Scott, who had never in his own childhood read specialised 'children's books', found it hard to achieve a synthesis of simple style and substantial content. James Ballantyne, consulted about the opening chapters, found them by turns too historical and too childish – a criticism which Scott countered by claiming that the style was for children and the content for adults. Once he had found his own way out of this impasse, however, Scott got on quickly, especially after he had persuaded the trustees that he should be allowed to keep the book's profits for himself, on the debatable grounds that he was writing it in his spare time.

The truth was that for all his determination to economise, Scott was incapable of living on a severely reduced income. His disability made it impossible to endure the discomfort of cheap travel. He still had to meet the expense of upkeep at Abbotsford and the rent of an Edinburgh residence, and had an unmarried daughter and son to provide for. Besides, he was unused to foregoing life's luxuries – wine, cigars, books and such antiquities as still took his fancy. Although he gave fewer dinners in Edinburgh than he had in Charlotte's lifetime, Abbotsford in the summer still drew visitors accustomed to being housed, fed and entertained liberally. Scott certainly worried more about his cash flow than he had before the crash, but he did not stop spending money.

The first series (there were to be four more before 1831) of *Tales of a Grandfather*, covering the period between the kingship of Macbeth (1040–57) and the Union of the Crowns in 1603, was published in December 1827, in time for Christmas shopping. Its dedication ran: 'Humbly inscribed to Hugh Littlejohn, Esq.' and it is by this name that the sadly short-lived John Hugh Lockhart was long remembered. At the time the little boy was gratifyingly pleased with his book and, according to James Ballantyne, so carried away by the rousing battle scenes that he tried to stab his little brother with a pair of scissors.

The possibility of being stabbed, or worse, was probably weighing on his grandfather's mind at the same time. In the *Life of Napoleon*, Scott had made some damaging and, to be fair, poorly substantiated remarks about General Gaspard Gourgaud, a distinguished artillery officer and close confidante of Napoleon who had followed him to exile on St Helena. The implication was that Gourgaud had leaked to the British government confidential information concerning Napoleon's claims of ill-usage by his captors and plans of escape, thus betraying the Emperor he had served with such distinction. Outraged, Gourgaud wrote and published a strong disclaimer; Scott fanned the flames with a defiant reply in the *Edinburgh Weekly Journal* on 14 September 1827. Gourgaud threatened to come over to London and challenge Scott to a duel, to which the 55 year-old replied, with a bravado reminiscent of his first bare-knuckle fight at the High School of Edinburgh in 1779. Not only would he accept the challenge, he announced, but defend himself with one of Napoleon's own pistols. Needless to say, he had a pair of these in his armoury at Abbotsford.

In the event no challenge was received, and Scott's horrified family breathed easily again. The worst the unrepentant biographer had to endure was the transitory indignation of the Paris newspapers.

# CHAPTER 30

# Past and Present

*Years rush by us like the wind. We see not whence the eddy comes,*
*nor whitherward it is tending, and we seem ourselves to witness their*
*flight without a sense that we are changed; and yet time is beguiling*
*man of his strength, as the wind robs the trees of their foliage.*

~ *Woodstock*, chapter 38, 1826 ~

SCOTT WAS FORTUNATE in the kindness of his trustees, particularly Sir
William Forbes, who got Abud & Son off his back by quietly settling his
debt. This generosity freed Scott from the very real danger of being
arrested and imprisoned, should he visit London. The trustees were
serious enough about recovering the creditors' money, but decently
reluctant to humiliate a man so widely popular and admired. They
turned a blind eye to Scott's little schemes for reserving some earnings
for his own use, wisely aware that he would work more efficiently
without undue pressure from them.

Scott's own seriousness was evident. *Woodstock* was finished in a
matter of weeks and, along with the first series of *Chronicles of the
Canongate* and *The Life of Napoleon*, had by the end of 1828 raised
£40,000 for the trust. Scott had the satisfaction of knowing that a small
dividend had been paid. In 1829 Robert Cadell received the creditors'
trust's permission to begin publishing the 'Magnum Opus' edition of the
novels, first proposed by Constable, with new prefaces by Scott and
illustrations by distinguished artists including Sir Edwin Landseer
(1802–73) and Scots Alexander Nasmyth (1758–1840) and Sir William
Allan (1782–1850). The 'Magnum Opus', published in 48 volumes by
Cadell between 1829 and 1833, was an inspired publishing venture
which paid rich rewards, enabling the trust to pay more dividends and
Scott eventually to reduce his debt by almost half. It would finally be

settled in 1847, when Cadell bought the remaining copyrights from Scott's heirs. The trustees must have been well aware too just how much Scott's determination was costing him. His gaunt appearance, sparse white hair and painful gait were plain to see; he saw himself in his late fifties as others saw him, a prematurely aged man. The generation preceding his had not, however, entirely passed away, and in 1828, while he was living in Walker Street, Scott had an encounter with the past which he found both poignant and unsettling.

Lady Jane Stuart, the mother of Williamina Belsches, had the misfortune to outlive by many years her husband and her only child, and in 1829 would lose her son-in-law, Sir William Forbes. In the autumn of 1827 this sad old woman wrote to Scott, asking his permission to give away some poems he had once written out for Williamina, and followed it up with another offering him a gift of Williamina's commonplace-book. 'The recurrence of these matters seems like a summons from the grave,' Scott noted in his *Journal*. Some months later he called on Lady Jane at her house in Maitland Street, and heard her confess to – and apologise for – sabotaging his relationship with her daughter. Scott found this raking up of the past distressing, but went on visiting out of pity. 'I am not clear that it is right or healthful to be ripping up old sorrows,' he admitted, 'but it seems to give her deep-seated sorrow words, and that is a mental blood-letting.' To Scott, Williamina was now little more than a melancholy shade, but Lady Jane's memories oppressed him, adding to his sense of time 'beguiling man of his strength' at a period when he had troubles enough of his own.

As soon as he had finished *Tales of a Grandfather*, Scott began to plan a second series of *Chronicles of the Canongate*. He intended another series of shorter stories and began confidently enough with an introduction featuring Chrystal Croftangry and two tales, 'My Aunt Margaret's Mirror' and 'The Laird's Jock'. Unusually he then found himself unsure how to continue and consulted James Ballantyne, whom he trusted as a shrewd critic. Ballantyne, harking back to the phenomenal success of *Ivanhoe*, was keen for Scott to write another tale of chivalry and, although he himself feared the format was becoming stale, Scott began a third tale along the lines Ballantyne suggested. 'The North Inch of Perth' was centred on a semi-legendary battle of 1396 and featured a duel between the chiefs of two Highland clans to settle a quarrel in the presence of Robert III. Scott thought he was getting along well until one day he received an unexpected letter from his publisher. Pointing out that the first series of the *Chronicles* had not sold particularly well (Scott claimed to be unaware of this), Cadell went on to state his dissatisfaction with the new Croftangry narrative and the two tales which Ballantyne had shown him.

This was not what Sir Walter Scott was used to, and no doubt the former Black Hussar of literature was sorely tempted to pull rank again. Once he had calmed down, however, Scott played a very cool hand. In a letter to Ballantyne, its tone more of sorrow than anger, he proposed that the best way forward was for him to take a couple of years' break from fiction. 'I hold a fallow break to be the only remedy for exhausted ground, and that is not always successful.' The implied threat that he might abandon fiction altogether was enough to bring Cadell and Ballantyne to their knees. Without Scott as cash cow, publisher and printer would collapse, and it took only a few days to come up with a solution. Scott agreed to withdraw the two short stories (which he subsequently sold to a magazine, allowing him to keep the money) and to concentrate on expanding 'The North Inch of Perth' into a stand-alone novel.

Subtitled 'St Valentine's Day', the springboard for the action of *The Fair Maid of Perth* is the attempted abduction, in the early hours of 14 February, of the eponymous maid Catherine Glover by Sir John Ramorny, a courtier in the service of the King's son, the Duke of Rothesay. The intervention of Henry Gow the armourer, who cuts off Ramorny's right hand in the street – the first of many bloody episodes – sets the scene for a novel with various strands; the initial rejection of Henry or 'Hal o' the Wynd' by the pious, pacifist and anachronistically Protestant-leaning Catherine; the revenge of Ramorny which leads to the murder of the hapless bonnet maker Oliver Proudfute and incarceration and death at Falkland of the Duke of Rothesay; the machinations of the Duke of Albany and Earl Douglas at the court of amiable but gormless Robert III.

The main action, however, concerns the rivalry of Henry Gow and Conachar, Simon Glover's apprentice, for the favour of Catherine, whose preference for Henry is qualified by her disapproval of his quick temper and distaste for his trade in arms. This enmity climaxes when Conachar, henceforth grandly known as Ian Eachin MacIan, is promoted by his father's death to be Chief of Clan Quhele. In this role he displays all the pomp and bravado of a hereditary chief, but at heart he is a quaking coward; Scott claimed his brother Daniel as the inspiration for this character. Eachin's moment of truth comes when he is called to lead thirty of his clansmen in a fight to the death with an equal force of Clan Chattan. Henry Gow joins the ranks of Clan Chattan, and when Eachin, having seen his foster-father and seven foster-brothers die to protect him, finds himself face to face with the angry armourer, he flees across the North Inch and jumps into the Tay. The pacifist Fair Maid marries Henry the armourer, finally accepting the reality of the time, that the peace-society she loves depends on the war-society supported by her husband's trade.

Scott was by 1828 a master in the art of conveying the divergence between the remote, sparsely peopled Highlands and the settled, community-based Lowlands, and their mutual distrust. He does full justice to both in *The Fair Maid of Perth*, a pageant of a story with a large and colourful cast. But its chief interest lies in Scott's making the city of Perth, in this medieval tale, a microcosm of his own ideal of a feudal community. At the top of the preordained order are the king and the nobility, and below them the burghers, proud of their artisan skills, secure in the protection of the aristocracy and unambitious of climbing the social tree – though not beyond the reach of patronage, as Scott makes hilariously clear in the final paragraph of the book. Below them are 'the poor', deserving and undeserving, villains such as the sinister leech Henbane Dwining and the murderous thug Bonthron, and virtuous peasants like the Glovers's servant Dorothy and the armourer's house-keeper Dame Shoolbred. Written in the shadow of looming political reform in Britain, *The Fair Maid* was above all about Scott's longing not only to keep hold of a past social order, but to show it could still work.

Sophia and Lockhart's last child, Charlotte, was born on 1 January 1828. In April, his private purse healthy with the proceeds of *Tales of a Grandfather* and reviews put his way by Lockhart for the *Quarterly*, Scott took Anne to London for several weeks. Apart from seeing his new granddaughter and meeting friends, Scott's chief business concerned the long – and ultimately futile – process of securing the money in Chancery for Lady Scott. He also met the Duke of Wellington and the Home Secretary, Sir Robert Peel, to solicit favour for Lockhart and young Walter. Despite being, he said, 'paralysed with rheumatism', he got out and about a lot, sat for his portrait to James Northcote (1746–1831) and Benjamin Robert Haydon (1786–1846), and was amused to see his waxwork, in full tartan splendour, at Madame Tussaud's. In what was to be their last meeting, he enjoyed a private dinner with the King. The dedication of the 'Magnum Opus' was offered and graciously accepted, and Scott met ten-year-old Princess Victoria, the King's niece and future Queen. 'I hope they will change her name,' he wrote.

Scott's visit was also the occasion of a family reunion. Charles, who had at last secured a government post as Foreign Office attaché in Naples, was in London, and Walter too turned up. All might have been happy but for the fact that Charles, along with Sophia, was showing symptoms of the rheumatic illness afflicting their father. Even more distressing was the deterioration of Johnnie who, halfway through the visit, was taken off to be cared for at Brighton by Sophia and Anne. It seemed that the boy was dying, but the alarm was premature. Although his decline was inexorable, Johnnie would live on for three painful years, and Scott, though he tried to be philosophical, was profoundly distressed. Gloom was deepened further by the bankruptcy that summer of Daniel Terry, in whose Adelphi Theatre Scott had invested £500 before the crash. The actor-manager returned briefly to the stage but died a year later, after a number of cerebral seizures. Scott noted fearfully that they had left him unable to remember his lines.

Terry's was the first of a number of deaths that would sadden Scott in the following months. His kinsman Scott of Raeburn died, as did his old friends Bob Shortreed, Lady Jane Stuart, Sir William Forbes, Sir Thomas Lawrence and – most grievously – his trusted friend and factotum Tom Purdie. Purdie's end came without warning as he sat in a chair by his own fireside at the end of October 1829. He had been in a privileged position at Abbotsford, Scott's ideal retainer, fiercely loyal, pawky and familiar, but never crossing the boundary between familiarity and respect. He was a key figure in Scott's vision of Abbotsford, and his master was shocked by his loss. His role as Scott's outdoor support was taken by the forester John Swanston and the supervision of the estate fell to William Laidlaw, but neither could replace Tom Purdie in Scott's affection or his increasing physical need.

*   *   *

On 5 February 1830, Scott suffered a second transitory ischaemic attack, more alarming than that of January 1826. By then renting a house in Shandwick Place owned by Walter's mother-in-law Mrs Jobson, he was in his study with an elderly lady from Hawick who had consulted him about the memoirs of her late father. With characteristic generosity, Scott had agreed to read the manuscript. He had been sitting over it for about half an hour when he rose abruptly from his chair and staggered next door to the drawing room where Anne was sitting with Lockhart's sister Violet. Before the horrified young women could rise to help him, he fell to the floor at their feet. A doctor was called, but some ten minutes passed before Scott was able to speak. The usual rituals of bleeding and cupping were performed and, recorded Lockhart, 'the occurrence being kept quiet, when he appeared again after a short interval, people in general observed no serious change'. Scott was told he had a digestive problem and was prescribed a near-starvation diet of gruel and water, but he was not deceived. Memories of his father's end haunted him; 'I am told it was from the stomach. It looked woundy like palsy or apoplexy,' he wrote grimly in his *Journal* on 26 May. A month later he heard of the death of the King and the succession of his brother, the Whig-supporting William IV.

Though the need to repay his debts and make money for himself drove him to write on, Scott was aware that something had to give. Although he swithered occasionally, writing that 'it is perhaps a violent change in the end of life to quit the walk one has trod so long', in the summer of 1830 he negotiated retirement from his clerkship in the Court of Session. His pension was fixed at £800 a year and, since he would no longer have to pay rent in Edinburgh, he reckoned that he would almost break even. Back at Abbotsford, he was writing at Lockhart's suggestion *Letters on Demonology and Witchcraft* (which disappointed many readers by its scepticism) for John Murray's 'Family Library', more *Tales of a Grandfather*, and a lengthy survey of Scottish history for Lardner's *Cabinet Encyclopaedia*. Having published *Anne of Geierstein* (a novel set mainly in Switzerland where he had never set foot) in 1829, he was also making plans to write another, *Count Robert of Paris*, set even more remotely in Constantinople in 1096, during the First Crusade.

Around this time, Scott's relationship with his old friend James Ballantyne was showing signs of strain. Ballantyne had offended Scott by his criticism of *Chronicles of the Canongate* and a frank lack of enthusiasm for *Anne of Geierstein*, and when Ballantyne's wife died in February 1829 he received scant sympathy from his former partner. Scott, whose stoicism in the face of Charlotte's death seems to have hardened into callousness in the intervening years, was disgusted by Ballantyne's failure to attend his wife's funeral and by the prostrating grief and religious doubts which afflicted the bereaved man afterwards. When after two months Ballantyne still had not returned to work, Scott's impatience boiled over, and he threatened the printer with the loss of the 'Magnum Opus' contract. Two days later Ballantyne meekly returned to the printing shop, but the old harmony had been shattered. It was soon to be put under further strain by political difference between them.

# CHAPTER 31

# Reform

*The Whig ascendancy in the British Cabinet killed Sir Walter. Yes, I say and aver it was that which broke his heart, deranged his whole constitution and murdered him .... From the moment he perceived the veto of a democracy prevailing he lost all hope of the prosperity and ascendancy of the British Empire.*

~ James Hogg, *Familiar Anecdotes of Sir Walter Scott*, 1834 ~

IT WOULD BE too easy, when reading of Scott's life in upper middle-class Edinburgh with its civilised law and literature, clubs and philosophical societies, and his experiment in feudal living in the pastoral Borders, to forget that all his adult life he feared malign forces bent on destroying the orderly world that he loved. His alarm was exaggerated, for all that throughout the period of the French Revolution, the Napoleonic conflict and the 1820s, the democratic aspirations unleashed in 1789 would not be silenced. A rumbling popular discontent with poor wages and conditions was widespread, erupting occasionally into acts of civil disobedience that chilled the heart of Sir Walter Scott. In the years after Waterloo, when demobilised soldiers arrived home in vain expectation of work, the level of unrest rose, fuelled by a fiercely reactionary Tory government. Trade unions were outlawed in 1816, and 1817 saw the banning of public meetings and the suspension of Habeus Corpus, the protection of every individual's basic rights since the thirteenth century.

Two incidents stand out in what were inflated by Tory propaganda into 'Radical Wars'. In August 1819, some 60,000 working men and women had convened at St Peter's Field in Manchester to hear the Radical leader Henry Hunt make a speech advocating Parliamentary Reform. A huge military force had been sent to keep order, including the Manchester Yeomanry, a heavy-drinking volunteer force with no experience of crowd control. Although the demonstration began peacefully, a provocative order from the city magistrates for Hunt's arrest caused a scuffle in front of the platform and a tremor of anger to run through the crowd. The amateur Yeomanry drew their sabres and in the ensuing panic killed ten and seriously wounded 400 people. Scott's reaction to this outrage is revealing: 'The Manchester Yeomen behaved very well, and notwithstanding the lies in the papers without any unnecessary violence.'

This 'Peterloo Massacre' was followed up by Acts of Parliament increasing the power of law enforcement, making prosecution easier and imposing a tax on low-priced periodicals, a reluctant admission of improved literacy among working people. But dissent would not be stifled, and in 1820, as Abbotsford was rising in all its retrospective splendour, insurrection broke out closer to home. On 1 April a plea for a general strike was made at a meeting in Glasgow. When this failed to materialise, a ragtag army of around fifty defiant Radical weavers, armed with pikes and a few muskets, left Glasgow Green to march to Carron ironworks, hoping to seize cannon. At Bonnymuir on 5 April they were charged by the Falkirk troop of Yeoman Cavalry, and in a brief, bloody encounter many of the Radicals were wounded. Nineteen were captured along with their leaders, Andrew Hardie and John Baird. All were sentenced to hard labour or transportation, except for the leaders, who were hanged at Stirling in August.

Scott's attitude to Radicalism had never changed since 1794, when he had watched the execution of Robert Watt at the Tolbooth of Edinburgh. Radicals were 'the enemy within' and must be treated without mercy. Scott in his Edinburgh Light Dragoons days had been eager to play his part in armed crowd dispersal – even if he had chickened out in the face of a starving man at Moredun Mill. In 1820 he was again feverishly sharpening his sword and roaring for a Border Volunteer Force to defend property against an imagined horde of armed Radicals piling in from the north of England. His reaction to the brutal repression of the pathetic insurrectionists at Bonnymuir was that 'the dogs' deserved all the punishment they could get.

The Whig party generally sympathised with the Radicals, and Edinburgh in the early nineteenth century was predominantly a Whig city. Henry Cockburn, the Whig son of a Tory reactionary related to the Dundas family, wrote indignantly in Memorials of his Time of the hereditary slavery inflicted within living memory on the colliers and salters of

Scotland. Although that practice had been abolished in 1779, gross injustices still existed, chiefly the shocking inadequacy of the franchise. The Scottish population was almost 2,500,000, of whom only 3000 were entitled to vote. In country areas only freeholders had votes, and half of these were 'paper barons' who did not actually own property at all. In Edinburgh, a city of 162,000 citizens, only 33 were enfranchised, and in other towns the situation was similar.

Such unfairness was indefensible to everyone except a minority of ultra-conservatives like Scott. He had personal friends among his political foes; indeed, he admitted rather plaintively in his *Journal* that he enjoyed the company of Whigs like Henry Cockburn and Francis Jeffrey more than that of members of his own 'set'. Their cordiality, however, covered a deep ideological divide. By 1830, when the clamour for Reform was sweeping the nation and Edinburgh's Whigs were scenting victory, Scott behaved as if Abbotsford was in imminent danger of having all its windows smashed.

The hardening of Scott's already extreme views on social and political structures in the 1820s was difficult even for his admirers to understand. The English essayist and critic William Hazlitt greatly admired Scott's genius in 'scanning the recesses of the human heart', but was angered by his ungenerous political opinions. In *The Spirit of the Age* (1825) he bitterly expressed his dismay:

> [Scott was a man] *who amiable, frank, friendly, manly in private life, was seized with the dotage of old age and the fury of a woman the instant politics was concerned – who reserves all his candour and comprehensiveness of view for history, and vented his littleness, pique, resentment, bigotry and intolerance on his contemporaries – who took the wrong side, and defended it by unfair means – who, the moment his own interest or the prejudices of others interfered, seemed to forget all that was due to the pride of intellect, to the sense of manhood.*

Such words are painful to those who love Scott, but the pain is in the truth. Hazlitt ascribed Scott's die-hard views of Reform to his 'dotage', no doubt unaware that Scott had held them all his life. James Hogg, less eloquently but just as bluntly, held that the prospect of Reform had 'killed Sir Walter'. Certainly Scott's *idée fixe* about the imminent collapse of civilisation darkened his last days, and did more harm to himself than to anyone else.

*    *    *

On 15 November 1830, the long Tory hegemony in Britain came to an end. Scott's hero, the Duke of Wellington, left office and was replaced by the Whig, Earl Grey, with a ministry committed to Reform. In Edinburgh Henry Cockburn became Solicitor-General and Francis Jeffrey Lord Advocate. Two days later, alone in his dressing room, Scott had another minor stroke. Unrest, particularly in the cities, now became more widespread and Scott, who had not told anyone that he had been unwell, decided that the time was ripe for publishing his deeply unpopular view of the national situation. Refusing to be discouraged by Robert Cadell and James Ballantyne, with whom he was in the huff due to their trashing of the opening chapters of his 'Byzantine Tale' *Count Robert of Paris*, he set to work on a lengthy political diatribe along lines of the *Malachi Malagrowther* letters.

On 18 December, Cadell and Ballantyne, both declared Whig sympathisers, arrived in trepidation at Abbotsford. The following morning in Scott's study, Ballantyne was obliged to read aloud the essay in which, Lockhart notes, 'Sir Walter attacked the principle of Parliamentary Reform *in toto*'. Although the Whig William Laidlaw, who was present, loyally praised Scott's 'bursts of indignant and pathetic eloquence', Cadell and Ballantyne were appalled. Again joining forces against their bestselling author, they roundly condemned a tirade which threatened to damage Scott's reputation and adversely affect his future sales. 'There ensued a very unpleasant scene' which culminated in Scott's losing his temper and throwing the manuscript into the fire.

So distressing did the participants find this episode that Cadell and Ballantyne, against their better judgement, encouraged Scott to go on with *Count Robert of Paris*. It seems that neither believed he would live to finish it.

*    *    *

In January 1831, Scott travelled to Edinburgh, where he made his will and gave it for safe-keeping to Cadell, rather than his son Walter or Lockhart. There seems no clear reason for involving the publisher in his private affairs; he may have done so on an impulse when, marooned in Edinburgh during a ten-day snowstorm, he was given hospitality by Cadell in Atholl Crescent. Yet since Scott had recently quarrelled with Ballantyne, who had had the temerity to write and publish an article in support of Parliamentary Reform, the matter of the will emphasises the increasing influence of the publisher over the author. On the same visit he acquired a brace to support his lame leg, but it did little good and he was obliged to use a sedan chair to carry him when he called on his friends. It was clear to everyone that his voice had weakened, his conversation become dull and his gait painfully slow. Back at Abbotsford, on March 23 he insisted stubbornly on attending an anti-Reform meeting in Jedburgh where he infuriated a restless audience of weavers by his scarcely audible, hesitating speech. But his conclusion was clear enough:

> My friends, I am old and failing, and you think me full of very silly prejudices; but I have seen a good deal of public men, and thought a good deal of public affairs in my day, and I can't help suspecting that the manufacturers of this new constitution are like a parcel of school-boys taking to pieces a watch that used to go tolerably well, in the conceit that they can put it together again far better than the old watchmaker …. I should not be much surprised if it were to turn out that their first step had been to break the main-spring.

These words were met by a fury of hissing and booing, but when the abuse had died down Scott had the last, contemptuous word: 'I regard your gabble no more than geese on the green,' he said, and as he left added the words made famous by the Roman gladiators: '*Moriturus vos saluto*' – 'I who am about to die salute you.'

On 5 April, Scott noted in his *Journal*, 'I have a hideous paralytic custom of stuttering with my pen and cannot write without strange blunders; yet I cannot find any failure in my intellect.' The blunders proved ominous. On the 17th, again in his dressing room but with the house full of guests, Scott became seriously ill. Anne sent for a doctor from Edinburgh who advised the visitors to pack up and go home. Scott afterwards described his illness as 'a distinct shock of paralysis affecting both my nerves and speech', although in a letter to Lockhart which he dictated to Anne soon afterwards, he again insisted that 'as far as I am conscious [there is] no alteration in the state of my mind'. Nonetheless, he had the symptoms of a stroke or 'cerebrovascular accident', in which blood vessels in the brain become blocked. Again he was bled and blistered and starved; the only treatment that suggests his doctors had a clue about such illness was the insertion of a seton or drain stitched into his neck to draw off excess fluid from his brain. That he was badly impaired was obvious to all around him; the Lockharts, arriving on 10 May, were shocked by his thin, haggard appearance and the distortion of one cheek, and the novelist Susan Ferrier described him with 'his face swollen and puffy, his complexion mottled and discoloured, his eyes heavy and dim; his head had been shaved and he wore a small black silk cap, which was extremely unbecoming'.

More distressing still was the personality change nowadays associated with dementia. This most good-humoured and hospitable of men withdrew into deep gloom, and was seized by an irritability which often erupted into rage. He had rows with Anne, who had to bear the brunt of his illness as she had borne her mother's; it is a sad reflection that, just as Walter Scott WS had worn down his hapless daughter in the 1790s, so Sir Walter wore down his thirty years later. But despite every attempt to distract him, he went on working, dictating his novel to William Laidlaw and keeping his *Journal*, its late entries a tragic testament to the breakdown of his spelling, omissions of words and the 'stuttering' which he had noticed himself.

\* \* \*

On 7 May, just as he was dragging himself out of bed, Scott received a stunning blow, a 'formal remonstrance' from Cadell and Ballantyne who, having encouraged him to continue, now condemned the third volume of *Count Robert of Paris* out of hand. 'God knows I am at sea in the dark,' wrote poor Scott, 'and the vessell [*sic*] leaky into the bargan [*sic*].' On the 12th he laid the book aside and, to the horror of his family, began another, *Castle Dangerous*, set in 1306 during the Scottish Wars of Independence. His hero was Sir James Douglas, the friend of Robert the Bruce, and to gather inspiration he invited Lockhart to accompany him on a visit to Douglas Castle and Church in Lanarkshire. In a one-to-one situation, the pitiful failing of his father-in-law's memory and speech became even more evident to Lockhart, and it is indeed astonishing that the man he described could actually finish *Count Robert of Paris*, write *Castle Dangerous*, and still be alive when they were published. Scott had no illusions about these novels; he thought neither of them 'sea worthy' and was amazed by Cadell's letter in January 1832, announcing that 'each sold off about £3400'. It revived his hope that he might even yet write himself out of debt.

Meanwhile, as one Reform Bill after another was thrown out in the early months of 1831, public anger rose to fever pitch and Scott's obsession with the political situation continued unabated. On 18 May, again ignoring the frantic pleas of both of his daughters, he insisted on going to Jedburgh to attend the last election held under the old system, to support the Tory candidacy of his kinsman Henry Scott. The ugly atmosphere in the streets was not calmed by the presence of two troops of dragoons. The burghers, who had not forgotten Scott's performance in March, were in furious mood, and as he left the hustings he was spat at and pelted with stones, to cries of 'Burke Sir Walter!' The verb 'to Burke', meaning 'to suffocate', was then fashionable, smothering having been the preferred method of the infamous murderers Burke and Hare. Scott had to be hustled into his carriage and driven away under a hail of stones. 'Much obliged to the bra' lads of Jeddart,' he wrote bitterly in his *Journal*, but for a man who believed so fervently in class distinction and respect for one's 'betters' the humiliation must have been hard to bear. Ever after, the words 'Burke Sir Walter' chilled him and haunted his dreams.

\* \* \*

It required three attempts between March 1831 and July 1832 before the Reform Act passed into Law. In Edinburgh, at the election in December, Francis Jeffrey and James Abercromby (who later became Speaker of the House of Commons) were elected to represent the city. Mrs Eliza Fletcher, widow of an idealistic Whig lawyer, who knew and loved Scott despite her ardour for Reform, wrote a luminous account of election night in her *Autobiography* (1875):

> *It was a glorious sight for us to see these truly honest men borne home amid the acclamations of tens of thousands of their grateful and emancipated countrymen. We stood by them on the balcony of Mr Jeffrey's house while they shortly returned thanks to the people. Few events ever excited me more than those which took place in Edinburgh at that time.*

On this night of joy and promise fulfilled, when the age of the 'common man' dawned and the patriarchal world he loved began its long retreat into history, Sir Walter Scott had been three months in his grave.

# CHAPTER 32

# A Voyage Out

*I neither regret nor fear the approach of death if it is coming. I would compound for a little pain instead of this heartless muddiness of mind which renders me incapable of anything rational.*

~ *Journal*, October 1831 ~

THERE IS A gap in Scott's *Journal* between May and October 1831, which he afterwards filled in with a summary of his sufferings during the period. For the first time he admits the feeling of mental confusion which he feared far more than any physical ill. His way of keeping the disintegration of his mind at bay was to go on writing, against the advice of his doctors, his family, and even, at last, his publisher. Scott was, after all, still Robert Cadell's greatest asset, and his death from overwork before all the 'Magnum Opus' introductions had been completed was an outcome to be avoided if possible. The falling away of Scott's old vigour in *Count Robert of Paris* and *Castle Dangerous* had been noted with concern by Cadell, but there was no question of his rejecting them for publication.

As the summer of 1831 slipped away, it seemed doubtful to all who cared about him that Scott could survive another biting Scottish winter. The first idea of the family, with Cadell's blessing, was to make a tour through Germany, pay a visit to Goethe at Weimar, cross the Alps and wind down through Italy to visit Charles at Naples. Scott himself, though gloomily mindful that his novelist predecessors Fielding and Smollett had gone abroad for their health and never returned, was for the first time willing to contemplate the possibility that he too would die in a foreign land. The idea of another five months of chilblains, rheumatic pain and stiff, unreliable legs, lacked appeal, and besides he could as well write his next novel in Italy as at Abbotsford. That he had this in mind is suggested by his choice of holiday reading, five volumes of *The Knights of Malta* by the French Abbé de Vertot which he had first read as a teenager. Presumably he kept his writing intention to himself.

The idea of an overland journey was sensibly discarded due to fear that Scott could not cope with its rigours. A sea voyage was next contemplated, and through a complicated web of connexions, including Lockhart's colleague John Wilson Croker, Scott's friend Captain Basil Hall, the First Sea Lord Sir James Graham, the Prime Minister Earl Grey and finally King William IV, Scott was offered a passage to Malta on the warship HMS *Barham*. Anne and Walter, who had been given leave from his regiment, would accompany their father. In view of Scott's vocal Toryism, it was an extraordinarily generous gesture from a Whig government, and displays a more magnanimous sort of politics than that espoused by Scott. The creditors' trust allowed him to borrow £500 to cover his expenses, and Cadell topped up his funds with a £1000 advance for the rights to Scott's travel journal. It was agreed that he and his party would travel to Portsmouth in time for the sailing of the *Barham*, planned for 22 October.

The last days at Abbotsford were poignant. William Laidlaw was given his instructions, and the poet William Wordsworth made the journey from Grasmere with his daughter Dora to say goodbye. The two writers drove together to Newark Castle, an excursion which inspired Wordsworth's fine poem 'Yarrow Revisited'. Friends called to take their farewells, aware that they might be seeing Scott for the last time. It is probable that Scott felt most pain at parting with his dogs. On 23 September he left Abbotsford with Walter, Anne and Lockhart, and after a halt at Rokeby and a final parting with Morritt, travelled on to London.

The capital, wrote Scott, was 'in a foam with politics', and he was gleeful when the second Reform Bill was thrown out on 8 October by the House of Lords, 'quoited downstairs like a shovel-board shilling, with a plague to it'. This rebuff to the plans of a government showing him such goodwill briefly perked Scott up, and he was quite cool on the following day when he saw a mob gathering in Regent's Park and 'roaring for Reform as rationally as a party of Angusshire cattle would have done'. As darkness fell, the frustrated crowd took to smashing windows in the West End, 'making work for the glaziers,' Scott noted laconically.

It was a disappointment that Lockhart could not go abroad because of the *Quarterly*, nor Sophia because of her children, but until the last moment Scott hoped that his daughter-in-law might join him. Apparently Jane called off because she was prone to seasickness, with the result that once again Anne was left to nurse her father without the support of another woman. She had developed gastric problems, no doubt exacerbated by stress, and had reason to feel aggrieved. Throughout the weeks of the voyage she fell out with Scott when he refused to stick to his diet, and made clear her resentment of Walter's showing off and choosing to dine out with other officers rather than *en famille*. They quarrelled constantly, and when they finally arrived in Naples, Charles, who was chronically unwell, found their discord hard to bear.

The voyage to the Mediterranean began badly. Due to a west wind blowing, the Scotts were obliged to hang about in the Fountain Inn at Portsmouth for a week in the care of the attentive Captain Basil Hall. The *Barham* eventually sailed on 29 October, but three days later was still beating off Land's End. All the Scotts were violently sick. Beyond the Bay of Biscay the weather improved, and Scott, who took easily to life on shipboard, enjoyed getting up on deck and talking to Captain Pigot and his officers. He was thrilled to see from the sea Cape St Vincent, Trafalgar and Gibraltar, and by the time the *Barham* reached Malta on 22 November he felt stronger in body and mind. After a slow start due to quarantine regulations – there had been cholera in London as they passed through – Scott took up residence at Beverley's Hotel in Valetta, where he spent three weeks sightseeing and being feted by British expatriates who even gave a ball in his honour. His most pleasurable contact was with John Hookham Frere, who had been British Minister to Spain during the Peninsular War (1806–13) and whom Scott had met in London more than twenty years before. He ate and drank too much, incurring the wrath of Anne, and began to write *The Siege of Malta*, doubtless to the despair of all around him.

On 13 December, the Scotts sailed on the *Barham* for Naples, arriving on the 17th. Charles, who had not been looking forward to the visit, was horrified by the gaunt, ruined appearance of his father, and before long the incessant squabbling of his siblings began to grate on his nerves. But he had organised entertainment, and although his father was in one of his periodic panics about money – one day borrowing from Walter for fear of having to 'try a begging box', and the next spending lavishly in the belief that all his debts were paid – he had happy moments. Scott admired the Bay of Naples, went to Pompeii, and appeared at a reception for the King's birthday. He had of course packed for just such an occasion, and appeared as a Brigadier General of the Royal Company of Archers, the bodyguard created in Edinburgh for George IV in 1822. This he described as 'a very decent green uniform laced at the cuffs and pantaloons, and looked as well as sixty could make it out when sworded and feathered *comme il faut*'. His fondness for dressing up at least was unabated.

On 16 January came the news that ten-year-old Johnnie Lockhart had died in December. No incident of his final year shows more clearly the blunting of Scott's capacity to feel; the passing of his best-loved grandchild was noted chillingly in the *Journal*: 'I could not have borne it better than I do now, and I might have borne it much worse.' That night he went to the opera. There is much other evidence that Scott's mental condition was deteriorating fast. He alternated between lucidity and confusion, serenity and fretfulness; his speech was often slurred and his memory for names fugitive. He could not remember Maria Edgeworth's, and referred to her as 'the Irish woman'. Those who saw him on a good day, however, were pleased with his conversation; Sir William Gell, who acted as his guide to the antiquities, recalled 'his conversation replete with anecdotes'. His children would have told a different story.

Walter's leave was up the first week in March, and he departed, probably with some relief, to England and his regiment. Three weeks later on the 27th, according to Lockhart, Scott heard news that Goethe had died, and his response – 'Alas for Goethe – but he at least died at home – Let us to Abbotsford' – has become a staple of the Scott legend. The scholar Donald Sultana, however, in *The Journey of Sir Walter Scott to Malta* (1986), claims there is no evidence that Scott knew in Naples about Goethe's death; Lockhart had made the incident up to give drama to Scott's homesickness. By now, though, the winter was almost past and the homesickness was probably real enough.

On 11 April, Scott left Naples with Charles, Anne and Sir William Gell. They travelled by Rome, where Scott was present for the Papal Blessing, *urbi et orbi*, on Easter Sunday, then on by Bologna and Florence to Venice. Scott still met people and took intermittent interest in the churches, castles, villas and abbeys to which the disabled but indefatigable Sir William escorted him. The last words in the *Journal* were written in the Roman lodgings where the Scotts arrived on the cold, moonlit evening of 18 April: 'We slept reasonably but on the next morning…'. The rest of the journey can be traced in a diary where Charles Scott made brief notes, mostly of arrivals, departures and the weather.

* * *

Scott's extreme irritability, which seems to have faded among the sights and society of Rome, returned with a vengeance as his painful bones were jolted in a carriage over the rough roads of northern Italy. Anne and Charles, both ill themselves, found his peevishness hard to bear. Now he talked of nothing but getting home, only brightening up when the Apennine scenery reminded him of Scotland. It was bitterly cold as they crossed the Alps into the Tyrol, and came north through Munich, Heidelberg and Frankfurt. Scott wanted to travel by night as well as all day, and his angry petulance convinced Anne and Charles that a crisis was approaching. The useless procedure of bleeding was inflicted on Scott by his manservant John Nicholson several times along the way.

A stage of the journey on a Rhine steamboat eased Scott's aching bones, and the landscape of German ballads and Byron's *Childe Harold* briefly animated him. But beyond Cologne the flat countryside again depressed Scott, and on 9 June, near Nijmegen on the Dutch Border, he suffered a major stroke with subsequent paralysis. Somehow Charles and Anne managed to get him to Rotterdam, and on the 13th they arrived in London. Since there had been no time to alert the Lockharts, Scott was put to bed in the St James Hotel in Jermyn Street, where he remained for three weeks in a stupor broken occasionally by flashes of recognition. Among his visitors there were his publisher Cadell, who had come hurrying down from Edinburgh, and his sister-in-law Mrs Thomas Scott, who came and stayed to help Anne. Otherwise Scott saw none but Lockhart and his children, including Walter who once again had to ask for leave.

Scott's stay in London was, however, as John Sutherland says, 'a kind of lying-in-state'. When news of his illness broke, crowds gathered outside the hotel, newspapers carried daily bulletins on his health, and even the Royal Family made regular inquiries. In his occasional lucid moments, Scott was still desperate to get home, and eventually the four doctors who had been attending him agreed that a journey could do him no more harm. On 9 July, in front of a crowd that had gathered at the docks to pay their silent respects, he was carried comatose onto a steamship, accompanied by Walter, Anne, Lockhart, the manservant Nicholson and Cadell. After two days at sea, his still unconscious body was unloaded into a carriage at Leith, on the spot where he and half of Edinburgh had greeted the King ten years before. The crowd was smaller but still sizeable, and the mood sadly changed. On the 13th, as his carriage entered the Vale of Gala, Lockhart writes that Scott began to rouse himself:

> *As we rounded the hill at Ladhope, and the outline of the Eildons burst on him, he became greatly excited; and when, turning himself on the couch, his eye caught at length his own towers at the distance of a mile, he sprang up with a cry of delight …. Mr Laidlaw was waiting in the porch, and assisted in lifting him into the dining-room, where his bed had been prepared. He sat bewildered for a few moments, and then resting his eye on Laidlaw said 'Ha! Willie Laidlaw! Oh, man, how often have I thought of you!' By this time his dogs had assembled around his chair – they began to fawn upon him and lick his hands, and he alternately sobbed and smiled over them, until sleep oppressed him.*

Revisionist critics of Lockhart have in recent times had a field day. It has been pointed out that Scott could not have seen Abbotsford from a mile away; the towers are visible only much closer to the house. Lockhart's famous account of Scott's last coherent words has likewise taken a battering. Yet the story of Scott's homecoming is deeply moving, and as with all legends the reader is left hoping that, after all he had suffered, it might in essence have been so.

\* \* \*

Scott, who had hoped for a quick death, did not have his wish granted. His agony continued for a further two months, and makes a harrowing tale. At times his mind seemed briefly to clear, and one day he even tried to write again. But his fingers refused to close around the pen and, with tears running down his face, he said, 'friends, do not let me expose myself – get me to my bed – that's the only place'. He struggled against those who were trying to help him, muttered 'Burke Sir Walter', and sometimes screamed for hours on end. Lockhart, who nursed him faithfully, wrote economically that 'the end was slow'.

In his description of his father-in-law's dying, however, Lockhart was not economical at all. In his account, Scott had a moment of lucidity a few days before he died, in which he called Lockhart to his bedside. 'I may have but a minute to speak to you,' he said. 'My dear, be a good man – be virtuous – be religious – be a good man. Nothing else will give you any comfort when you come to lie here.' The truth about this pious and improving scene was revealed by Herbert Grierson, whose book *Sir*

*Walter Scott, Bart.* is subtitled *A New Life, Supplementary to, and Corrective of, Lockhart's Biography*. Grierson had unearthed a damning letter to Lockhart from an evangelical lady urging him, for the spiritual encouragement of his readers, to invent just such a story. It is unlikely that Scott was ever fully conscious during the last days of his life. He died in the presence of his children on 21 September, 1832.

*   *   *

For a man of such stature and reputation, Scott's funeral was a relatively modest affair. On 26 September, after prayers 'in the usual Scotch fashion', his coffin was carried by his own servants and foresters from the house to the hearse and driven by way of Darnick, Melrose and Bemersyde to Dryburgh Abbey. There Scott was buried beside Charlotte, as he had desired. Lockhart described the silent crowd in the forecourt at Abbotsford, the cottagers dressed in black standing at their doors to watch the cortège pass by. He said the train of carriages covered more than a mile, and all Scott's friends attended. That the followers of Scott to his grave were many is unquestionable, although Robert Chambers, who attended, remarked how few of Scott's Edinburgh friends made the journey to Dryburgh. It was half-past five before all were accommodated and the Episcopal burial service read. Memorably, Lockhart records the weather: 'The day was dark and lowering, and the wind high.'

# CHAPTER 33

# A Life in Story

*Walter Scott is a writer who should just now be re-emerging into his own high place in letters.*

~ G. K. Chesterton, *Twelve Types: A Collection of Biographies*, 19 January 1902 ~

WHEN HE DIED, Sir Walter Scott was among the most celebrated people of his day. His novels were bestsellers, stage versions and operas of his work were sold out, and public curiosity about his own life story was intense. Naturally keen to control ill-informed speculation, the Scott family eagerly agreed with the publisher Robert Cadell that John Gibson Lockhart should write an 'authorised' biography. In many ways he was an obvious choice. He had been intimate with Scott for the last twelve years, had the confidence of his children, knew his friends and had privileged access to his father-in-law's journals, private papers and correspondence. Lockhart began his monumental task by encouraging Scott's friends to send him their recollections, and so acquired, among many others, the testimonies of Will Clerk, James Skene, Adam Ferguson, Joanna Baillie, Mrs Mary Ann Hughes, William Laidlaw and James Mitchell, who had been the Scott boys' tutor fifty years before. The sheer bulk of his material, however, made Lockhart's *Memoirs of the Life of Sir Walter Scott, Bart.* long in the writing. The public was impatient and others jumped in to fill the gap.

First up was Robert Chambers, the Edinburgh bookseller who had become one of Scott's many protégés. With his brother William, Robert had founded the publishing house of W. & R. Chambers, and launched, in the year of Scott's death, the periodical *Chambers's Edinburgh Journal*. Here, in serial form, Robert published his friendly, moderately indiscreet reminiscences in 1832–33; they were not published in book form until

1871. A less benign biography, begun by William Weir and completed by George Allan, appeared in 1834, but by far the liveliest of the pre-Lockhart publications was by James Hogg, the 'Ettrick Shepherd', who had known Scott since the days of the *Minstrelsy* in the early 1800s.

That there was real affection between the mercurial and blissfully egocentric peasant Hogg and successful, affably condescending Scott is not in doubt. Scott promoted Hogg's poetry, fixed jobs for him, petitioned the Duke and Duchess of Buccleuch on his behalf when his farming enterprises came unstuck, and bailed him out even in the time of his own desperate financial need. On his part, Hogg admired Scott and was anxious for his approval; he boasted of their friendship but, although he believed sincerely in the brotherhood of writers, was not above resentment and class envy. When, after Scott's death, he sat down to write his *Anecdotes of Sir W. Scott* and *Familiar Anecdotes of Sir Walter Scott*, the last thing he intended was to cause offence to the Scott family, but given his natural candour and willingness to spill beans, it was inevitable that he would. Even now, the reader's reaction to Hogg's indiscretion and self-projection is a mixture of discomfort and hilarity, but as entertainment, *Anecdotes* is hard to beat.

Hogg was deeply hurt by Lockhart's fury and blatant attempts to suppress his freedom of expression; their always uneasy relationship, defined by satirical contempt on Lockhart's part and resentment on Hogg's, quickly deteriorated into acrimony. Three of Hogg's indiscretions in particular roused the ire of Lockhart, busy with his own carefully crafted account: Hogg's open claim that Lady Scott had been a drug-addict, his amused incredulity at Scott's deference to the bearers of titles, and his observation that, for all his virtues, Scott 'told lees'. Hogg was not accusing Scott of general mendacity; his reference was to Scott's long refusal to acknowledge the authorship of his novels, which had patently involved him in subterfuge and denial. He was telling his truth about Scott as he saw it, and that it was different from Lockhart's truth brings to the surface a very important question about the reliability of biography.

There are really three stories of Sir Walter Scott. One is the story he told about himself in the *Memoirs* of his early life, the *Journal* he kept in his last years, and in the prefaces and appendices he wrote for the 'Magnum Opus' edition between 1829 and 1832. Another is the story told by Lockhart, and yet another exists in the astonishing body of revisions and additions to these core narratives over almost two centuries since Scott's death.

If we accept the essential subjectivity of human experience, that confession is selective and that no one bares the soul without self-protective reservations, it follows that autobiography should be approached with caution. Scott's initial wish to give the public what they were entitled to know may have changed as his fame grew, but in his personal writings he remained in control of his text; he chose to reveal or conceal. If sometimes he embroidered plain fact, it was because, like all human beings he fantasised, and, because he was a creative writer, the line between literal and imagined truth in his mind was probably a finer one. He was not deliberately trying to mislead, but could not resist the temptation to spice up his story.

Essentially, Scott's story was one self-invention; of the sickly child who became a tough, popular schoolboy, a teller of tales and doughty street fighter, morphing in turn into an establishment figure with a gentleman's access to aristocratic circles, a soldier, a passionate lover, a patriarchal landowner, a famous poet and novelist, noble in ruin and stoical in pain. Despite the disarming, self-deprecatory tone of his letters and *Memoirs* and, in his *Journal*, his searing honesty in revealing his own pain, the Scott who was steeped in legends of heroic deeds was never less than the hero of his own tale. It was this version that Lockhart published, using Scott's own *Memoirs* as the first chapter, in his biography of 1837–38.

The book sold steadily enough, despite the fact – for a work that has been compared favourably with James Boswell's *Life of Samuel Johnson*, the greatest biographer of the pre-modern age – initially it received little critical attention. Perhaps Lockhart had taken too long to publish; by 1837 Scott had been dead for five years, politically and socially times had changed, and critical interest had shifted to the work of the living. The *Edinburgh Review* and Lockhart's own *Quarterly* carried no reviews, and the only substantial piece of contemporary criticism was Carlyle's typically sweet-and-sour essay in the *London and Westminster Review*.

During the almost two centuries that separate the publication of Lockhart's work from today, opinion about its merits has been divided. Privately, Lockhart was much criticised by his contemporaries for an unbecoming frankness in revealing his father-in-law's foibles, and there was shock in Edinburgh about his dealings with Constable and the Ballantynes. Lockhart did not entirely whitewash Scott, but he clearly blamed James Ballantyne for Scott's ruin. The Ballantynes responded indignantly, and the ensuing all-too-public row provided both scandal and diversion for the citizens of Edinburgh. Despite a less than favourable start, however, Lockhart's work prospered, and set a pattern for Victorian biography until 1884, when James Anthony Froude brought a swarm of hornets about his own ears by revealing the marital problems of Thomas and Jane Carlyle.

Modern scholars generally have not been kind to Lockhart. They find his sanctimonious tone grating and his snobbery and animosities unpleasant. More seriously, they have picked holes in his best-known anecdotes, many of which are now revealed as inventions. A work once seen as too candid is now regarded as hagiography, its presentation of Scott evasive and unreliable. There is no doubt that many of these accusations are true, but in Lockhart's defence it may be said that he was obliged to consider the sensitivities of Scott's family, and to note that between his time and ours the art of biography has undergone a massive change.

To Lockhart, modern candour, particularly about sexual matters, would have been abhorrent. He was not alone in believing that a biographer's duty was to present his subject as favourably as possible, and it is wrong to think of him as deliberately mendacious. Lockhart was a classicist, and his theory of biography probably influenced by the theory of the Greek philosopher Plato of the 'noble lie', which suggested that an untruth might be justified if its intention could be seen as serving the common good. An extension of this concept was the 'pious myth' where it was permissible to clothe fact in fiction, provided that the intention was not to mislead, but to provide spiritual uplift. However questionable, these ideas – which underlie much religious myth-making – do give a clue to Lockhart's mindset as he set about his task. And it says much about the power of myth that, for all the scholarly research undertaken in more recent times to unpick the embroidery and lay bare the truth about Scott, for the ordinary reader the legends have proved remarkably durable. We love the stories of the finding of *Waverley* among the fishing tackle in the attic; the whirlwind journey to Polton through the winter night; Scott's last homecoming and deathbed, not exactly as they were but as Lockhart wanted us to remember them.

\* \* \*

Scott was not commemorated only in words. He was not long dead before committees were formed to plan his memorials. Already immortalised in portraits as striking in their dissimilarity as in their fidelity to their subject, and at Abbotsford, which first opened to the public in 1833, he was destined to be remembered in stone and bronze throughout the English-speaking world. An eighty-foot column, surmounted by a statue, was unveiled in Glasgow's George Square in 1838, well ahead of the Scott Monument in Princes Street, Edinburgh, in 1844. This vast Gothic structure, as integral now to the city's image as the Castle, has never been universally admired; it was described disdainfully in 1929 as 'perhaps the most naively philistine structure in the country'. Other memorials were unveiled in towns made famous by association with Scott, such as Perth, Galashiels and Selkirk. New York's Central Park's Literary Walk paid tribute to Scott in 1872, and all over the world fountains, plaques and inscriptions recalled him. In London, where money originally raised for a national memorial tribute had sensibly been used to reduce Scott's remaining debt, a bust was placed in Westminster Abbey's Poets' Corner in 1897.

Meanwhile, all over Scotland, mini-Abbotsfords were built in suburban roads, Edinburgh's main station was named 'Waverley', streets and villas were labelled 'Ivanhoe', 'Kenilworth' and 'St Ronan's'. Even Balmoral Castle, built for Queen Victoria and Prince Albert in the early 1850s, gives a nod to Abbotsford. Scott's face appeared on bank notes, stamps, crockery and biscuit tins, and the idea that his popularity might ever fade seemed far-fetched. Edward Bulwer-Lytton, author of *The Last Days of Pompeii*, could state confidently in 1832 that 'the most commanding genius of modern times has left us to seek for that successor to his renown which, in all probability, a remote generation alone will furnish forth'.

In fact, the decline in Scott's popularity was not as swift as G. K. Chesterton's 1902 plea for his reinstatement suggests. Throughout the Victorian period, Scott's inspiration can be traced in the work of George Eliot, the Brontës and Edward Bulwer-Lytton, a prolific writer in his day. The 'Waverley' novels were translated into languages as diverse as Portuguese and Polish, Italian and Greek, and Scott's influence on European writers such as Fyodor Dostoevsky, Gustave Flaubert, Alexander Dumas and Honoré de Balzac is well known. In the United States, where an exasperated Mark Twain blamed *Ivanhoe* for a glamorisation of chivalry that precipitated the Civil War, Scott remained colossally popular throughout the century.

It was in the bleak aftermath of the First World War of 1914–18 that Scott's reputation really toppled dramatically. In an age weary of slaughter, his tales of medieval chivalry were deemed distasteful, and his preoccupations no longer seemed relevant to modern life. Although the 'Waverley' novels, particularly *Old Mortality* and *The Heart of Midlothian*, remained part of the Scottish Higher syllabus for the next fifty years, and were widely distributed as school prizes, new styles of writing, sparer, more elliptical and less concerned with narrative, became fashionable at the expense of Scott. Taking their cue from *Ivanhoe* and *Treasure Island*, some critics administered the kiss of death, dismissing him, along with Robert Louis Stevenson, as a writer for children. 'It is impossible to believe,' sniffed Ford Madox Ford in *The March of Literature* (1938), 'that any grown man could take seriously the adventures of Ivanhoe or Rob Roy.'

As the twentieth century rolled on, bringing the cinema and television to challenge reading as a pastime, Scott became a name better known through film than literature, although now even that second-hand fame has faded away. As for the books, in the age of the internet and sound bite, we are told, attention spans are short and no one has time to read Scott any more. He is too wordy, too far removed from modern concerns, and his references, especially since the decline of Latin, too taxing and obscure. And, unlike Robert Burns and James Hogg, in the egalitarian age he dreaded Scott is perceived as too posh.

Recently, however, at a time of political discussion on the future of the United Kingdom, Scott's attempts to reconcile Unionism with a distinct Scottish identity have become relevant again, and in some small ways he has returned to public attention. This change does not appear to be driven by any great desire to re-engage with his work, but rather plugs into a contemporary need to celebrate 'Scottish heroes' of one kind or another. Abbotsford has been given a makeover, a new railway line is publicised as a link between Edinburgh and 'The Scott Country', and Waverley Station has been decorated with quotations from the works of Scott. All of this is commendable enough, but rather misses the point. That there were heroic aspects of Scott's life is not in question, but if he had not been a great writer they would for ever have remained private virtues. He would have lived his life as a moderately prosperous Edinburgh lawyer and spare-time antiquarian, married, had children and died. Without the books, his name would be lost. There would be Princes Street without the monument, and Scott's life of no interest to anyone.

So why should modern Scots make an effort to break into Scott's world? To discover our greatest author in his love of his country, his exuberance, humour and humanity. To enjoy the haunting evocation of city and landscape, and encounter our language in the 'last purely Scotch age', with its abundant vocabulary and sublime echoes of the King James Bible. Above all to experience the joy of the stories, enchanting and heart-breaking, atmospheric, comic and tragic by turns, to see a steady light shone on our history, and dignity conferred on the rich and poor of our nation.

\* \* \*

Scott's hope of passing on his baronetcy and founding an Abbotsford dynasty through Walter and his children was sadly unfulfilled. It must have been clear to him in the last years of his life that Walter and Jane were unlikely to have a child, but he could never have imagined the dreadful incidence of early death in the rest of his family. Despite their outdoor upbringing and apparent robustness in childhood, the Scott children were not destined to grow up healthy. Anne Scott, who had chronic gastric illness and was weakened by the stress of nursing her parents, died in the Lockharts' London house in 1833, having survived her father by only eight months. Aged only 30, she was buried far from home in the New Cemetery in the city's Harrow Road, now called Kensal Green. There she was joined by her sister Sophia, who died after a long illness, probably precipitated by influenza, in 1837. She was 38.

Charles Scott, plagued for most of his adult life by rheumatic pain, returned from Naples to London on the retiral of the Ambassador he served, where wet winters made his condition worse. In 1841, he was sent on a diplomatic mission to Persia, but the long journey on horseback through Turkey proved too taxing for his frail body. He died, Lockhart records, of an 'inflammatory disease' and was buried in Tehran, aged 36. It is not surprising that after the deaths of his brother and sisters, the second Sir Walter Scott dreaded returning to Scotland, and especially to Abbotsford. It was not a journey he was to make alive. Now a Lieutenant-Colonel in the 15th Hussars, he was posted in 1839 with his regiment to India where, following a tiger hunt, he contracted a tropical fever. On his way back to England to recuperate, he died on board HMS *Wellesley* near the Cape of Good Hope in 1846, aged 45. His body was returned to Scotland by his widow and, alone of Scott's children, he was buried with his parents at Dryburgh Abbey.

It was now that the grasping Robert Cadell, who had published Lockhart's *Memoirs of the Life of Sir Walter Scott* and gained extraordinary access to the affairs of the Scott family, bought the last copyrights they held, ostensibly to settle Scott's debts once and for all. Since Lockhart had more altruistically donated the proceeds of *Life* to the creditor's trust, this sale meant that the remaining family never received a penny in royalties from Scott's once great literary estate. Robert Cadell died in 1849, a very wealthy man.

Scott's only living heirs were now the surviving children of Sophia; Walter and Charlotte Lockhart. Although the baronetcy had died with his uncle, Walter Scott Lockhart inherited Abbotsford. But the curse of early death continued to dog the family; this third Walter was a dissolute young man who quarrelled bitterly with his father and died at Versailles, aged only 27, in 1853. John Gibson Lockhart himself did not long survive this tragedy; he died at Abbotsford the following year and was buried at Dryburgh at the feet of Sir Walter Scott. All hope of posterity now rested on the shoulders of 25-year-old Charlotte Lockhart, who married James Hope, a prominent member of the High Church of England, and with him converted to Roman Catholicism. This couple took the name of Hope-Scott, and it is from them that all of Sir Walter's present-day family are descended.

# Select Bibliography

The authoritative texts of Scott's work are to be found in the Edinburgh Edition of the Waverley Novels, published by Edinburgh University Press 1993–2012, under the general editorship of David Hewitt. Paperback editions of the best-known texts, with scholarly introductions and annotations, are published by Oxford University Press and Penguin Books. Most of Scott's less widely-known novels can be found through online booksellers.

The best reading edition of *Journal of Sir Walter Scott* is edited by W. E. K Anderson (OUP 1972, Canongate Books 1998). Quotations in this book are taken from the edition of 1891 edited by David Douglas. Quotations from Scott's letters are taken from *Letters of Sir Walter Scott 1787–1832*, edited by Sir Herbert Grierson (1932–37).

### Secondary sources

ANDERSON, W. E. K (ed.) ( 1972): *The Journal of Sir Walter Scott* (Oxford).

BUCHAN, JOHN (1932): *Sir Walter Scott* (London).

CARLYLE, THOMAS (1888): *Critical and Miscellaneous Essays* (London).

CARSWELL, DONALD (1930): *Sir Walter: A Four-Part Study in Biography* (London).

CHAMBERS, ROBERT (1872): *Memoir of Sir Walter Scott* (Edinburgh).

_____ (1868): *Traditions of Edinburgh* (Edinburgh).

COCKBURN, HENRY (1856): *Memorials of his Time* (Edinburgh).

CRAWFORD, T. C. (1965): *Scott* (Edinburgh).

DAICHES, DAVID (1971): *Sir Walter Scott and his World* (London).

_____ (ed.) (1993): *The New Companion to Scottish Culture* (Edinburgh).

FORSTER, E. M. (1927): *Aspects of the Novel* (London).

GARSIDE, PETER (2015): *The Oxford History of the Novel in English*, vol. 2, 1750–1820 (Oxford).

GIFFORD, DOUGLAS (ed.) (1988): *The History of Scottish Literature*, vol. 3, The Nineteenth Century (Aberdeen).

GRIERSON, HERBERT (1938): *Sir Walter Scott, Bart.* (London).

_____ (1932): *Letters of Sir Walter Scott 1787–1832* (London).

HAYDEN, JOHN O. (ed.) (1970): *Sir Walter Scott: The Critical Heritage* (London).

HEWITT, DAVID (ed.) (1981): *Scott on Himself* (Edinburgh).

HOGG, JAMES (ed. Jill Rubenstein) (2004): *Anecdotes of Scott* (Edinburgh).

JOHNSON, EDGAR (1970): *Sir Walter Scott: The Great Unknown*, 2 volumes (New York).

KAMM, ANTONY (2009): *The Jacobites* (Edinburgh).

KELLY, STUART (2010): *Scott-land: The Man who Invented a Nation* (Edinburgh).

LANG, ANDREW (1906): *Sir Walter Scott* (New York).

_____ (1910): *Sir Walter Scott and the Border Minstrelsy* (London).

LOCHHEAD, MARION (1954): *John Gibson Lockhart* (London).

LOCKHART J. G. (1838): *Memoirs of the Life of Sir Walter Scott, Bart.*, 7 volumes (London).

LUKÁCS, GEORG (1967): *The Historical Novel* (London).

LUKACS, JOHN (2005): *Remembered Past: A Reader* (Wilmington).

MICHAELIS, RICHARD (ed.) (2014): *The Life of Napolean Boneparte by Sir Walter Scott* (London).

MILLER, KARL (1976): *Cockburn's Millenium* (London).

_____ (1983): *Doubles* (Oxford).

MILLGATE, JANE (1984): *Walter Scott: The Making of the Novelist* (London).

MUIR, EDWIN (1936): *Scott and Scotland: The Predicament of the Scottish Writer* (London).

_____ (et al.) (1950): *Sir Walter Scott Lectures 1940–1948* (Edinburgh).

OMAN, CAROLA (1973): *The Wizard of the North* (London).

PEARSON, HESKETH (1954): *Sir Walter Scott* (New York).

PREBBLE, JOHN (1990): *The King's Jaunt* (London).

QUAYLE, ERIC (1968): *The Ruin of Sir Walter Scott* (London).

REPPLIER, AGNES (2005): *On Sir Walter Scott*, quoted in LUKACS (2005).

ROCHESTER, RALPH (2001): *For Love of Williamina* (Bridport).

ROYLE, TREVOR (1993): *The Mainstream Companion to Scottish Literature* (Edinburgh).

SULTANA, DONALD (1986): *The Journey of Sir Walter Scott to Malta* (New York).

_____ (1993): *From Abbotsford to Paris and Back* (Stroud).

SUTHERLAND, JOHN (1995): *The Life of Walter Scott* (Oxford).

WILSON, A. N. (1980): *The Laird of Abbotsford* (Oxford).

WORDSWORTH, DOROTHY (1894): *Recollections of A Tour Made in Scotland in 1803* (Edinburgh).

## Online resources

The National Library of Scotland – Millgate Union Catalogue of Walter
Scott's Correspondence and John Murray Archive
www.nls.uk

Edinburgh University Library – Walter Scott Digital Archive
www.walterscott.lib.ed.ac.uk

Abbotsford House, Melrose
www.scottsabbotsford.com

Rokeby Park, Barnard's Castle
www.rokebypark.com

Scott Monument, Edinburgh
www.edinburgh.gov.uk

Project Gutenberg – ebooks of Scott's works
www.gutenberg.org/ebooks/author/59

The Edinburgh Sir Walter Scott Club
www.walterscottclub.org.uk

# Index